God
and
Country

God
and
Country

*How Evangelicals
Have Become
America's New
Mainstream*

Monique El-Faizy

BLOOMSBURY

Author's Note: Some of the names in this book have been
changed to protect the privacy of persons involved.

Published by Bloomsbury USA, New York
Distributed to the trade by Holtzbrinck Publishers

All papers used by Bloomsbury USA are natural, recyclable products made from
wood grown in well-managed forests. The manufacturing processes conform to
the environmental regulations of the country of origin.

Library of Congress Cataloging-in-Publication Data

El-Faizy, Monique.
God and country : how Evangelicals have become America's new
mainstream / Monique El-Faizy.—1st U.S. ed.
p. cm.
Includes bibliographical references and index.
ISBN-13: 978-1-58234-519-2 (alk. paper)
ISBN-10: 1-58234-519-8 (alk. paper)
1. Evangelicalism—United States.   2. Christianity and culture—United States.
3. Christianity and politics—United States.   4. United States—Church history.
I. Title.

BR1642.U5E42 2006
277.3'083—dc22
2006013324

First U.S. Edition 2006

2 4 6 8 10 9 7 5 3 1

Typeset by Westchester Book Group
Printed in the United States of America by Quebecor World Fairfield

For Theo and Xander
and, of course, for Oliver

Contents

Prologue

I BEGAN THIS project reluctantly. It was at the urging of an insightful friend that I first considered writing about evangelical Christianity. I would likely never have come to it on my own, having turned my back on my fundamentalist upbringing in college. But when I revisited the world of my youth, I saw a vastly different place, one that had grown to resemble the secular world—in style, if not in substance. It was clear those changes had expanded the influence of the evangelical subculture, though not yet to what degree. At the time, President Bush was in the early months of his first term in office, the details of his religiosity were only beginning to emerge, and the impact evangelicals were having on American culture had not yet come into focus.

I also saw the bias the press carried against evangelicals as it chronicled their ascent—a bias I, in fact, shared. I had rejected evangelical Christianity when a cross-country move to attend the University of Pennsylvania widened my world and I had come to see born-again Christians through the same lens as that of my peers. I considered the religion oppressive, its believers closed minded, and I did so with the kind of fervor only a former adherent could muster. And yet, I was unable to completely dismiss evangelicalism, because there were people I loved and respected who belonged to its ranks.

I had assiduously avoided church since my early days in college, and any encounter with Christianity made me uncomfortable. Shortly before the conversation that prompted me to write this book,

I had given birth to my first son. I realized that, since my husband was Jewish, if I wanted my child to have any understanding of my family's beliefs and customs, I'd have to overcome my aversion. I thought that undertaking this project might help me do that. Approaching it with journalistic detachment would give me cover.

So the writing of this book has, inevitably, been a personal journey as well as a professional one. I have tried to put aside my own negative feelings about the evangelical world and look at it with fresh eyes. Clearly the religion appeals to millions of people. I set out to overcome my own biases and figure out what it is about evangelicalism that people are drawn to. I have come to appreciate that evangelical Christianity can provide a warm, comforting, and, at times, even stimulating community. I have also seen the flip side: that it can be judgmental and closed minded. But in forcing myself to be more open minded about the people I was meeting than I was naturally inclined, I have come to know evangelicals who are genuine, interesting, intellectually curious, and engaged with the world in which we all live. They just happen to believe in something I don't.

Along the way many of the people I interviewed told me they thought God was using this project to bring me back to him. That hasn't happened, and I sincerely doubt it will—there are too many beliefs at the core of evangelical Christianity that I can't see myself ever accepting, and I have too vivid a memory of the shortcomings of the earthly Church to want to be part of it again. Still, I've met many believers whose intellects I respect and whose kindness I admire.

I see my role in the writing of this book as neither judge nor apologist. I wish simply to shine a spotlight on a world little understood by those on the outside. Just as leaving the church two decades ago allowed me to broaden my horizons, revisiting it has helped me open my mind and deepen my understanding of a phenomenon that has seized America and is affecting all of our lives. I hope anyone reading this book will come away similarly enriched.

Introduction

SATURDAY EVENING, THIRTY-THIRD Street and Seventh
Avenue. Make your way up the escalators, past the pictures of
Muppets, rock stars, and sports heroes and toward the Theater at
Madison Square Garden. You'll encounter several smiling greeters
along the way, handing out schedules and donation envelopes. As
you ascend the final bank of escalators, you'll hear snippets of hand-
clapping, stomp-inducing music. Round the corner into the upper
level of the theater, and spread out before you will be thousands of
people of all ages and races waving their hands in the air, swaying
and dancing and singing praises to Jesus.

Not exactly what one might expect on a Saturday night in the
heart of Gotham, perhaps, but it's happening all over. In the midst
of New York City, emblem of fast living and vice, is a vibrant world
of evangelical Christianity. You can find it at these weekly services at
Madison Square Garden, preached by prosperity-doctrine evangelist
Creflo Dollar, who flies in from his home in Atlanta. You'll discover
it at Times Square Church, which meets in a converted theater and is
visited by eight thousand people each week. It will be apparent in the
speed with which appearances by evangelists like Billy Graham and
Texas pastor Joel Osteen sell out or fill up. And you'll uncover it in
hundreds of smaller churches that meet in apartments, schools, and
renovated storefronts across the city. If you know where to look,
you'll see it everywhere: a growing city-within-a-city of evangelical
Christians, right under the nose of the city's intellectual elites.

While liberals and secularists still operate the levers of power in New York, on a national level evangelicals have become the new establishment. In the planks of our culture—politics, publishing, music, and entertainment—evangelicals have risen to prominence. The 2004 presidential election opened the eyes of many so-called blue state Americans to the importance of evangelical Christianity (red state Americans were already aware of it), but its reach still hasn't been fully realized. Throughout the country—even in blue America—evangelical Christians exist in significant numbers. In the five boroughs of New York City alone there are at least eighteen evangelical megachurches—defined as a congregation with more than two thousand members—and at least three of those are in the ultraliberal borough of Manhattan. Democratic stronghold California not only has a sizable evangelical population but is the birthplace of some of the most critical developments in the religion and home to many of its most important churches. Some of the fastest-growing congregations in Massachusetts and New Hampshire are evangelical, and New England as a whole has come to be regarded by evangelicals as one of the most promising mission fields in the country.

Over the course of the past several years, America has undergone a realignment and is now a country in which evangelical Christians are no longer a fringe group but instead make up its core. It's a transformation that has taken place largely unnoticed by the East Coast media and Hollywood, but the fact is that nine out of ten Americans believe in God, and roughly one in three is evangelical. And while the rest of the country has finally woken up to the importance of evangelicals in American society, their understanding of them remains superficial. Alarmist media reports generally portray a unified, monolithic, right-wing bloc, and while there are factions—important factions—in the community for which that characterization is accurate, evangelicals cannot be painted fairly with such a broad brush. They are more diverse and, in many areas, more moderate than those outside of the fold realize, which is why they have become so influential.

While estimates as to the size of the evangelical community range from 44 million to more than 100 million, depending upon how pollsters phrase the question, evangelicals can be found in every Christian denomination and in nondenominational churches. In a May 2006 Gallup survey, 44 percent of American adults identified themselves as born-again or evangelical, about 86 million people. While the Gallup number bumps up and down in each poll, over an extended period of time it has been essentially flat. A January 2006 sampling conducted by the Barna Group indicated a significant spike in the number of born-again Christians, but it is unclear if that is the beginning of a trend. While it remains to be seen if evangelicals are growing in number, it is clear they are growing in might.

The strength of evangelicals comes in part from their sheer numbers and partly because they have learned to adopt the look and feel of secular America. Instead of living an isolated, parallel existence, as they once did, they are making the country over in their own image. Like other groups before them, including women, homosexuals, and African Americans, evangelicals have learned to straddle two worlds—their own and the one that the rest of us live in. They have blurred the lines once drawn between them and us, and in doing so, the evangelical community has become America's new mainstream. While some of the country's most visible and prestigious institutions are still left leaning and secularist, they no longer represent the center of American life.

The evangelical community derives its might from a local, grassroots base. In many parts of the country meetings of the school board and other local governances begin with prayer—not because it's legal, but because it's so accepted that it has never been challenged. The foundation of evangelical power is also widespread. Evangelicals don't sit in our nation's ivory towers or on the editorial boards of our major newspapers, but they wield sizeable clout over school boards, speak loudly through hometown papers, and, for the moment, run the United States government. Many reporters have, in the years since Bush was elected to his second term, been writing "gee whiz" stories about evangelical Christians that, in their incredulous tone, sometimes seem worthy of the cover of *National Geographic* magazine. As large and powerful as the evangelical community may be, it is still a mystery to those on the outside.

Evangelical dominance has been sped along by the proliferation of different types of media, such as blogs, Internet sites, and a burgeoning number of cable channels, all of which have helped break the influence monopoly held by a trio of TV networks and a handful of newspapers. As the number and types of media outlets increased, evangelicals found new ways to be heard. But despite their power, many evangelicals still feel that they are a persecuted minority whose beliefs and sensitivities are consistently under attack by the greater culture, a dynamic that creates a volatile situation. Evangelicals are upwardly mobile but they don't get the respect they desire and they feel their morals aren't reflected in the greater culture to the degree they think they deserve. The result is a resentment that helps explain the fervor with which many of them push to impose their values.

But that feeling is slowly beginning to change. In July 2005 *Christianity Today* posted an editorial on its Web site entitled "We're Prime Time, Baby!" The editorial noted that *Newsweek* had dubbed 1976 the Year of the Evangelical. "If 1976 heralded the birth of the media reckoning with the crowd that took the Bible at least as seriously as did Carter, evangelicalism's persona has come of age in 2005. Now we're on during prime time," it read. The editorial identified a few recent articles and most editorial boards as exceptions, but concluded that "we're no longer overlooked, persecuted, discriminated against, and misquoted in the mainstream media." The last line of the editorial summed it up: "So, we've been mainstreamed. Now what?"

What indeed. Over the past few decades evangelicals have become better educated and more affluent and thus have amplified their power. When they began to mobilize, they already had a network of well-placed business and political leaders who had quietly ascended to the tops of their fields. The growing preeminence of evangelicals has also been fueled by the demise of mainline denominations.

America's elite used to be culled from denominations with roots that reach centuries back, such as the Episcopalians and mainline Protestants. In the past, as people from other religions climbed up the socioeconomic ladder, they would move into those denominations. Today that is no longer true. Successful evangelicals now choose to remain in evangelical churches, both raising the status of those churches and expanding their congregations. As a result more and more of this country's most influential figures call themselves evangelical—and they're not content to stop there. The movement's leaders are now training talented youth and encouraging them to enter areas of society in which there have previously been few who belonged to the faith. They want to expand their reach.

In most places in America, people consider their lives through the prism of their faith and speak about the role of God in their lives in the same concrete terms others use to talk about the weather. Those who are not religious tend to gloss over those statements as inconsequential. After more than a year of interviewing, I realized I was doing exactly that, and it was preventing me from fully understanding the people I was writing about. When people explained the success of various books or movies as "a God thing," I'd think, "Okay, but what's the real reason?"

I became conscious of this tendency during an interview with a woman who had struck me with her insightfulness and intelligence. Partway through our conversation she started talking about seeing the forces of Satan working in the world, and I felt myself tuning out. The next day I was interviewing the former president of a major American retailer who was telling me that she consulted God before she made any decisions about her career. She opted to take a lower-ranking job for half her previous salary because she felt this was where God was leading her. These two encounters led me to rethink the way I was approaching the evangelical community. For those of us who are not believers it is almost impossible to grasp how essential an evangelical's spiritual experience is in his or her life. God is a living, tangible, and daily presence.

Those not part of the evangelical 44 percent will likely recall the Moral Majority and the pushy fundamentalists of the 1980s when they think of born-again Christians. The doctrines held by today's evangelicals are similar (the difference between evangelicals and fundamentalists is more one of attitude and terminology than of belief), but they have changed their approach. The fundamentalists of twenty years ago were about political confrontation and societal isolation, but there's been a paradigm shift since then. Today's evangelicals take a much softer line of attack and have carefully broadened their appeal.

Their core beliefs remain the same, but evangelicals have undergone a remarkable stylistic transformation over the past several decades. While you can read articles and books about Dominionism and secessionist groups, these evangelical factions lie at the fringe of the movement, and even most of their Christian brethren think they're peculiar. To focus exclusively on such groups is to define the evangelical community by its outer edges; in this book I concentrate instead on its core, a group that looks surprisingly like the rest of America. In this book you will read about people doing things you would never do, things you might find downright strange, but, aside from their faith, many of the people I met during the course of my research were not all that different from me and the people in my social circle.

This is by design. No longer isolated and "other," evangelicals have learned to put forward a visage both welcoming and relevant. This change is apparent before one ever walks through a church door. The religious symbols and white clapboard buildings with bell towers have been replaced by rambling complexes that are inoffensively neutral. They have every amenity, from coffee bars to gyms to volleyball courts, but don't telegraph their purpose with obvious signs such as crosses or the hollow fish symbol believed to have been used to identify the early Christians. It's easy to be fooled, but no matter how warm and welcoming they appear, the essential belief of evangelicals remains the same: Without the salvation Jesus Christ provides, man is guaranteed an eternity in hell.

I am not an evangelical Christian, and yet I know the religion like an insider, having grown up as a fundamentalist and having considered myself a committed born-again Christian for more than a decade. I will use that insight to shine a spotlight into this little understood but crucially important facet of American society. In this book I'll go beyond the stereotypes and into the lives of evangelicals across the country. It's only through awareness that the rest of us can know how to appropriately respond to the considerable progress evangelicals have made in shaping the world in which we all live.

WHO ARE THEY AND WHAT DO THEY BELIEVE?

There have been thousands of news stories about evangelicals over the past several years, yet the group remains largely misunderstood. Just the word—*evangelical*—is a source of confusion. The Greek roots of the word mean "good news," and the sharing of that news, the Gospel, is a central tenet of evangelical Christianity. Evangelicals feel they have an imperative to spread the story of Jesus Christ. They also believe that unless one accepts the salvation bought by Christ's death on the cross, one is doomed to eternal damnation. Finally, they believe that the Bible is God's authoritative word on earth. Anyone who shares in those three beliefs I have considered an evangelical for this book. The evangelical body is a very diverse one, so my grouping encompasses many seemingly different groups, but they all share one other crucial characteristic: They have an individual relationship with Jesus Christ. Their faith is private, rather than institutional. They believe that because of Adam's sin in the Garden of Eden man is condemned to eternal death, but that the crucifixion of Jesus Christ atoned for that sin. They have, at some point, made a decision to accept that forgiveness and in doing so gain eternal life. At that point, they entered into a personal relationship with Jesus.

There are many denominations that are primarily evangelical, particularly in Protestantism, but evangelicals can be found everywhere.

There is, for example, a robust movement of evangelicals in the Catholic and Episcopal churches. Many evangelical churches do not belong to any specific faction. Indeed, evangelical Christianity is notable in that it transcends affiliation. Its rise marks the death of denomination.

For the sake of this book, what unites these people is more important than what divides them. Defining evangelicals is tough, since even those who proudly wear the badges disagree about what they mean, so I have been intentionally general and treat their differences as largely stylistic. Not everyone whom I term a fundamentalist will agree on every point of doctrine; equally, a fundamentalist may, theologically, be in lockstep with someone I term an evangelical.

For the rest of America, these internecine doctrinal distinctions (biblical inerrancy versus biblical primacy, the timing of the Second Coming of Christ, etc.) are generally of little importance. The most succinct clarification of the difference between the two comes from Notre Dame historian George Marsden, who writes: "A fundamentalist is an evangelical who is angry about something."

The term *evangelical* can be used to describe people with the set of beliefs I previously laid out, or simply to define a style of Christianity. When I refer to evangelicals, I will generally mean someone who belongs to that broad group, which will also encompass fundamentalists and born-again Christians. I will, on occasion, use the term *evangelical* as a contrast to *fundamentalist*; in those instances I will be referring to the stylistic differences between the two. Evangelicals and fundamentalists often simply use the word *Christian* to refer to a person who has had a born-again experience, someone who made a sentient decision to accept Jesus Christ as his personal savior. (Those of us who haven't are "pagans.") Evangelicals and fundamentalists share a lot of common ground doctrinally; where they differ is in their relationship to society. Fundamentalists are militant and antimodernist. (Though, ironically, since the latter part of the twentieth century it has been the fundamentalists who have been most active in the political arena.) Evangelicals believe they have a responsibility to reach into the larger culture, rather than provide a critique from the sidelines.

Over the past twenty-five years fundamentalism (as opposed to evangelicalism) has been on the wane. The dominant message in fundamentalist churches was one of the hell and damnation that awaits those who lack a relationship with Jesus Christ. Today's evangelicals have moved their attention from God's wrath to God's love. This change has made them more palatable to outsiders, and their willingness to involve themselves with popular culture has enabled them to affect it.

Because evangelicals have become the dominant Christian force on the cultural landscape, I have focused on them, largely to the exclusion of fundamentalists, some of whom, including Jerry Falwell and James Dobson, are already well known to American readers. While they still wield considerable influence in the political arena, they represent the old guard of evangelical Christianity, not its future, and are therefore of decreasing importance. In the hundreds of interviews I did over the course of researching this book, I found few, if any, Christians who said these most conservative leaders of Christianity spoke for them. While most evangelicals agree with the Christian Right's position on issues such as abortion and gay marriage, the average evangelical has an agenda that is much broader and an attitude less confrontational.

I have also chosen to exclude several high-profile and highly controversial figures, including Trinity Broadcast Network owner and founder Paul Crouch and charismatic faith healer Benny Hinn, both of whom have been the subject of several exposés in the media. While they have gigantic followings, the intention of this book is to focus on the mainstream of evangelical culture and its impact on society. The vast majority of evangelicals I spoke with expressed varying levels of discomfort with both Hinn and Crouch who raise questions with their lavish lifestyles and refusal to disclose financial documentation. In addition, neither has made much of a mark on the landscape of American secular culture.

CULTURAL ENGAGEMENT: PAST, PRESENT, AND FUTURE

While evangelicals have valued societal involvement at other points in their history, the current trend toward cultural engagement took root in the mid-twentieth century, about the same time the community started to move its focus from the consequences of sin to the grace of God in an attempt to be more appealing to nonbelievers. I will use that refocusing as a jumping off point and will chart the community's progression to its current state of participation. Most of the churches I visited are megachurches, not because evangelicals don't attend smaller churches but because such large congregations are very visible and their superstar pastors can claim a disproportionate amount of sway over the body of evangelical Christianity as a whole.

Today's evangelicals may look and sound like the rest of America, but their very act of adapting to the culture around them ties them to their forefathers. The tussle between fundamentalists and modernists is almost as old as the country itself. The community has a history of reinventing itself to find new ways to appeal to outsiders and draw them in. Indeed, outreach is a key component of evangelical Christianity, and most churches of a certain size place an enormous emphasis on spreading the word. That, in large part, is what keeps the religion vibrant: New members are always being added.

But it's one thing to attract converts and quite another to keep them. Evangelical Christianity has been successful because churches have become adept at creating all-encompassing, embracing communities that serve to shelter insiders from the influences of the outside world and provide a safe, nurturing environment for the whole family. You can drink your coffee in a Christian coffee shop and shed unwanted pounds at your church's weight-loss group. There are even Christian Yellow Pages for many areas.

"Be in the world, but not of the world," we were often exhorted at my church youth group. When I was a teenager growing up, that meant living the majority of my social life within the confines of the church. I went to a Christian camp in the summers and for spring and winter retreats, to youth group on Wednesday nights and Sunday mornings, and on Friday nights I often went dancing at a local church that showcased the latest Christian bands. Aside from family holidays, the vast majority of the trips I took growing up—camping on the beach, hiking through the forest—were taken with my church youth group. I lived a large part of my life in a separate Christian universe. Churches today provide even more social opportunities for youth.

In the decades since I left, that world has undergone an astonishing shift, one so transformational that it's now tough to differentiate the evangelical world from the secular one. Particularly in the entertainment arena, the lines that separate the Christian from the mainstream have blurred significantly.

For the past several years, evangelical Christianity has been bursting through cultural boundaries at an amazing clip. The music of born-again bands, sometimes nearly indistinguishable from the secular competition, is routinely played on MTV and on Top 40 stations throughout the country (everything from Lifehouse to rap-star-turned-preacher-turned-rap-star-again, Mase). Christian films have flickered on silver screens from coast to coast (including Mel Gibson's *The Passion of the Christ* and preacher T. D. Jake's *Woman, Thou Art Loosed*). God-friendly television programs can be accessed from virtually every living room in America (*7th Heaven* and *Joan of Arcadia*, to name just two), and evangelical books (the Left Behind series, *The Purpose-Driven Life*) fly off bookstore shelves. But evangelicals feel there are still aspects of the culture that portray them unfairly and don't reflect their values. It is to those areas they are turning their attention.

If a look to our youth is any indication, the evangelical impact is liable to intensify. Not only are Christian universities increasing in number and in influence but evangelical groups are mushrooming on such esteemed campuses as Harvard and the other Ivy League schools.

While it's the kinder, softer, hipper face of evangelical Christianity that's attracting the youth and selling books and records, it's the conservative old guard that's driving the political agenda. Evangelicals have become adept at adopting the grassroots tactics their liberal opponents used decades ago and at finding hot-button issues that will motivate their base. Realizing that all politics is local, as the adage goes, and that today's hometown leaders are the national leaders of tomorrow, evangelicals have packed school boards, courts, and town halls with people who share their faith. One fringe group, Christian Exodus, has taken that to such an extreme that it is coordinating an effort to get evangelicals (they use the term Christian constitutionalists) to move to two key counties in South Carolina where they believe they can fill the city council, county council, elected law enforcement positions, and elected judgeships with their candidates. They plan to continue on a county-by-county basis until they control the whole state, at which point they will turn their attention to the next state.

Some pastors, such as Rod Parsley in Ohio, have taken a leading role in injecting Christian values into the political arena, and his grassroots organizing was credited with helping put his state in the "Bush" column on election day in 2004. He has since broadened his efforts, merging evangelical outreach with voter registration, but has also come under scrutiny from the IRS for possibly crossing legal lines that prohibit pastors from endorsing specific candidates. The outcome of Parsley's case is likely to determine how deeply into politics pastors are willing to wade in the future.

Evangelicals have also applied pressure on the president who, as a devout evangelical himself, doesn't need much prodding to fall into line. He has obliged the Christian community by appointing conservative judges—some shoehorned in by recess appointments—and the administration has given millions of dollars to evangelical groups through its faith-based initiative, most often to the exclusion of other religious groups. Evangelicals are agitating for a role in foreign policy as well and have been able to push their agenda of fighting

AIDS in Africa onto the front burner. The 2006 National Prayer Breakfast showed how far evangelicals have gone in mainstreaming their foreign policy goals—the annual address by the president was preceded by a speech by rock star Bono, in which he urged the faith community to keep up the fight to eradicate the deadly disease.

The evangelical agenda is broadening to areas traditionally considered the domain of Democrats, such as poverty and global warming. On their hot-button issues, though, evangelicals remain as conservative and as passionate as ever. They will not rest until abortion has been banned, and with his two appointments to the Supreme Court, Bush has given them a chance of finally accomplishing that goal. They continue to work tirelessly for state legislation to ban gay marriage and to agitate for a federal marriage amendment. How all this will play out on the national stage has yet to be seen.

As evangelicals move out of the trenches of the far right and onto more moderate ground on some issues, new questions arise. What will be the effect of their adopting a broader agenda? Will the Republican Party try to keep up with the new evangelical program and thus be changed, or will evangelicals begin to move toward the Democratic Party, a shift that is already, to some degree, under way? The Democrats have been making a concerted effort to reach out to evangelicals, but the only way they will be able to do that on a large scale is by being more open to pro-life candidates. Will evangelicals also be able to transform one of the last places liberals feel relatively safe—in the Democratic fold? The next few election cycles are likely to reveal the answers to many of these questions. Americans, particularly secular Americans who feel threatened by the evangelical agenda, need to understand these forces so they can be ready to respond.

I
Belief

CHAPTER ONE

The Triumph of Engagement

I N A DIMLY lit former warehouse that has been converted into a church sanctuary a diminutive blond in a black-and-white bouclé suit and high heels whips her 4,200-person audience into a frenzy. This is perhaps the most diverse church body I've ever seen, with elderly white women in floral dresses sitting next to young black women wearing shimmery blouses. A man a few rows behind me has on a purple satin shirt under a lavender-and-white print knee-length jacket. A well-coiffed platinum blond with a southern accent sits to my left. The pastor, Paula White, is preaching to her home congregation here at Without Walls International Church in Tampa, Florida.

The sermon is about letting go of relationships that are holding you back and learning to build ones that help you grow. "Somebody say 'Let it go!' " she urges. "Let it go!" the audience responds in unison. White preaches as if she is channeling Aretha Franklin. She stands behind a large wooden pulpit as she starts each new point of her message, then steps to the side as she begins to crescendo. By the time she reaches each oratorical peak she is perched on the edge of the stage leaning toward the audience and making sweeping gestures with her French-manicured hands. The crowd is in her thrall, and some people rise to jump up and down in front of their seats. Once she's made her point, she goes quiet, returns to her lectern, and pauses before launching into the next theme.

White cites a passage in the Gospel of John in which Jesus met a woman at a well and offered her living water. The woman dropped her water pot and ran to town to tell people she had spoken to a man who might be the Messiah. White sees the woman dropping her water pot as a sign that she has severed ties with her previous life.

"Don't revisit what God has ended," White says. "When God says it's done with, you've got to drop the water pot." She starts migrating toward the front of the stage. "Please let me break it down for you. You ready? Somebody say 'bring it on, bring it on.'"

"Bring it on!" her audience forcefully replies, launching White into a rhythmic monologue.

"You gotta drop the water pot.

"What are you doing still going down to the Mad Dog? You gotta drop the water pot!

"'Oh Paula, I'm just going down—I know those are my old drinking buddies.'" White plays her own interlocutor. "You've got to drop the water pot. Make no provision for that entry that Satan had in your life. You have to bring closure to that.

"'Oh, but now he's just a friend.'

"No. I'm gonna tell you, I'm gonna tell you all you need is one Barry White song playing and he ain't going to be a friend at two a.m. in the morning telling you 'Baby, you looking so good.' Come on. Drop the water pot. Break the Barry White CD. Bring closure to that thing that keeps pulling you back that God said, 'I'm finished with.'"

White and the congregation she pastors with her husband, Randy, break through the barriers that historically have separated churches along the broad evangelical spectrum. She is a white woman who preaches as if she's black. Her congregation is Caucasian, African American, Hispanic, and Asian. Services are attended by some of Tampa's most affluent, including, at times, New York Yankee Gary Sheffield and former Yankees Ramiro Mendoza and Darryl Strawberry, and also by residents of local housing projects who are picked up by buses each week. The church bears many of the hallmarks of a Pentecostal church, but I didn't see anyone speaking in tongues. The Whites have violated most of the rules of church growth along the way—including meeting in tents with no climate control and not providing convenient parking—yet according to megachurch researcher John Vaughan, Without Walls is among the top five churches in the country, in terms of both growth and size.

On the surface, Without Walls has little in common with the ultraconservative, isolationist existence I remember from my youth, in which we were warned to "be in the world but not of the world" and to make sure that our closest friends were Christians. The church I attended, Grace Community Church, was founded when its pastor left his Presbyterian congregation because of pressure to ordain women as elders, something he believed the Bible prohibited. In that environment and at that time, no one would have dared consider a female pastor like White.

White's sermon, too, is very different from those I remember from my church days. I'm sure no one was talking about extramarital sex—at least not without a brow furrowed in judgment and a very liberal dose of verbal finger wagging. The messages in my church were stern and solemn and much less engaging. I recall one sermon, after I had already walked away from the faith, in which our pastor commended people who were chaining themselves together in front of abortion clinics. But that was unusually political for him. Normally his lessons honed in on a passage in scripture and taught the congregation how to live a more godly life, including, for instance, instructions to women on submitting to their husbands.

Of course, I had come to Tampa expecting to see something very different from the fundamentalist churches I grew up in, having had breakfast with White months earlier at the Trump International Hotel on the edge of Central Park. Donald Trump is a personal friend of White's, and she regularly stays at his hotel during her frequent visits to New York. The staff there know her and greet her warmly and deferentially. As we spoke I realized she and her congregation defied any classification I could think of. She, along with her husband, runs one of the largest churches in the country in a world where women are traditionally not allowed to be pastors. She has a TV show that airs both on Fox and BET, among other networks. She counts some of the country's richest people as friends and leads a Bible study for the Yankees, but also has a vibrant inner-city ministry. On top of it all she is a perky, polished blond who, on the morning I met her, was wearing a body-hugging tiger-print dress that highlighted a figure befitting the Playboy Bunny she aspired to be when she was younger.

The diversity of her congregation, her ability to minister to the down-and-out one day and hang with Donald Trump and the Yankees the next, and, indeed, White herself, illustrate just how fluid the world of evangelical Christianity has become and the degree to which it intersects with secular America. The evangelical subculture has become more sophisticated and now, in many instances, looks like secular culture. By adopting the look and feel of the mainstream, evangelicals have been able to have an effect on every aspect of American life from entertainment to education to politics. No longer intent on disseminating doom and gloom and the wrath of God, evangelicals are now emphasizing the redemptive message of the Gospel and have become more savvy about getting it out. White could be the poster child for the demise of doctrinal distinction and for the new, more accepting, more attractive face of evangelical Christianity. Watch her weekly television show and you'll see that her ministry is firmly Bible-based, but meet her on the street and you'd be unlikely to guess that she's a preacher.

The meteoric rise of White's church and the dominance of megachurches on the American religious landscape seemed to signal the demise of the fundamentalist churches I grew up attending. I decided to find out if that was indeed the case by returning to see what had become of my home church and to visit some of the institutions that have played the greatest role in transforming evangelical Christianity into the powerful force it is today.

The washed-out logo that greets visitors to Grace Community Church in Lake Forest, California, is a harbinger of the changes that have taken place inside the sanctuary's walls. The mountains, cross, fish, seagull, sun, and sea once painted in vibrant hues are now faded to dusty pastels. The upper parking lot, built more than twenty years ago to accommodate the line of cars that backed up onto the road-way as their drivers waited patiently to find a space before one of the two jam-packed Sunday services, now sits almost empty. The sand-colored adobe is stained, the paint on the white gazebo peeling.

I slip my car into an empty spot right in front of the main entrance—a near impossibility when I attended this church in the 1970s and 1980s. I expect to see clusters of people chatting on the paved area between the main building and the Sunday school class-rooms, even though the service started several minutes ago. Instead, a lone woman opens an umbrella as she makes her way to the parking lot on this gray, drizzly morning. Inside, the seats that were once filled with forty-somethings and their teenage children are primarily occu-pied by senior citizens listening to a seemingly inexperienced pastor preaching an uninspiring sermon. Several dozen interlocking chairs with brown padded seats are stacked in an unused wing, superfluous.

My family moved from New York to Orange County, California, in 1974, just in time to catch the crest of the wave that was the Jesus People movement, a revival of artists, intellectuals, and hippies who had come to live along the beaches of Southern California. Their look may have been countercultural, but the doctrines they espoused were anything but. They took their disillusionment with society and zeal for change and applied it to traditional Christianity, creating a radical, relevant new form of worship. The movement helped revital-ize even those churches into which these long-haired hippies would never dare set foot.

Grace Community belonged in the latter category. It was founded in the mid-1970s when the pastor of the Presbyterian church we attended left to start his own, doctrinally conservative, nondenominational church. At first the membership consisted of just a handful of families who met in each other's homes. In a pat-tern common to independent churches, the congregation quickly got too big for that and began meeting in the local high school, where it continued to grow rapidly. After a few years the church was successful enough to buy a plot of land and break ground on a building of its own.

This start-up fundamentalist church struck me as an odd choice for my immigrant parents when I first started reflecting upon my religious upbringing. My father is Egyptian, from a Coptic—or Orthodox Christian—family, although his mother took him as a child to a Presbyterian church. He left Egypt after Gamal Abdel-Nasser rose to power and made life difficult for Copts, and moved to Amsterdam, where he met my mother. My mother attended a Dutch Reform church when she was growing up. When my parents moved to New York shortly after getting married, church was a matter of convenience—they went to whichever happened to be nearby. First it was Dutch Reform, then a Presbyterian church, where I also went to preschool. When I started kindergarten, they put me in Catholic school. They didn't strongly identify with any particular brand of Christianity. After we moved to Southern California in 1974, they started going to a Presbyterian church that was near our house. When the pastor left to start his own congregation, they liked him enough to follow him to Grace Community. As I thought about it more, though, their decision to enter into this fundamentalist world began to make sense. My mother has talked about being drawn to a spiritual experience that is immediate and personal—a distinguishing feature of evangelical Christianity—and my father grew up with a very strict interpretation of scripture similar to Grace's theological vision, which included a literal reading of the Bible.

Grace lay somewhere toward the fundamentalist end of the evangelical spectrum, though not as far in that direction as the school I attended. My Southern Baptist school, which was modeled after Bob Jones University, was even more socially and theologically conservative than Grace. My parents sent me there because they were worried that if they sent me to the public school in Dana Point, the surfer town we'd moved to, I'd wind up using drugs, and Capistrano Valley

Christian School was the nearest private school. The Wednesday morning chapel services there were mostly forgettable, but there are some that cling stubbornly to my memory, such as the annual screenings of *A Thief in the Night*, a classic end-time film made in 1972 that left me with nightmares for years. The story line is similar to that of the blockbuster Left Behind series, starting with the rapture—the moment when born-again Christians are whisked away to meet Jesus in the heavens—and continuing to the rise of the Antichrist and persecution of all those who refuse to take the mark of the beast, 666. The screenings of *A Thief in the Night* (and eventually of its sequels, *A Distant Thunder* and *Image of the Beast*) always ended with an altar call, in which we were invited to come to the front of the auditorium and accept Christ as our savior to ensure we'd be raptured when the time came. Kids flooded forward, year after year.

The fun didn't end there. We were also treated to a yearly showing of the pro-life propaganda flick *Silent Scream*, a twenty-eight-minute film that documents an actual abortion. At one point the doctor holds the feet of an aborted fetus between his fingers, an image so indelibly seared on my psyche that decades later when my husband and I were choosing birth announcements I could hardly look at the one with the two little footprints. Other services featured someone playing Led Zeppelin's "Stairway to Heaven" backward so we could hear the phonograph hiss "Sssssatan, Ssssatan."

Those early days at Grace were heady, exciting ones. The Jesus People movement had broken through as a national phenomenon, Bible-based, nondenominational churches were popping up everywhere, and fundamentalists were developing a voice in the political arena. Grace was growing at a healthy pace, and its members were united in the stimulating work of starting something new. It wasn't long before they were adding services, Bible studies, and youth events. By the time I left for college a decade later, Grace was vibrant and well established.

I have only dim memories of my early childhood years at Grace, but I recall my junior high and high school years vividly. As with many evangelical churches, Grace had a lively youth program that filled up our social calendars. We had Wednesday night Bible studies, sleepovers at the youth pastor's house, and the requisite camping trips. I remember making s'mores on an overnight at the beach and examining scorpions during a trip to the mountains. I recall my times at Grace as happy ones, but as I grew older I struggled to conform to its strictures. When I went away to college and left the shelter of Grace and Christian school behind, I met for the first time people who were smart, ambitious, and driven and who didn't believe what I believed. I realized I didn't know which of those beliefs were truly mine and which I had simply inherited, and that sorting them out would be a messy, painful business, so I turned my back on all of it. In the end, leaving the church was a relief.

The Grace I found on this return visit was a faded reminder of more dynamic days, which was probably to be expected. Grace's current state is the same as that of fundamentalist Christianity as a whole. The churches that are thriving these days are certainly not the ones that focus on the "don'ts" of Christianity, as Grace did, but rather the inclusive evangelical churches that stress the doctrine of God's love. These successful churches adapt to modernity rather than shun it and draw on a characteristic of American evangelicalism that historian Mark Noll calls "culturally adaptive biblical experientialism." It's a tradition that predates the Declaration of Independence. In the early eighteenth century, British actor-turned-evangelist George Whitefield used the skills he had learned as a young thespian to woo huge crowds. He also crossed racial and socioeconomic lines, preaching to anyone from Native Americans to British-born bluebloods and was deliberate in his efforts to speak to slaves. From that point on, American evangelicals have continued to adapt to cultural trends, including learning how to popularize the Gospel and how to use technology to disseminate their message.

That tendency to engage the larger culture on its own terms lay largely dormant for much of the twentieth century. It showed stirrings of life beginning as early as the 1960s, but Paula White's church and the ascendancy of evangelical Christianity as a whole are indications that it has reemerged in full force. How did the more moderate face of evangelical Christianity triumph over its isolationist fundamentalist counterpart, and what does that victory ultimately mean? A handful of churches had been instrumental in changing the look of evangelical Christianity. They made the church more casual in its approach and deinstitutionalized it; they infused it with the vernacular of the self-help movement and led it to abandon many of the trappings of organized religion, all in a bid to become more appealing to outsiders. I decided to visit those influential churches to see how they had helped transform the evangelical world. My journey began with a short trip up California's I-5.

CALVARY CHAPEL: COME AS YOU ARE

It's a perfect Southern Californian evening in early September and nearly a hundred people have clambered over a sandstone promontory onto a crescent of sand in Corona Del Mar known as Pirate's Cove. Newport Harbor is visible in the distance as late-summer's amber sun hangs above the horizon. The band sets up while kids climb on the rocks and explore the caves that line this secluded, waveless beach. Eventually the lead guitarist starts strumming and the crowd joins in. "Sing praise, sing praise," they croon, swaying and holding their arms in the air while toddlers giggle gleefully and dart in and out of the ocean.

After a few songs the serious business starts. A handful of pastors wade waist-deep into the gently lapping waters as dozens of people line up on the shore. They have come to be baptized, to declare their commitment to Jesus Christ with their friends and families as witnesses. For some this is the first time, for others this is a rededication of their lives. After they are dipped, the newly consecrated emerge, dripping, from the salty water, some smiling, others tearful, into the embrace of their loved ones who are waiting at the water's edge. From where the audience stands the quiet conversations and prayers going on in the water are inaudible. It's a mysterious, intimate rite. As dusk darkens the sand is dotted with clusters of euphoric people congratulating each other and taking pictures. It reminds me of the aftermath of a graduation ceremony.

These baptisms are still a ritual here, though the numbers have dwindled since Calvary Chapel's founding pastor, Chuck Smith, began them more than thirty years ago. Back then it was surfers and hippies who had migrated south from Haight-Ashbury who were being dunked into the sea, many hundreds at a time. In his book *Harvest*, Smith writes that in a two-year period in the mid-1970s more than eight thousand people were baptized in the waters off this short stretch of sand. These beach baptisms were such a phenomenon that *Time* magazine included a photograph of them in its 1971 cover story on the Jesus revolution.

Beach baptisms are just one of many ways churches have taken their business into the places where people live and work. Smith helped deinstitutionalize religion and made worship something people could incorporate into their everyday lives, not just something they dabbled in for an hour or two on Sunday morning. Pastor Chuck, as he is called, is considered one of the godfathers of the Jesus People movement that began in the late 1960s and reinvigorated evangelicalism, and his influence on the way people worship is evident today in nearly every evangelical church in America.

The birth of the Calvary movement sounded an early death knell for the isolationist tendencies of fundamentalists because it pushed Christians to engage people in their own language and on their own terms. The atmosphere at Calvary evolved out of Smith's own background as a pastor in the charismatic Foursquare Church, started in 1922 by Aimee Semple McPherson after she'd had a vision from God. Charismatic churches are those, generally speaking, that embrace the "gifts of the Holy Spirit," which include speaking in tongues and healing, and they tend to have a participatory style of worship, with clapping and hand raising. Smith took what he liked from the Foursquare Church and created a new, nondenominational mode of worship, which eventually spawned so many offshoots that it became its own pseudodenomination. Smith took over Calvary Chapel in Costa Mesa, California, in 1965 when the struggling church had just twenty-five members and seemed on the verge of closing. Just two years later the congregation numbered more than two thousand and soon Calvary was spawning offshoots. Today there are more than five hundred affiliate churches globally, and more than thirty-five thousand people call Calvary Chapel Costa Mesa their home church.

Many megachurches today are nondenominational, either in name or in fact, but at the time Smith started at Calvary, the mainline denominations were still dominant. Evangelicals now move freely between churches of different denominations and also between churches with no denominational affiliation.

Calvary initiated the praise-and-worship movement that culminated in the singing sessions and Christian band performances that now launch the services in evangelical churches across the country. When I was growing up we still read from hymnals and sang songs that had been written more than a century earlier. Today, the vast majority of evangelical churches sing contemporary songs, the lyrics of which are usually projected on screens behind the lectern. Music was so important to Calvary that Smith helped found a record label, Maranatha! Music, which recorded and distributed albums made by the bands that regularly performed at the church. Maranatha! gave birth to today's multimillion-dollar Christian music industry.

When I was a teenager and didn't want to go to church with my parents, I would occasionally attend services at what was then my local Calvary Chapel in Dana Point—now run by Chuck Smith Jr. I remember being struck by how different it was from Grace Community. Services at Grace began with traditional hymns; at Calvary the music was contemporary, usually a selection of Christian ballads with something with a harder beat thrown in. Xeroxed sheets with the lyrics were handed out before services so everyone could join in. At Grace, people stood rigidly in front of their seats while they sang, an occasional sway the biggest display of expression one would see. At Calvary, people moved around, closed their eyes, held their arms in the air, and even spoke in tongues. As a teenager, my well-scrubbed sensibilities were taken aback at such free-spirited displays. Now, the culture of Calvary Chapel has been so widely adopted by evangelical Christianity that such manifestations are commonplace even in much more conservative churches.

Smith didn't have such a long view when he started out. He didn't even intend to minister to the era's dispossessed youth when he first took over the tiny church in Costa Mesa—far from it. "Actually, at the time of the hippie movement, these long-haired, bearded, dirty kids going around the streets repulsed me," Smith wrote in the fall 1981 issue of *Last Times,* a Calvary publication. "They stood for everything I stood against. We were miles apart in our thinking, philosophies, everything."

But Smith and his wife, Kay, couldn't stop thinking about the flower children and how they could reach them. They'd drive to Huntington Beach or Laguna Beach and watch the hippies walking up and down the streets and pray for them. Eventually, through a young man their daughter was dating, they met a hippie who had become a born-again Christian. "I wasn't prepared for the love that came forth from this kid," Smith wrote. "His love for Jesus Christ was infectious. The anointing of the Spirit was upon his life, so we invited Lonnie [the young man] to stay with us for a few days." He invited a few friends, and soon the Smith household was overrun with newly converted hippies. With their rebellion against the establishment and materialism of their parents' generation, the youth of the sixties were seeking a transcendent experience, making religious revival an unexpected but natural outgrowth of the decade's upheaval. Some of these countercultural revolutionaries turned to drugs, others to spiritual exploration through transcendental meditation and Eastern religions, but many found the fulfillment they were looking for by entering into intimate, personal relationships with Jesus Christ. Smith was moved by the zeal with which they embraced their newfound religion and through them began to understand the disillusionment that had gripped their generation.

Smith didn't want to send the kids back to the drug-ridden pads they'd come from, so he rented a two-bedroom house for the youth who had moved from getting high on drugs to getting "high on Jesus," as they put it. By the end of the first week there were twenty-one kids living there. A week later there were thirty-five of them. The house was so crowded that someone was even sleeping in the bathtub. The numbers continued to grow and soon they had houses all over Orange County and the surrounding areas. It wasn't long before there was a network of these houses growing as quickly as the Calvary Chapel church itself.

Smith took the church well beyond the building's four walls and Sunday morning service to address people's physical concerns in addition to their spiritual ones. While there is considerable precedence for the church's focus on material needs in American evangelical history—the Salvation Army is but one example of an evangelical organization with a service mandate—Smith can be seen as beginning the return to practical outreach programs. Smith's orientation toward service was reinforced by the very people he was helping. As the countercultural youth became Christians and part of the church body, they brought with them a sensitivity to concerns such as the civil rights movement and the plight of the underclass. Smith's legacy is manifest today in churches that do things like build affordable housing and offer drug rehabilitation programs.

Smith was also one of the first to embrace the casual come-as-you-are Christianity found in most evangelical churches today. His was the original aloha-print shirt, which has become the unofficial uniform for pastors, although he himself was a traditional man who traded in short sleeves for a suit and tie on Sunday morings. In one often told story, someone in the church who had grown sick and tired of the mess left by the scores of unwashed long-haired kids turning up each Sunday posted a sign prohibiting bare feet as a means of keeping them out. Smith tore the sign down and said that if the church needed to rip up the carpeting and put in cheap folding chairs so the kids could come, that's what they would do. That willingness to accept people as they are ran contrary to the ethos that prevails in many churches. "Often, in American evangelicalism, what people want to do is clean up people first to bring them to church, rather than save them," says Bob Wenz, vice president of national ministries at the National Association of Evangelicals. "Chuck Smith brought a profound example of a church that really embraces the disaffected and the unchurched who don't fit the typical Sunday morning evangelical stereotypes of the fifties and sixties. He got rid of dress codes, he didn't worry about hair lengths, he didn't worry about guys who came with tattoos and body piercings and all those kinds of things." In most churches today people feel comfortable attending Sunday services in anything from jeans to suits, allowing those who don't want to dress up on the weekends or who don't own fancy clothing to participate. By eliminating the dress code, Smith enabled people to better integrate their church lives with the rest of their lives.

Calvary was also an early adopter of the anti-intellectual element that's found in many churches today, when a seminary degree is no longer a prerequisite for taking the pulpit. A suspicion of secular intellectualism is a legacy of fundamentalism, but an extensive network of Bible colleges and seminaries turned out a class of clergy that was well schooled in the intricacies and original languages of the Bible. Calvary lessened the importance of education. "I know of only one pastor of a large Calvary Chapel here in California who has, I believe, two advanced degrees, one seminary degree and a doctorate," says Ron Enroth, a sociology professor at Westmont College and one of the first academics to write about Calvary. "That's very, very unusual."

GOD WANTS YOU TO LIVE THE GOOD LIFE: POSSIBILITY THINKING

The dominant voice in evangelical Christianity today is decidedly kinder and gentler than the one I grew up with—and it sounds a lot like that of the Reverend Robert Schuller, the spiritual granddaddy of the seeker-sensitive church. Schuller started preaching his soothing message in the mid-1950s from the tar-paper roof of the snack bar at a drive-in movie theater in Garden Grove, California. He had been sent by his denomination to open a new church in Orange County, but with only five hundred dollars in assets he had to be inventive in his thinking about where to meet. So, adapting to the culture of California, he went to the people where they lived—in their automobiles. On the first Sunday he held services, one hundred people pulled their cars into the Orange Drive-In and rolled down their windows to hear him speak.

His message was as inventive as his location. Schuller borrowed liberally from Dr. Norman Vincent Peale, the famed pastor of Marble Collegiate Church in New York City who wrote *The Power of Positive Thinking,* a twentieth-century self-help classic. Even before he penned that volume in 1952, Peale was marrying psychiatry and psychotherapy with religion and spirituality. In 1937 he and Dr. Smiley Blanton started the Freudian- and Jungian-steeped Blanton-Peale Institute in the basement of Marble Collegiate. Schuller adapted Peale's approach and invented a doctrine of "possibility thinking" that blended the self-help movement with Christianity. His son and successor, Robert Schuller II, describes "possibility thinking" as "not only thinking positive thoughts but making positive plans." One of Schuller's primary objectives was to help people feel good about themselves. He wrote books with uplifting titles such as *God's Way to the Good Life*, *You Can Become the Person You Want to Be*, *Peace of Mind Through Possibility Thinking*, and *Self-Esteem: The New Reformation*. Schuller changed the lexicon of the evangelical church and his legacy can be seen in the feel-good, make-your-life-work-better sermons that have become pervasive.

Schuller opened the door to the liberal use of pop psychology and the self-help format that many of today's pastors rely on to draw the wounded and needy to evangelical Christianity. It's the same language that Oprah and Dr. Phil speak, with a good measure of God thrown in. If you remove references to Jesus, many of the books written by today's superstar pastors are tough to distinguish from their secular counterparts, which makes them palatable even to people outside the church and thus widens their sphere of influence. "Some people would say [Schuller] is really on the edge of what's appropriate evangelicalism," said Edith Blumhofer, director of the Institute for the Study of Evangelicals at Wheaton College. And yet, Schuller's influence can be seen in many respected evangelical works today, including the best-selling book by pastor Joel Osteen, *Your Best Life Now*. With chapter titles such as "Enlarging Your Vision," "Developing a Prosperous Mindset," and "Happiness Is a Choice," Osteen, like Schuller, preaches a motivational message of positive Christianity and suggests that we allow ourselves to be limited by our own thoughts and attitudes. To achieve all that God wants for us, the two men argue, we have to be able to envision ourselves living that enriched life. The two preachers share a Christian version of creative visualization that holds that it's not enough to wait for God to work in your life; if you have a dream or a goal you have to be willing to take the initiative and, putting faith in God, take a first step toward attaining it. As Osteen puts it in his book: "If you don't think you can have something good, then you never will. The barrier is in your mind. It's not God's lack of resources or your lack of talent that prevents you from prospering. Your own wrong thinking can keep you from God's best."

Schuller and Peale may have brought the touchy-feely approach to twentieth-century churches, but the inclination toward self-analysis and self-growth is hardwired into this ruggedly individualistic country's DNA. America was founded on the decidedly un-European notion that an individual's rights supersede those of a group or institution, and ever since we Americans have been wearing our emotions on our sleeves. A focus on self is permitted here to a degree not generally accepted in other cultures. We weren't only home to the "me generation," we are a "me country," reliant on motivational books and therapists' couches. The impulse has been around as long as the republic—Benjamin Franklin's *Autobiography* is an early example of the self-help genre, in which he set out to show how a person could improve his or her life and character through constant self-assessment.

That focus on one's deficiencies dovetails well with the message of Christ. Many evangelicals first explored the Gospel because they felt broken and were looking to be healed. Schuller's emphasis on empowerment appeals directly to people's felt needs. He, like many in evangelical Christianity, melds American therapy culture with something much more enduring, an eternal God. The therapeutic element in evangelical Christianity is, again, a demonstration of cultural adaptation and was well evident by the late-nineteenth century when preacher Henry Ward Beecher sprinkled his sermons with motivational messages.

That both Schuller and Smith were based in Southern California is not surprising. The area has been the birthplace of many of the new movements in evangelical Christianity. With its spread-out exurban communities and long solitary car commutes, nowhere is the alienation of modern life more evident. It's also made up of a transitory population that, like my family, migrated west in search of opportunity and better weather and is cut off from families and religious traditions. The church was where my mother found her new friends when we moved to California and it gave her a place to focus her energies, an experience typical of transplants to the exurbs.

Schuller further disseminated his ideas through his Institute for

Successful Church Leadership, which educated other pastors. "We were the original seeker church," Schuller II says. Seeker churches rely on advertising and other marketing tactics to lure people who otherwise probably would not go to church. "When we first started our ministry it was very, very modern, contemporary. It was the hippest thing around. What happened then, my father's teaching in the Institute was picked up by [megachurch pastors] Bill Hybels and Rick Warren and I could name probably fifty other guys."

"His was the first church I had ever seen that was unashamedly focused toward reaching nonchurched people," Bill Hybels told me. "In the church I grew up in everything was to reinforce the already convinced. Here Schuller builds a church and redesigns almost everything on his campus and at his services to make it visitor friendly and to put the message at a level that a first-timer could understand its relevance."

Schuller's sell-'em-what-they-want attitude was evident in a conversation recounted by Calvin Tomkins in his 1977 *New Yorker* profile of architect Philip Johnson, who at the time was designing the building that became Schuller's Crystal Cathedral in Garden Grove, California. "We don't call them 'penitents,' Philip. We call them 'new seekers,'" Schuller told Johnson. Tomkins also pointed out that Schuller "likes to say that he is in the business of retailing religion, and he describes the church that he commissioned Richard Neutra to build as 'a twenty-two-acre shopping center for Christ.'" The retailing analogy is apt—evangelical Christianity is all about selling Jesus Christ to people who don't necessarily know they need him—and one that has caught on both in substance and in form. Televangelists and pastors share the urgent, insistent techniques of telemarketers (the mop with the telescoping handle that's just $19.99 if you act now and the free gift of eternal life are both limited-time offers), and megachurches everywhere have come to resemble shopping centers, with their clusters of buildings surrounded by seas of asphalt parking lots. Churches are stand-ins for the mall, which in its own turn replaced the town square as the hub of centralized convenience, a single place where a person can drop off the kids for some fun, grab a snack and a cup of coffee, chat with the members of her community (in exurbia, this is as close as many get to community), buy a book or two and, in the sermon, get some practical information for living one's life.

Once again drawing on a long evangelical tradition, the elder Schuller was a pioneer in the use of the media. He started transmitting the *Hour of Power* broadcast of his weekly service (tagline: "God loves you and so do I!") in 1970, taking note of every little detail. "We have several things that we have started, things you won't find written down in any religious history books," the younger Schuller says. "One of the things we started was gray robes. Prior to our *Hour of Power* nobody wore anything but black robes . . . The reason we did it was for television. [Black] just looked too stark for television." By 1980, when Schuller dedicated the three-thousand-seat church that Johnson built for him, the *Hour of Power* had a viewership of more than 3 million. The television show was all the more awe-inspiring with Johnson's dazzling Crystal Cathedral as a backdrop, a four-pointed star built of latticed steel and ten thousand panes of mirrored glass. At the time of his retirement in 2006, the white-haired, avuncular Schuller had the largest Sunday morning audience of any preacher on TV, with an international broadcast audience of 30 million in 156 countries.

The Crystal Cathedral looms over a cultural and aesthetic wasteland that sits in the crook of the intersection of I-5 and I-22, just a few miles from Disneyland. The arrival of such a notable architectural addition to the landscape was not widely welcomed—at least not in the Christian community. In the dour fundamentalist circles I grew up in, the 14-million-dollar project was roundly criticized for its lavish audacity, with Schuller's many detractors (his portrayal of a beneficent, loving God was not yet a popular one) arguing he could have better spent the money by giving it to the poor. At the time the project was seen as crass and commercial, though in comparison with today's megachurches, with their lakes and gyms and video games and playgrounds and volleyball pits, the Crystal Cathedral looks almost modest.

I was still carrying a bit of acquired distaste when I went to visit the Crystal Cathedral for the first time. It was a scorching hot summer day and the two ninety-foot retracting doors behind the pulpit were closed so the searing winds wouldn't blow in. But even without an open wall, the building was airy and filled with light. Johnson initially had balked at building a transparent structure that would look out onto an ugly parking lot and rows of cars. "I want God in the cars, because that's where *they* are," Schuller insisted. Staying true to the church's roots, an area of the parking lot is outfitted with transmitters for people who want to listen to the sermon in their cars.

Far from what I expected, the sanctuary is not gaudy, but inspiring and uplifting, and its sparkling openness compels visitors to look heavenward toward the 128-foot glass ceilings. One gets a hint of the wonder that must have filled thirteenth-century visitors to Chartres cathedral. But where the soaring ceilings and magnificent stained-glass windows of gothic architecture were tempered by the cold austerity of the stone structure, modern engineering has freed the Crystal Cathedral from such constraints and allows the entire edifice to be transparent. The heavier material, namely, the honey-colored wood used for the ends of the pews, the organ, and throughout the auditorium lends a sensation of warmth. Palm and ficus trees are planted liberally throughout, creating a garden ambience. On bright days congregants are bathed in sunlight. The feeling is nothing short of idyllic. And despite housing one of the five largest pipe organs in the world, a seventeen-foot-tall gold-leaf cross, a rose-granite altar, and a fountain, the sanctuary cannot be called garish.

Schuller occupies a curious place in the world of evangelical Christianity. His Institute for Successful Church Leadership counts among its graduates some of the biggest names in the movement, including Bill Hybels, Rick Warren, leadership guru John Maxwell, and megachurch pastor Kirbyjon Caldwell. But despite a statement of faith on the Crystal Cathedral's Web site that hits all the major points, many evangelicals don't count Schuller among their ranks because they feel he isn't doctrinally conservative enough—although he considers himself one of them. They dislike his willingness to embrace nonevangelicals and his statements that we are all God's children, and feel that his loving message dilutes the critical tenet that we are all sinners and require redemption through Christ. Yet Bill Hybels credits Schuller as having had a bigger impact on his church than any other figure in Christianity, and the seeds for the obfuscation of both doctrine and denomination in today's evangelical world were sown at the Crystal Cathedral.

Internecine squabbles aside, even those who object to Schuller's doctrine acknowledge that he was one of the primary influences on today's seeker-friendly movement. "I credit Robert Schuller as the key person to have orchestrated this previously unimaginable change in evangelical Christianity," wrote pastor Bob DeWaay. "It was Schuller's bold move, beginning in 1955, to integrate the positive-thinking philosophy of Norman Vincent Peale with savvy, business-oriented marketing techniques." By considering the way people live and reaching out to them on their own ground, Schuller brought the church into the world where the rest of America is.

WILLOW CREEK: CHURCH FOR THE UNCHURCHED

In the mid-1970s, roughly the same time that Grace Community was born, a twenty-one-year-old man named Bill Hybels went knocking on doors in Palatine, Illinois, to find out why church attendance had fallen. Some people told him church was irrelevant to their lives, others said it was boring, some complained about judgmental pastors, and still others grumbled that churches were always asking for money.

Hybels set out to start a church that would address those grievances and bring people back to God. So for the next six years he held services in a local movie theater that were designed to appeal to

"Unchurched Harry and Mary" and helped launch the seeker-sensitive movement of churches that eschew overtly religious language and symbolism so as not to scare off potential converts. In a then-groundbreaking format that expanded the Calvary model and has since become a template for churches around the country, Hybels began his services with contemporary, sometimes secular, music and included skits, artistic performances, and multimedia slide shows. They required little mental effort from the audience.

Hybels's experiment was the spark for the megachurch movement. Today, Willow Creek Community Church occupies a huge, swanky campus in South Barrington, Illinois, that includes a lake and acres of parking lots. The church has six thousand members and is attended by twenty thousand people each week. It also has influenced the more than 10,500 other churches that are members of its Willow Creek Association.

Despite the now-obvious appeal, other Christians didn't initially approve of Hybels's methods. "People on both sides of us on the continuum were suspicious," he told me during a visit to Willow Creek. "People on the liberal side were quite concerned that we were too Bible oriented, that we were trying to lead people into a personal relationship with Jesus Christ, we took heaven and hell seriously, we took the issues of scripture so seriously I think the liberals were saying, 'Hey, loosen up.' And yet the fundamentalists saw our use of the arts and our relevant communicating style and they were worried that maybe we were being too superficial or not serious enough about things of scripture because of our methodology."

Willow Creek doesn't fall particularly far toward the liberal end of the evangelical spectrum in theological terms, but it is antifundamentalist by virtue of its inclusiveness and modernity. Whereas fundamentalists traditionally live in a parallel universe with institutions that mirror secular ones, Willow Creek believes not only in going out into the non-Christian world but in inviting those non-Christians into its own world, allowing a cross-pollination of ideas and influence.

By making his church nonthreatening and undemanding, Hybels

gave people a place where they could feel good about going to church, rather than judged or inadequate. Willow Creek and other megachurches like it are appealing places, even for those not particularly interested in religion. For starters, they offer free child care. People are always looking for a safe place for their kids to hang out—especially by Sunday morning when they've been home for half the weekend. Parents worry about what their children are being exposed to, and youth programs like those at Willow Creek provide wholesome entertainment. And in an exurban society where people spend hours in their cars each week isolated from one another, an inviting church like Willow Creek offers a sense of community to people who otherwise have none. It's no coincidence that the states with the most megachurches are California and Texas, the country's largest and among the most sprawling.

The visual language of Willow Creek has become standard in the modern megachurch, where the church building has been neutralized and desanctified. Visitors begin by driving in to a huge parking lot and most likely are directed to a spot by a church volunteer. The feel is that of a business complex in an industrial park. At Willow Creek one enters through double glass doors into a wide atrium; in warmer parts of the country, such as California and Florida, the buildings tend to be freestanding and public spaces are in the open air. Willow Creek's lobby features a huge water wall whose soothing sounds dampen any din created by the thousands of people walking through the area. This central space is a conduit to Dr. B's Café, a cozy Starbucks-style coffee shop named for Hybels' mentor Dr. Gilbert Bilezikian. There is a guest-services booth, a main auditorium, a smaller auditorium, and an activity center that houses Seeds bookstore and a cafeteria where people can watch the service on TV monitors while they eat. There are seating areas with comfy chairs throughout the complex. Unlike many megachurches, Willow Creek doesn't have an ATM in the lobby because they don't want people to feel pressured to give money during the offering (evangelical churches survive on members' tithes—the Bible commands Christians to give

10 percent of their earnings back to God). The 7,200-seat auditorium, while plush, is more subdued than those of some of the other megachurches I have visited. At Willow Creek there are no hymnals, no stained-glass windows, and no visible religious symbols that might be off-putting to the uninitiated; other megachurches have a simple cross hanging behind the pulpit. The architecture and décor are of a style that visitors of all stripes are familiar with. "That's been a strategy since the early days of the church," Cally Parkinson, director of communication services at Willow Creek, tells me. "The auditorium—we don't call it a sanctuary—and its surroundings are designed intentionally to resemble more of a college campus than a traditional church."

Similarly, the scale of the complex puts guests at ease: It's spread out enough that newcomers don't feel like outsiders among clusters of people who all know each other, but not so rambling as to make them feel lost. Even during services people can be found sipping lattes at Dr. B's or perusing the shelves of the bookstore and are never made to feel that they *should* be somewhere else, like in the auditorium or at a Bible study. It's an easy place to hang out. The smiles aren't too big, the greetings aren't too warm. The down-to-earth attitude feels more authentic than forced.

Sensitivity to individual reactions has been another trademark of American evangelical Christianity since this country's earliest days. In Europe where each nation had a state church, ministers didn't have to compete for a crowd. But with no official religion, worshippers in America have many options, so preachers need to be conscious of individual reactions—which is why American services have always tended to be light on theological sophistication and heavy on practicality. That's even truer in the present-day evangelical world, where institution and denomination are of little importance and people change congregations freely. Given that, churches need to be responsive to worshippers' preferences and it is usually the pastor who draws people to a particular church, not the institution itself. All of the churches highlighted here and, indeed, the preponderance of in-

fluential megachurches today are presided over by a charismatic figure and are built, to a large degree, on a cult of personality.

The Sunday of my visit to Willow Creek, the service included a
visit from Stephen Baldwin, a member of the famous clan of actors
who became a Christian and turned evangelist. Baldwin was now
touring the country promoting his skateboard ministry, Livin' It,
and recounting the story of how he found Jesus Christ. After the requisite singing, Hybels, clad in his usual button-down shirt and khaki
pants and looking more like a Silicon Valley executive than a member
of the clergy, took the podium to deliver his message. In the popular
style inspired by Schuller, it was as much self-help and how-to as it
was sermon, a primer on communicating with teenagers with a measure of God thrown in. Sunday morning services are not intended to
be grist for the spiritual mill but rather "an introduction to the basic
truths of the Christian faith," according to the literature handed out
at the service. For real spiritual nourishment, the church encourages
people to attend one of the many meetings held throughout the
week. Serious Willow Creek members no longer bother to show up
on Sunday mornings and instead opt for meatier fare at one of the
church's other services.

Hybels is an engaging and entertaining speaker, not because his
sermons are filled with bells and whistles, but because he seems to
have so much fun doing what he's doing. This particular Sunday he
starts by telling stupid-teenager stories, beginning with the time he
stole a new golf cart the staff had bought the elderly director of his
Christian summer camp. "It's the middle of August, I can't sleep,
I'm in my cabin, I'm about fifteen years old and I get an idea in my
head," he says. "I just can't shake it. I get up, I started getting dressed
and one of my buddies goes, 'What are you doing? It's the middle of
the night—where are you going?' I said, 'I'm going for a ride in that
golf cart.' They were like, 'No way. You are not going to do that.' I
said, 'Yeah, I . . . I . . . I just have to.' We crawl through a window,
fire up the golf cart and go all over the camp, cruising, in the golf
cart. Pitch black. We're having a great time."

Hybels goes on to tell the packed auditorium that he and his co-horts turned the cart around to return it to the maintenance area near the beach when Hybels had another brainstorm. "I thought, I'm going to give these guys a thrill they'll never forget. So I turn and head toward the beach. I've got this thing going almost full speed. I go right out on the pier and I'm going real fast and I think, I'm going to stop right on the edge. But there was some condensation on the dock and I slammed my foot on the brake. We didn't even slow down. Right off the end. Okay?" Hybels continues with the saga. The golf cart sank ten feet down to the bottom of the lake, but his friends managed to get out. "They're like, 'We're dead, we're so dead.' I'm like, 'No, just give me a minute here . . . All we need is a pickup truck and some chains.'" Hybels and his buddies stole a truck, backed it onto the beach, dove down and wrapped chains around the cart, and pulled it out with the truck. They returned the truck, dried off the cart, and went back to bed. "I kid you not," Hybels assures the laughing crowd.

The congregation is right there with Hybels, enjoying his lark. "No one ever found out about that," he confides. "And if you tell . . ." His audience erupts into laughter. As Hybels launches into his next story, he seems momentarily derailed by his own mirth. "I'm laughing just thinking about it," he chuckles. Hybels is having a casual conversation with his audience. Once they are thoroughly entertained, Hybels starts his message, entitled "The Elephant in the Room." "You want to know what the elephant in the room is with a lot of these teenagers?" he asks the crowd rhetorically. "We stopped listening to them." He proceeds to tell parents they should plan fun activities so their kids will want to spend time with them, should give their teenagers space to exert their independence, should ignore the little things like messy rooms and hair lengths. He talks about his own struggles with his son and daughter: "From the time he was in seventh grade to the time he was a freshman in college, his hair was so long he had it in a ponytail. My dad never stopped turning over in his grave. We just never made that a big deal. Seana's room, her bedroom, looked like a landfill. It needed Superfunds from the government to clean up. Finally we decided we're not going to die on that hill. We just asked her to close the door . . . But when it came to things like character, truth telling, integrity in relationships, respect and faith issues, we went to the mat on those every single time. We would die on those hills but not on these other hills . . . gang, be careful. Go to the mat over the right things. Let the law of consequences happen in other things."

The message—with so little overt religious content it's tough to call it a sermon—continues along a common-sense path worthy of Dr. Phil. "Affirm any manifestation of maturity wholeheartedly," Hybels urges. "Catch your kid doing something right. You may have to look for a while . . . Every time your teenage kid makes a wise safety choice or does something right with character or relationships or something about their faith or so, applaud it, celebrate it, say, 'Way to go. I'm so proud of you.'" It's the kind of message that any parent could use. Christian or non-Christian, raising kids is hard—just take a look at the number of child-rearing books available at any bookstore—and raising teenagers is harder. Hybels figured if he could get people in the door by giving them advice they could apply to their own lives, they would eventually be receptive to the other part of his message, the Gospel of Jesus Christ.

It is only near the end of his homily that Hybels delves into the spiritual, but even here he doesn't assume that he is talking to a Christian crowd. "Finally . . . pray fervently. And that's just not a spiritually correct final point, friend," he says. "You want a big elephant in the room with a lot of Christian parents? A lot of Christian parents don't pray for their kids very much." Every church service I have ever attended ended with a prayer, but Hybels treats his closing invocation like it is an idea that just popped into his head. "We're over time and I thought maybe the appropriate way for us to end would just be to pray. Would you stand now and we'll do some praying for our kids?" He sums up with a quick, basic prayer. And that is it. At no point did he open a Bible, quote from the Bible, or even refer to the Bible. At many churches, regulars are distinguished from outsiders by the Bibles they carry. I have at times brought one to church services so as not to be immediately recognized as a nonbeliever. Here at Willow Creek, Bible ownership isn't an issue.

That's one of the main contributions of Willow Creek to evangelical worship today: It taught churches to consider services from the perspective of non-Christians, and that pragmatism is a big part of what fuels the growth of megachurches across the country. It's a point noted by preachers all along the spectrum, from Paula White, who works as a life coach to the powerful and famous, often without ever mentioning Jesus, to Pat Robertson, whose daily news show features diets, fitness tips, and weight-loss challenges.

For better or for worse, Hybels created a new vernacular, the language of the seeker-sensitive church. He took the openness of Calvary and pushed it a step further by cutting way back on religion. "Whether or not people adopt the Willow Creek style fully in their own churches, people feel strongly about it one way or the other," says Blumhofer. "Do churches want to be seeker sensitive, and what does that mean? Do we want not to offend people who come in, or is there something nonnegotiable about the evangelical message?" Hybels's approach stirred controversy among those who felt that he was watering down the message of the Gospel—and many still feel that way—but it's a technique that is widely copied. Ted Haggard, president of the National Association of Evangelicals, sees value in what Hybels has taught the church. "Willow Creek's message to the overall body is, 'Speak in ways that non-Christians can understand. Worship in ways that non-Christians can relate to.' And that is impacting everybody," he says.

SADDLEBACK: PUTTING IT ALL TOGETHER

It's almost Easter, and as I jump out of my car and climb the first of many sets of steps between the parking lot and the sanctuary, the

Southern California sky is a glittering blue. I've been efficiently guided into an empty space by a member of the Parking Ministry making sweeping arm signals and am now trying to make my way past the forces of the Greeting Ministry, whose smiling ranks are welcoming me with the aggressiveness of department store holiday-time perfume spritzers. Finally, I push through one of the many sets of double doors and am directed to a seat—presumably by a member of the Seating Ministry. Worried that I'm late, I'm too rushed to read his name tag.

I needn't have fretted. Though it started several minutes ago, I'm by no means the last one to arrive to this Sunday morning service of Saddleback Church in Lake Forest, California, just a few miles away from Grace Community, the church of my childhood. The service starts with a good dose of Calvary-style music, and people trickle in as the band plays.

Finally, the singing is over, and Rick Warren takes the stage. Warren, America's most famous pastor, is a gifted synthesizer who has blended elements from Schuller, Hybels, and Smith to concoct a church recipe that exemplifies today's brand of evangelical Christianity. Saddleback is friendly and convenient, and offers a sense of community. No longer legalistic, Saddleback, and indeed, the larger world of evangelical Christianity, conforms to the user, rather than demanding adherents adopt a stringent set of rules to live by. Saddleback embodies the best—and sometimes the worst—the evangelical world has to offer. It is built on a formula that is easily franchised, which makes its offspring inherently inorganic. Churches have been created in Saddleback's image hundreds of times under other names by pastors across the country. Warren's sermons, which are available online for other church leaders, hearken back to the early days of *USA Today* in their digestibility. Saddleback has been likened to McDonald's in its transportability.

This Sunday, Warren is flanked by palm trees, clad in the aloha-print shirt trademarked by Chuck Smith, and looking disconcertingly like a Jimmy Buffett fan. He is going to great lengths to convey that he is an ordinary guy, just another one of us. "I don't understand art," he says at one point, taking Calvary's easily accessible anti-intellectualism a step further. "To me art is a picture of Elvis on velvet." Warren's image is projected onto massive screens behind him so he is visible to everyone in the huge worship center, as this, the biggest of Saddleback's multiple-service venues, is called. Saddleback resembles Willow Creek and Calvary in that it has no apparent denominational affiliation. It is, in fact, a member of the Southern Baptist Convention, although Warren himself often obscures the connection.

As he gives his sermon, Warren is careful to appeal to the lowest common denominator, delivering a message that could hardly be called scholarly although, unlike Hybels, Warren reads from and refers to the Bible. But there is no parsing of scripture, no considering the original language, no discussion of the different ways a particular word can be translated. Instead, there are movie clips and self-deprecating jokes. The message is fun and easy to follow. Following Schuller's lead, Warren encourages people to take in his sermon from wherever they are most comfortable. Some people sit outside on plastic lawn chairs, soaking up the sun as Warren is projected to them via video screens and speakers mounted on the outside of the sanctuary (the sermon is even piped in to the restrooms). I see women in dresses and others in running shorts. Kids play on the grass nearby and teenage girls amble past with sodas they've purchased from the café.

Halfway through the service I leave the worship center to wander around the campus and peek into some of the different tents, each of which, over the course of the weekend, has a service in a different style, leaving no potential subgroup overlooked. This is a church where individual choice is sacrosanct and no personal preference need be subjugated to someone else's idea of God. In the main worship center that I just left is "Saddleback Classic . . . full of music and inspiration," according to a brochure from the information center. "Overdrive" in Venue Tent 2 showcases hard rock. "Praise!" in Venue

Tent 3 has Gospel music and more singing, "Unplugged" meets in room 404, and the music is acoustic. "Passion" provides "a more intimate atmosphere and a younger feel," according to the brochure. "Elevation" is the Saturday night singles service. The contemporary music trend that began at Calvary has culminated in a plethora of options here at Saddleback, making attending church an even easier proposition since most people can now come and listen to a good twenty minutes of the kind of music they like.

When the service is over, I explore the 120-acre campus, designed by some of the same people responsible for Disneyland. There are plenty of places to hang out, from the coffee shop to the burger stand next to the sand volleyball courts. Orange County is a sprawling, often superficial place where people smile at each other in the grocery stores but often don't know the name of the person living next door to them. At Saddleback people greet each other warmly and feel they are there for a shared purpose. They have something in common by virtue of attending the same church.

Still, with a population in the tens of thousands, the sense of community is diluted. That's where small groups come in. By joining a group of ten people or so, as everyone here is urged to do, Saddleback's members can forge real intimacy with people who share their interests or circumstances. There's an upside for the church as well. People so emotionally invested are likely to remain, and become more deeply, involved. The thousands who belong to small groups at the church make up a committed army that reaches out into the local community and into the world at large.

It may be fun, but is it church? Is there any spiritual nourishment being offered? Critics of Saddleback and the seeker-friendly movement as a whole say it's too easy, too watered down to provide spiritual sustenance. It is certainly true that Sunday morning services are far from demanding. The first time I went, I brought my Jewish husband, who has never been comfortable inside a church. But after twenty minutes of soaking up the sun on Saddleback's patio, listening to music, and taking in the easy sermon which, that morning, included clips from *Meet the Parents*, he pronounced Saddleback bearable. While that's exactly what Warren and other seeker-friendly pastors are going for, a sermon that is pleasant for my husband is de facto devoid of any strong Christian content.

Of course, even Warren admits that Sunday services aren't particularly weighty—and that, in large part, is the point. Seeker-sensitive churches don't want to do or say anything that could scare away the uninitiated. Sermons are designed to promote growth: They are short and punchy. These churches want to be a place where anyone can feel comfortable. On that front, they succeed. Warren sees church involvement as a progression through a series of concentric circles: community (the unchurched), crowd (regular attendees), congregation (faithful Christians and members), committed (those who are dedicated to growth, i.e. attend small groups), and core (those who actively serve in the church). So for the "community" to be able to make the move to "crowd," the barriers to entry must be quite low—though the committed and core groups are surprisingly large, indicating that the church is quite good at hooking people who wander through its doors.

Criticisms aside, Warren, largely as a result of the fame and funds he obtained as a result of his best-selling books, *The Purpose-Driven Church* and *The Purpose-Driven Life*, has had immense impact on pastors who want to emulate his approach and has considerable access to politicians who want to court his constituency. He has made a massive push into humanitarian work in Africa and around the world that has helped raise awareness of AIDS and global poverty throughout the evangelical community. Warren has become the most visible pastor in America and Saddleback has become, for many, the gold standard of the twenty-first-century church.

It's a formula that has worked time and time again across the country, but also one that many old-school Christians continue to feel threatened by. Some time back, Grace Community imploded when a sizable portion of the congregation and governing body, taken with the phenomenal growth Saddleback was seeing just down the road, wanted to make Grace over in Saddleback's image. Others, though, were less impressed with the casual, easy-going but ultimately insubstantial sermons. Unable to come to an agreement over the direction Grace should take, a sizable chunk of the church left. Many of them are now members of Saddleback.

Saddleback is thriving while Grace stagnates. The conservative brand of Christianity that ruled the day at Grace didn't stand a chance in the face of the kind and loving God who lives at Saddleback, and the fate that met Grace is one that befell fundamentalism as a whole. It's more fun to be a part of society and to take advantage of all it has to offer. The appeal of an isolated Christian existence is waning. The era of the angry fundamentalist is over.

CHAPTER TWO

A Brief History of
Evangelicals in America

I see the destiny of America embodied in the first Puritan who
landed on those shores, just as the human race
was represented by the first man.

A LEXIS DE TOCQUEVILLE wrote those words as part of an explanation for the continued existence of democracy in America, but they apply just as well to a study of evangelical Christianity on these shores and of the dichotomy that has characterized American Christianity for almost as long as it has existed. The Puritans came to America in 1620 to escape persecution for their efforts to scrub ornament, liturgy, and other traces of Catholicism from the Church of England—an inherently isolationist move. When they arrived in America they worked to establish a New World in which their beliefs played a role in every aspect of civic life and culture. The New England colonies came to be known as "Bible Commonwealths," because their laws were based on religious principles.

The Christianity that was planted in New England emphasized biblical supremacy and the sacred relationship between God and the individual. It placed a premium on spiritual renewal and the notion of a living, personal religion—elements that remain hallmarks of evangelical Christianity today. The churches were, for the most part, congregational and under local control, so they were free to evolve as their members wished. By the 1730s the focus on a "true religion of the heart" had so deepened that revivalism had seized the American colonies, having earlier taken hold of the British Isles the settlers had left behind. The Great Awakening, as that period came to be called in America, first broke out in Northampton, Massachusetts, when hundreds of people joined Jonathan Edwards's church. The style of Christianity that we now identify as "evangelical," with its essential new birth experience, emerged during this period.

Edwards's most famous sermon from this time was called "Sinners in the Hands of an Angry God" in which he likened the human situation to that of a spider or other "loathsome insect" being held over a fire, such has God's wrath been provoked by our sinfulness. And yet, he preached, it is God's hand that prevents us from being cast into the fires of Hell, and God who will grant us grace if we turn to him. The scolding and frightening sermon was infused with urgency. Edwards exhorted his listeners to make a decision for Christ at that very moment to spare themselves God's fury, and asked them to consider the transformation they saw evident in the lives of people sitting around them who had already accepted God's love.

The revival was further spread by John Wesley and George Whitefield, whose preaching was also bolstered by the moving accounts that individuals gave of their religious conversions. Indeed, giving one's testimony, the story of how one became a Christian, remains a popular tool in evangelical outreach today. It is common in Christian forums for people to talk about the journey that led them to Christ, much in the same way that alcoholics and drug users tell the stories of their sobriety in support groups. Actor Stephen Baldwin became a Christian several years ago and has been invited by hundreds of churches and gatherings to share the story of how he found Christ.

As we saw in the previous chapter, one of the characteristics of evangelical Christianity in America today is its ability to adapt to the culture around it—a trait that was already evident in the religion's earliest days in this country. During the Great Awakening, Whitefield gave theatrical sermons in England's marketplaces and roamed across the American colonies, earning the titles the Grand Itinerant and the Divine Dramatist. Whitefield had dabbled in acting when he was younger and brought all he had learned on the stage to bear in his preaching. Benjamin Franklin was particularly impressed with Whitefield when he came to Philadelphia, despite their religious differences. "The multitudes of all sects and denominations that attended his sermons were enormous, and it was matter of speculation to me, who was one of the number, to observe the extraordinary influence of his oratory on his hearers, and how much they admir'd and respected him, notwithstanding his common abuse of them, by assuring them that they were naturally half beasts and half devils," Franklin wrote in his autobiography. "It was wonderful to see the change soon made in the manners of our inhabitants. From being thoughtless or indifferent about religion, it seem'd as if all the world were growing religious, so that one could not walk thro' the town in an evening without hearing psalms sung in different families of every street."

Whitefield was an egoist and a shameless self-promoter (not unlike some of today's preachers), but was also unparalleled as an evangelist. He was as concerned with the salvation of slaves and coal miners as he was with that of the rich and powerful. Crowds numbering in the tens of thousands gathered to hear him deliver his messages, and thousands converted. While a great deal of his success can be attributed to his talent for preaching, what truly distinguished him was his ability to adapt to his audience. Whitefield was constantly on the lookout for new ways to share the Gospel and spread the revival.

Edwards had been stunned by the fervency with which the Great Awakening began in Northampton, calling it "a surprising work of God." Whitefield, on the other hand, was more calculating in his approach. For starters, he abandoned the pulpit and went outdoors to where people gathered, enabling him to reach many who wouldn't dream of setting foot inside a church. He shared the Gospel in markets, in open fields, and in coal mines, and tailored his message accordingly. In those settings, Whitefield realized, the traditional method of sermonizing would never be able to hold people's attention, so he preached in a manner that made it difficult to ignore him. He stopped at nothing. He climbed trees. He cried. He embodied biblical characters. As much entertainer as evangelist, he popularized the Bible and targeted people's emotions. Today's megachurch pastors such as Rick Warren and Bill Hybels tear a page straight out of Whitefield's book when they punctuate their sermons with skits and film clips. Whitefield also relied on the media of his day to spread his message, learning how to use the newspapers to get positive publicity and lure even more people to his events. He printed the first of his autobiographical *Journals* when he was only twenty-five years old and two years later launched a monthly newsletter called "Christian History" that reported on his and other revivals. He solicited donations from wealthy individuals to support his efforts.

The Great Awakening inflated the membership of the denominations that embraced it, specifically the Presbyterians, Methodists, and Baptists. But even as souls were being won for the kingdom of God, the Enlightenment and the ideals it embodied were gaining traction both in England and in America. In this new way of thinking, rationality trumped the supernatural and truth was what could be observed or proven. Marx introduced the notion of a secular utopia that didn't depend on God or biblical guidelines, and the idea sparked a revolution. The widespread adoption of these new standards dampened the enthusiasm for evangelicalism. By the end of the eighteenth century there were many people for whom Christian beliefs were no longer of central importance. And yet, evangelicalism in its varied forms remained the unofficial national religion of the Republic and revivals were common occurrences throughout the first half of the nineteenth century. New England became consumed by the Second Great Awakening, while Kentucky fell into the throes of the Great Revival, made up largely of outdoor camp meetings. For the evangelists of the day saving souls was at once a work of spiritual merit and a patriotic act necessary for the survival of this new America.

The great preacher behind the Second Great Awakening was Charles Finney, who in 1836 founded Broadway Tabernacle (known today as Broadway United Church of Christ) in lower Manhattan. Stylistically, Finney borrowed heavily from Whitefield and expanded on his predecessor's methods, at the same time laying the ground-work for modern America's greatest revivalist, Billy Graham. Like Whitefield, Finney used the newspaper to disseminate word of his appearances. Like Graham after him, Finney used music to put peo-ple in an emotional state where they would be open to his message and positioned believers in the crowd who could counsel the newly converted once they had made their decisions for Christ.

This round of spiritual renewal ushered in a wave of social ac-tivism that coalesced around benevolent societies whose primary purpose was creating conditions in which souls could be saved, so, for example, they promoted sobriety through temperance societies and literacy through education groups. In fact, evangelicals were one of the primary forces behind much of the social reform of the day (throughout American history societal advances and retreats have been linked, in some way, to the strength of evangelicals, either di-rectly or inversely). They fought to end slavery; to reform prisons; and to care for the mentally ill, the orphaned, and the handicapped, an agenda that was an explicit rejection of the emphasis on the individual—both in politics and in religion—that had been perva-sive at the turn of the century. Finney shared in the activism of his day as a committed abolitionist who used his sermons to denounce slavery and who refused to administer communion to slave owners.

By the end of the Civil War, the growing Christian community was organized around the entrenched denominations—Methodist, Baptist, Presbyterian, to name but a few—groups that shared a general sense of unity. But even as, on the surface, Protestant Christianity seemed to rule the day, a subtle countertrend of secularism was afoot and the rise of Darwinism was triggering an intellectual crisis. In higher education, for example, most college presidents were still clergymen, but curricula were no longer based on biblical precepts. Society retained a religious veneer and many went to church on Sunday, but religiosity was be-coming less of a factor in people's day-to-day lives.

Those circumstances may have been quietly eroding the core of Protestant Christianity, but outwardly the evangelical community was still vibrant, with a strong emphasis on service and missions. Over the next several decades, evangelicals continued to be concerned with many of the same issues that had been important to the community before the Civil War, such as temperance and literacy, and their agenda came to be known as the social gospel. Rapid industrialization and urbanization had created deplorable conditions in the inner cities, and Christians went into the slums to address the societal ills that were endemic there, while at the same time spreading the word of God. The rescue mission movement was born out of their efforts, which included the founding of the Salvation Army in London in 1865 by Methodist pastor William Booth. By the 1880s that organization was aiding the poor in America as well and populism had emerged as a major political force on these shores. American society was, as a whole, progressive.

Despite the great number of social advances made during this time, a backlash was brewing among evangelicals who felt that the social gospel took attention away from the important task of winning souls for the kingdom of Christ. The roots of this disagreement were political as well as theological, and eventually it deepened into a rift that split Protestant Christianity into two distinct movements. The social-gospel advocates, who were more liberal theologically, adopted liberal politics and emphasized social reform and responsibility; those who were theologically more conservative adopted conservative politics and emphasized revivalism and an individual responsibility for one's own salvation.

One of the ways this fissure was manifest in theological terms was in the area of eschatology, or the interpretation of scripture detailing the end-times, chiefly the book of Revelation and the Old Testament book of Daniel. Speculation about the Second Coming of Christ has always played an important role in the religion; the first Christians believed Jesus would return during their lifetimes. Christians read the book of Revelation in various ways, and a key area of divergence is in the interpretation of what is described as a thousand-year period during which Christ will rule on earth. That millennium has been calculated and recalculated countless times. Saint Augustine in the fourth century understood the Bible to mean that the temporal church represented God's spiritual kingdom on earth and he believed the millennium was a figurative one, a point of view that came to be known as amillennialism. Finney and the social activists of his day were motivated in their efforts by a view called postmillennialism, which held that the reformation of society could usher in the millennium, after which Christ would return. Temperance and blue laws, fighting prostitution, and, most important, banning slavery—all of these reforms were undertaken in the hope that in creating a more godly society they could hasten the Second Coming.

The competing view about the end-times, now dominant among theologically conservative evangelicals, is called premillennialism and holds that Christ will come first to rescue believers from a Godless earth and then, after visiting judgment upon the world, rule for the thousand years mentioned in the Bible. This view gained in popularity as the nineteenth century progressed and Americans strayed further away from spiritual ideals, causing people to lose hope that they could bring about Christ's return through social reform. Premillennialism, while evident in the antebellum period (most notably among the followers of Baptist preacher William Miller, who was popular until the date in 1843 and then the revised 1844 date he predicted for Christ's return passed uneventfully) became more prominent after the Civil War. With premillennialism, Christians didn't need to feel responsible for the moral condition of the world, since Christ's return was no longer linked to the state of society. This allowed them to become more inwardly focused and to emphasize personal salvation rather than their collective responsibility for social progress—a frame of mind that, over time, helped the community skew Republican.

The variation of premillennialism that Americans have become familiar with through apocalyptic entertainment was formulated in England in the 1850s by a pastor named John Nelson Darby, who concocted a complicated system known as dispensational premillennialism. Dispensationalism divided history into ages, or "dispensations." In each, mankind is tested through the provision of a new means of salvation and judged for its failure. The first dispensation is the Age of Innocence, which begins with the creation of Adam and Eve and ends with their expulsion from Eden. Next is the Age of Conscience, which extends until Noah's flood. The third dispensation is the Age of Human Governance, which ends with God punishing man for building the Tower of Babel by introducing different languages. The fourth period, which begins with God's covenant with Abraham, is known as the Age of Promise and ends with Israel's bondage in Egypt. The fifth is the Age of Law, which runs from Moses to Jesus Christ. The death of Christ ushered in the sixth dispensation, the Age of Grace, which is the age in which we are now living. This age will extend until the rapture, the day when Jesus will descend into the sky and believers will be swept up to meet him in heaven. The next dispensation is the Age of Christ, when he will reign for a thousand years.

The rapture and the judgments that will accompany the end of the current dispensation have captured the American imagination. In the 1970s they were the subject of Hal Lindsay's best-seller, *The Late Great Planet Earth,* as well as of the film we watched in my school, *A Thief in the Night.* They were more recently fictionalized to great commercial success in the Left Behind series by Pastor Tim LaHaye and his cowriter Jerry Jenkins. These works of fiction open with the rapture, which triggers a seven-year period known as the tribulation. During the tribulation, the Antichrist will rise to power and institute a single global government and one world religion. Evangelicals have, at times, considered both the United Nations and the European Union possible vehicles for the Antichrist's ascension. Terrible plagues will be visited upon the earth, including famine, locusts, pestilence, and death. There will be a great earthquake, deadly hail, and fire storms, and water will turn to blood. A third of the earth's trees and grass will be destroyed, and a third of the stars will go dark. Burning mountains will plummet into the sea, and the sun will scorch the earth. The Antichrist will be killed and resurrected, after which he will emerge even more powerful and will demand to be worshipped. He will require everyone to take "the mark of the beast," which has been interpreted as the number 666 or some variation thereof. It's generally thought the mark will go either on the hand or on the forehead, and those who refuse it will be sentenced to die. After witnessing the rapture, many people will have become Christians and will refuse the mark in the knowledge that taking it would lead to eternal damnation. But in declining to take the mark these new Christians will condemn themselves to a life of persecution and will be forced to go underground, much like the early Christians. Many of them will become martyrs, but eventually all this will culminate in the battle of Armageddon, at which Jesus will defeat the Antichrist and his armies. Christ will then reign on earth for a thousand years, after which Satan will stage one last unsuccessful uprising and be judged and sent into a lake of fire. Jesus will then establish a new heaven and a new earth and all humanity will face the final judgment. It's pretty fantastical stuff, but very real to evangelical Christians, many of whom believe it will all, literally, come to pass.

Darby devised his complicated system at roughly the same time the horror novel was coming to prominence in England, and both stem from a distrust of reason, science, and the mechanization of society. Both, with their turning to the supernatural or fantastic, were in some part a reaction to the industrial revolution and the Age of Reason. *Frankenstein,* first written in 1818 but better known for the revised version of 1831, was intended as a warning about the hubris of modern man. In *Dracula,* written in 1897, the advances of modernity make it easier for the horrific count to prey on his victims, because people were looking to science for the cause of their affliction, not to the otherworldly. Similarly, it is only by using modern technology that the Antichrist is able to institute his evil plot of world domination. (In another subtle link, LaHaye's Antichrist hails from the Carpathian Mountains, as did Count Dracula.)

The widespread acceptance by evangelicals of Darby's systemization of scripture contributed to their eventual decision to abandon society at large. The escapist aspect of premillennialism provided—and continues to provide—a haven for evangelicals in times of stress. In the mid-nineteenth century it was the rapid societal changes wrought by the industrial revolution that left people feeling nervous. In 1970 when Hal Lindsay again popularized the theories in *The Late Great Planet Earth*, America was in the midst of the cold war and still reeling from a decade that had brought them the Cuban Missile Crisis, cultural revolution, race riots, and the Vietnam War.

Premillennialism was yet another sign of the deepening rift in Protestant Christianity that eventually resulted in the mainline churches placing an emphasis on social morality and the evangelical churches placing it on personal morality. At the time when Darby was writing, that rift was just beginning to crack the community, but it eventually became a chasm that divided fundamentalists and evangelicals for much of the twentieth century. The Christian leaders who adopted and disseminated Darby's teachings were the same men who became the leaders of the Bible institutes that formed the backbone of the network of institutions that would be built by fundamentalists during their eventual withdrawal. These men were strongly against modernism and modernists, particularly those within the church.

The word *fundamentalist* gained its current meaning in the early twentieth century, eventually coming to denote the most conservative and isolationist of evangelicals. The term is derived from a series of twelve pamphlets published in 1909 by oil barons Milton and Lyman Stewart. Entitled "The Fundamentals," the booklets highlighted several doctrines that are essential to conservative Christianity and at the core of fundamentalist theology, including the inerrancy of scripture, the divine nature of Jesus Christ and his virgin birth, the doctrine of substitutionary atonement (the idea that through his death Jesus Christ paid the price of our sins, thereby absolving us of guilt), the authenticity of miracles, the literal resurrection of Christ, and the literal return of Christ. The Stewarts distributed three million free copies of the pamphlets to ministers, missionaries, Sunday school superintendents, and others involved in evangelism.

But fundamentalists didn't emerge as a discrete group until the 1920s. World War I and the Marxist revolution had dramatically changed society, and by the middle of that decade conservative evangelicals felt under siege, a state intensified by the rapid advances and the societal excesses associated with the Roaring Twenties. The tensions between Christians who wanted simply to withdraw from an increasingly secular world and those who wanted to remain a part of it were nearing fever pitch. The antimodernist sentiment was frequently manifested in attacks on Darwinism. By the mid-1920s a handful of southern states had passed laws against the teaching of Darwin's theories, with similar legislation pending in several others. In 1925 Tennessee's statute was tested when a high school teacher named John Scopes was prosecuted for teaching the theory of evolution. The case garnered national attention and both sides pulled out their big guns. The famously eloquent lawyer Clarence Darrow was a member of the defense team and three-time Democratic presidential candidate (this was before the Republican Party had a stranglehold on the fundamentalist constituency) and fundamentalist Christian William Jennings Bryan aided the prosecution. The whole thing was memorialized by the esteemed *Baltimore Sun* journalist, H. L. Mencken, whose paper was also paying part of the defense team's expenses.

Although the antievolutionary forces won the first round in court (the conviction was later overturned on a technicality), in the press and particularly in Mencken's accounts, the trial was reduced to a fight between progressive scientific thought and backward religious forces, with the modernists emerging victorious in the court of public perception. The trial dealt a major setback to the image of fundamentalists, and they reacted by withdrawing from public view and remaining largely disengaged from civic life for several decades.

They may have been hiding in the shadows during their hiatus, but fundamentalists were anything but idle. During their absence from public life—what Pew Forum on Religion and Public Life director Luis Lugo calls "the desert years"—fundamentalists were regrouping and setting up a robust world of their own. They built a dynamic alternate universe by constructing parallel institutions. There are now fundamentalist versions of just about every cultural and societal institution one can imagine, from colleges to publishing houses to grassroots political networks, a great many of which were started during that period. It was from this base that fundamentalists would eventually organize their reincursion, first into politics and eventually into popular culture. As, over time, they have become increasingly evangelical and integrated, so, too, have their organizations. For example, what was once the Bible Institute of Los Angeles (and whose first president was fundamentalist Lyman Stewart) is now simply called Biola University. But all that was still to come—by the 1930s the fundamentalist community, particularly in the North, had completely realigned itself, having moved out of liberal denominations and into more conservative or independent churches.

While they may no longer have been prominent on a national level, fundamentalists continued the all-important work of winning souls. All this time, evangelists were speaking to the faithful through Christian publications, radio, and television, enabling some of them to develop reputations far beyond their local areas and, in cases such as those of Robert Schuller and Oral Roberts, to attain considerable levels of fame even outside the Christian community. The fundamentalists eventually reemerged in the 1970s and 1980s, as we will later see in this chapter, but the divisions that tore apart the greater evangelical community early in the twentieth century have yet to be entirely overcome.

Other developments further fragmented the evangelical community. On January 1, 1901, Agnes Ozman, a student at Bethel Bible College in Topeka, Kansas, began praying in tongues, the heavenly language that many Christians believe is the Holy Spirit speaking through humans, and thus the modern Pentecostal movement was born. (The Holy Spirit is the third member of the Trinity, which includes God the father, Jesus Christ, and the Holy Spirit. It is the latter member of the triumvirate who is a presence in the daily lives of Christians.) Speaking in tongues is one of the gifts of the Holy Spirit, first given to the early Christians when, on the first Pentecost after the resurrection of Christ, the Holy Spirit came down upon the disciples in the form of tongues of fire and they began speaking in a dialect that speakers of all languages could understand. Today, the language of tongues is generally indecipherable except to those with the gift of interpretation, also granted by the Holy Spirit.

The Pentecostal movement blossomed with the Azusa Street revival of 1906, when a Los Angeles gathering led by an African American preacher named William J. Seymour started speaking in tongues. For the next three years the run-down industrial building they met in became a place of pilgrimage. A *Los Angeles Daily Times* story called the event "A Gurgle of Wordless Talk." By the end of 1906, Seymour had incorporated as the Pentecostal Apostolic Faith Movement. Throughout the next decade the gift of speaking in tongues spread to other small denominations. The Assemblies of God was especially touched by this phenomenon.

The practice of speaking in tongues spread to mainline denominations in the 1960s through the Charismatic Renewal. The movement brought the gifts of the Spirit—in particular speaking in tongues and divine healing—into, initially, mainline Protestant churches, whose adherents were generally more educated and more affluent than the Pentecostals. Dennis J. Bennett, the rector of St. Mark's Episcopal Church in Van Nuys, California, sparked the renewal when he began speaking in tongues, along with many of his parishioners. Bennett decided to remain inside the Episcopal Church rather than start a distinct movement as Seymour had, marking one of the primary differences between Pentecostals and Charismatics. Pentecostals tend to have their own denominations in which the gifts of the Holy Spirit play a central role. Charismatics, rather than joining a separate movement, become more Catholic, more Lutheran, etc. and incorporate the spiritual gifts into the traditions to which they belong. When I use the term *charismatic* in this book, I intend it as an umbrella label that encompasses both Charismatics and Pentecostals. I am referring both to an embracing of the gifts of the Holy Spirit, and of a more participatory style of worship in which congregants are more likely to raise their hands and clap.

When speaking in tongues, communication with the divine, which all evangelicals believe in, is tangible. Thus the stress on the individual's relationship with God is even more pronounced in the charismatic tradition. The infusion of charismatic elements into the larger church body also increased the focus on the therapeutic aspects of Christianity and taught that people could look to God for health, happiness, and material success—a doctrine that has been taken to an extreme by today's proponents of the contentious prosperity gospel, which teaches that God wants his children on earth to have material riches.

In the 1950s Pentecostal Holiness preacher Oral Roberts held huge revivals in which divine healing was a centerpiece. In 1955 Roberts took to the air with a weekly show that was so widely watched that by 1987 89 percent of the public reportedly recognized his name. Roberts changed the way Christians thought about God, and those changes are evident throughout evangelicaldom today. Before Roberts, speaking in tongues was unacceptable except in the narrow Pentecostal stream, the idea of God being good was not dominant and to pray for the sick to be healed was unusual. Today, praying for the sick is commonplace in even the most traditional of churches, and speaking in tongues is practiced in one out every four churches in America.

As bizarre as it can seem to outsiders—and even to other evangelicals—Pentecostalism is the largest Protestant group in the world and it continues to grow by leaps and bounds. I visited a Pentecostal church in Mission Viejo, California, with a friend to see what it was all about. As we walked into the former movie theater that is now the Life Church, the first thing I noticed was that tissue boxes were perched on the end of every third aisle. My friend assured me I would soon understand what they were for. Within minutes, most of the people in the dimly lit room were lost in worship, swaying and singing with their eyes closed and their hands raised heavenward in gestures of submission to the Holy Spirit. Many of them—including one of the vocalists on the stage—punctuated their singing with speaking in tongues, something which, at that point, I had never before witnessed. It sounds like a strange, ancient language. In most cases, the person doesn't understand what he or she is saying. According to the commonly accepted reading of scripture, people may pray in tongues, but if the utterance is intended to be publicly heard, someone must also interpret it.

The congregants of the Life Church were practicing other spiritual gifts as well. The long session of worship music was followed by a call to the altar, at which point it became clear why the boxes of tissues were there. The Life Church believes in spiritual healing for ailments both physical and emotional, and the area in front of the stage was soon filled with people being hugged and ministered to by the prayer team. They huddled in small clusters, often weeping, with their heads bowed. A young girl so handicapped that she was unable to bend her legs or turn her head was pushed in a wheelchair to the front of the church and quickly encircled by people who anointed her, laid hands on her, and prayed for her to be healed. The heartbreak and hope of the people in front of the stage was palpable and members of the audience joined in with tears and praise.

A line of men stood in wait behind all the hustle and bustle—the catchers, my guide explained. Another common event at charismatic services is people being "slain in the Spirit"—something anyone who's tuned into a Benny Hinn crusade has seen. It's quite dramatic to watch. Hinn will pray with someone then touch the person on the head as he shouts something about "Jesus!" and the person will fall backwards. The belief is that the power of the Holy Spirit descends on a person with such force that he or she is knocked to the ground; the catchers break the fall to prevent injury.

While the rise of Pentecostalism and other developments fragmented the larger evangelical community, there were cohesive forces at work as well. One of these was the vast network of Christian radio. Fundamentalists and evangelicals throughout the country were listening to the same evangelists and were thus digesting the same messages—just as the larger evangelical community does today through Christian radio and television. (Focus on the Family leader James Dobson has an estimated radio audience of 4 million listeners occupying different points on the evangelical continuum.) The call to proselytize remained as strong as ever, and by the 1940s when Billy Graham first took to the pulpit, fundamentalists were reemerging with new vigor. Graham soon became the public face of the community and all factions rallied around him—at least temporarily. A deep fault line reemerged in 1947, when theologian Carl F. Henry, who came to be closely associated with Graham, published *The Uneasy Conscience of Modern Fundamentalism,* in which he argued that fundamentalists needed to bring their faith to bear on contemporary culture.

The book was a bombshell dropped on the greater evangelical community. Henry was by no means a proponent for liberal modernism but he did want to temper the rigidity and anti-intellectual leanings of the fundamentalist body. Henry was pushing for a more engaged form of the religion but his urgings were largely rejected by the fundamentalists he hoped to reform. Although Graham had started out as a staunch fundamentalist who opposed modernism, he supported Henry and eventually stopped using the fundamentalist label. During an interview given around the time of his 1955 crusade in Scotland, Graham said he didn't call himself a fundamentalist because of an aura of bigotry and narrowness associated with the term. Although he still held most of the same beliefs, culturally he had become an evangelical.

Henry's book drew an indelible line between the two traditions; now one was either a fundamentalist or an evangelical. By the time of the famous 1957 crusade in Madison Square Garden, which ran for sixteen weeks, fundamentalists had come out openly against Graham. They were upset that he had accepted the sponsorship of the liberal Protestant Council of Churches for that crusade, that he looked favorably upon modernists within the church, and, indeed, that he rejected the doctrine of separation. The result was the deepening of the earlier rift, with the fundamentalists rejecting the modernizing impulses that were at the root of the mainstreaming of evangelical Christianity that we see today. Graham and his fellow proponents of an engaged evangelical body came to be called the "new evangelicals." The fruit of that disagreement were so enduring that as late as the 1980s my school taught us that Graham was not a true Christian.

Despite the fundamentalists' rejection, Graham emerged as the preeminent evangelical leader, and his enduring broad-mindedness has helped him retain that informal title. Graham's efforts to be engaged with the culture were still evident in what may prove to be his last U.S. crusade, held at Flushing Meadows Corona Park in June 2005. Each night, Graham interspersed his speech with cultural references. Over the course of the three-night crusade, Graham mentioned *Star Wars*, Madonna, the Rolling Stones, *Blender* magazine, the Yankees and the Mets, and a visit U2's Bono paid to Graham at his home.

Divided though it was, the evangelical community soon found a new rallying point in the perceived moral decay that took hold after the cultural earthquake of the 1960s. Even Henry's engaged wing of evangelicaldom found the sixties and seventies too dissolute to bear, and the Vietnam War brought out their nationalistic and militant streak. But the evangelical community also benefited from the

spiritual seeking that characterized this era, when many newly religiously inclined youth turned to Christianity. Their suspicion of the
establishment led them to the locally organized churches of evangelicals. The evangelical community came out of this era with new
strength and helped elect an openly born-again Christian, Jimmy
Carter, to the White House. Carter's 1976 victory could have unified
evangelicals and marked a high point for them as a whole. Instead, it
just made public the tussle between rival factions in the movement.
Carter proved to be generally too liberal for evangelical tastes, but the
powder keg of discontent was ignited when the IRS rescinded the tax-
exempt status of hundreds of Christian schools. After that, the born-
again bloc turned vehemently against Carter (and, by extension, the
Democrats) and started to organize. It was then that Jerry Falwell
founded the Moral Majority, specifically to mobilize conservative
Christians to register and vote. The organization couldn't get rid of
Carter quickly enough and threw its weight behind Ronald Reagan.
Falwell's desire to be a force on the political landscape hearkened back
to the earlier revivalist impulse to clean up society. He and his politically engaged fundamentalist backers drew on a Manichean view that
colored their theology as well as their politics. Everything was cast in
terms of a struggle between light and dark that played well during the
cold war, when Americans were inclined to see things starkly in us-
and-them terms.

The Reagan administration marked a coming of age for evangelicals, giving them unprecedented access to a White House that routinely consulted them about appointments and policy. Reagan spoke at
the National Association of Evangelicals annual convention in both
1983 and 1984, the first time a U.S. president had ever attended an
NAE function. It was at the 1983 convention in Orlando that Reagan
gave his "Evil Empire" speech about the Soviet Union. Evangelicals
were also beginning to have an impact on Congress, having successfully pushed for the passage of bills on drunk driving and for equal
access to public school facilities for religious groups.

The fundamentalists were as extreme politically as they had been theologically, and by the time the late 1980s rolled around they were so out of touch with the mainstream of American society that they had become a joke to those outside of the fold. (That negative image still dogs them in many quarters.) For much of that, they have only themselves to blame. First there was Oral Roberts, who in 1987 announced to a broadcast audience that God told him if he didn't raise $8 million in a matter of months—through viewer contributions, of course—God would "take him home," presumably through death or by direct ascension to heaven. The statement was so ludicrous that the satirical comic strip *Doonesbury* started a deathwatch. Then came the televangelist scandals. First Jim Bakker (husband of the heavily made up Tammy Faye, now a gay icon) was revealed to have paid off his former secretary to keep quiet about sexual favors she had granted him, and then it was revealed that Bakker had made more than $3 million by defrauding his followers. Next in the parade of disgraced evangelists was Jimmy Swaggart. He had gone on the Larry King show and denounced Bakker's sexual misconduct as "a cancer on the body of Christ," but a short time later a private investigator, hired by a rival evangelist who had been fired after Swaggart made known that he was having an affair, came forward with pictures of Swaggart meeting with a prostitute. Swaggart weathered that storm—albeit with a much reduced audience—by saying he had been possessed by demons but Oral Roberts had cast them out over the phone. (The idea of demon possession is a very real one for evangelical Christians. When I was a kid I was afraid to watch movies about the occult, such as *The Exorcist,* for fear that I, too, would become demon possessed.) Swaggart's exorcism didn't seem to have been successful, though—a few years later he was found with a prostitute in his car when he was pulled over by police for driving on the wrong side of the road.

After Reagan's second term, the Christian Right organized around televangelist Pat Robertson. When he lost the Republican presidential nomination to George Bush in 1988, conservative Christians found themselves without a credible national leader and the community fragmented, although Robertson tried to keep it together by founding the Christian Coalition. Given the reputation of his fellow televangelists it could be considered a minor miracle that Pat Robertson's failed presidential bid did as well as it did. While he hasn't been dogged with the same level of sexual scandal as Bakker or Swaggart (though he has not been without accusation), a bad case of foot-in-mouth disease was Robertson's affliction. Even though he is a charismatic and his core audience is likely to consist of firm believers in the power of prayer, he lost mainstream listeners when he claimed, on several occasions, that his prayers helped steer the course of a hurricane. He was on thinner ice, though, with some of his other proclamations—when, for instance, he called feminism "a socialist, antifamily political movement that encourages women to leave their husbands, kill their children, practice witchcraft, destroy capitalism, and become lesbians," or when he suggested that the State Department's headquarters in Foggy Bottom be nuked and that Venezuelan president Hugo Chávez be "taken out." He became fodder for comedians once again when he said that the stroke Israeli leader Ariel Sharon suffered in early 2006 was God's punishment for giving up Israeli territory. "If you are playing along at home, this is Pat's first idiotic statement of the New Year," comedian Jay Leno quipped.

After Robertson's loss, the term *born-again,* widely used during the heyday of the Christian Right, was largely abandoned as the label of choice because it was associated with all that was negative about that era. The phrase comes from John 3:3, in which Jesus said, "Except a man be born again, he cannot see the kingdom of God." It can be used to describe anyone who has had a moment of personal salvation in which he accepted the absolution of sin bought by the death of Jesus Christ. That forgiveness is believed to secure eternal life; without it one cannot enter heaven. Many of the people I knew growing up no longer call themselves born again, although their beliefs have not fundamentally changed. As the term began to connote religious zealotry, many self-described born-again Christians dropped the moniker in favor of "evangelical."

This is the label the community wore when it reemerged as a political force after the Clinton presidency. The Clinton years had been decidedly less sunny for evangelicals. While Clinton welcomed them into the White House and courted them by inviting the leadership to state dinners, prayer breakfasts, and the like, evangelicals had become closely aligned with the Republican Party and the Clinton administrations' agenda was one of which they largely disapproved—although Clinton himself is a born-again Christian. Still, during those years of irrational exuberance the evangelical community, like the rest of America, grew more affluent and less eager to rail against the ills of society. It emerged after the Clinton presidency showing off a softer, less-confrontational face, more centralized around megachurches, and, in many quarters, pushing a decidedly temporal prosperity doctrine. Evangelicals had come to the realization that in order to alter the culture they needed to belong to it. In the ongoing cycle of involvement and withdrawal that has marked their arc through history, the evangelical community is perhaps more engaged than it has been at any point since the Civil War, and as such has been able, once again, to mold American society. In the following chapters we'll look at how, and where, they are doing that.

CHAPTER THREE

How They Get You: Outreach

W HAT? YOU WANT to clean *what?*" Dee Hu is trying, rather unsuccessfully, to wrap his mind around the question two volunteers from Vineyard Community Church in Cincinnati have posed him. His confusion is understandable, given the odd request. They would like to come in and clean the bathrooms at USA Nails, the manicure salon Hu manages. "Why?" Hu demands, still trying to figure out what these people really want from him.

"We just want to show you God's love," replies Josh Harney, the rugged young man leading the bathroom-cleaning team, part of the church's outreach program.

"It's just so sudden . . ." Hu replies falteringly. Since he doesn't go as far as throwing them out, Harney and his covolunteer Dori make their way back to the restroom. It's pretty clean, just a single stall reserved for staff use. Harney leans over to tackle the toilet and Dori pushes her blond hair away from her face as she starts in on the sink and mirror. "This is an easy one," Harney tells Hu while he works. "You should see some of the gas station restrooms." Hu watches the duo in action, still bewildered and asking questions. Where are they from? Why are they doing this? Is it an organized program? "I'm just kind of suddenly curious why they want to help somebody do something," he says, swiveling around to address me.

"So basically, the principle is what?" Hu demands, turning back to Harney. His question is exactly what the team is looking for. "The principle is, we believe God loves everybody, really," Harney explains.

"And that's with no strings attached, but we think people might not always understand that on a deep level. So we want to show that in a practical way." The bathroom clean, Harney says his good-byes and exits, leaving Hu with a little card that says "This is our simple way . . . of saying that God loves you. Let us know if we can be of more assistance." Vineyard's address and phone number are on the back, along with service times and a map to the church.

The bathroom cleaning is part of the church's monthly ServeFest, when scores of volunteers spend Saturday morning, Saturday evening, and Sunday morning fanning out across the city meeting people's small needs. They clean toilets and pass out hand warmers and hot chocolate in the winter and ice water in the summer. Around Christmas they set up a booth in a local mall and wrap presents for free. They put together bags of food and deliver them to people in need. The program's architect, Steve Sjogren, said that when he's out, he regularly buys lunch or coffee for the person behind him in line, and there are even special cards one can print out that say "This Meal's on Us!" The church has been at it so long that they are well known in the area, and Sjogren, who estimates Vineyard volunteers have "touched" about 6 million people, has been given a key to the men's restroom in City Hall in recognition of his service.

Sjogren calls this "servant evangelism," which he defines as "the idea that Jesus is better shown than talked about . . . servant evangelism is taking the idea of God and putting wheels on it." Sjogren believes the church shouldn't be inward focused (existing to serve only its members) but outward focused (reaching out to the community at large). The church should define itself "not by what we believe, but by what we do," Sjogren told me over lunch the day before I went out with the toilet cleaning crew. Years ago, when he was first starting Vineyard, he decided the church would do nice but insignificant things over and over again to demonstrate the love of God and to portray Christlike traits such as kindness and generosity. "We're trying to build an atmosphere of the kingdom of God," Sjogren said. What they're not trying to do is the old-fashioned, bottom line–oriented outreach that I grew up with, where Christians go out and talk to people about the consequences of a life without God (hell) and try to get them to accept Christ. Servant evangelism is pressure free and, instead, is all about creating a moment that will make people stop and think about who God is. The idea is that they will become so attracted to Christianity they will be swept up in what Sjogren calls "the God Blob," a reference to the 1958 horror movie classic *The Blob*. "You get pulled into it and it just gets larger than life," Sjogren said. Sjogren is so concerned about not coming across as church-y that he doesn't even call himself a Christian, preferring instead to describe himself as a "Christ follower." If you ask him what his profession is, he won't say "pastor" but will answer "atmosphere architect" or sometimes "motivational speaker." Of course, saving souls is Sjogren's goal, too, he just goes about it in a different way.

Outreach is one of the primary directives for evangelical Christians. In the Gospel of Matthew, Jesus tells his followers to "make disciples of all the earth," a dictate called the Great Commission. Because of their belief that anyone who has not accepted Jesus Christ as his personal savior will go to hell for eternity, evangelicals feel an imperative to spread the word. Nearly every evangelical church sponsors missionaries abroad, but domestic missions are equally important. This proselytizing often seems inappropriate or even offensive, but evangelicals regard it as lifesaving work in the most literal sense. And while the notion of a God who condemns those who don't see things in a narrow, specific way may feel draconian to the rest of us, evangelicals regard the stance as one of love. God gives us the liberty to choose redemption from sin, instead of forcing it upon us. Evangelicals also believe in a seemingly contradictory doctrine of predestination, which is why they don't place an emphasis on the numbers of people they guide to Christ. Their role is to make the most convincing case possible for the need to accept Jesus. The rest is up to God.

Sjogren is incredibly earnest about all this, and carries an attitude of servant evangelism with him wherever he goes. He has a kind, boyish face and an expression that seems to mask an inner sadness; he has the look of someone who would be easy to talk to. It's not surprising, then, that he often finds himself engaged in intimate conversations with complete strangers. He told me the story of a salesclerk he started talking to one day in a superstore who aspired to go to medical school. Sjogren asked the young man if he could pray for him. When the man agreed, they prayed together in the middle of the store. I didn't think much of the story until, as I was packing up to leave, Sjogren asked me if he could pray with me. I felt that it would be easier to acquiesce than to decline, so I bowed my head as he and his wife Janie held my hands. The three of us sat huddled at our table in the middle of the restaurant for what seemed like an eternity. I was wishing the prayer would end when Sjogren brought up my book. "Lord, let her sell not tens of thousands of copies but hundreds of thousands of copies," he prayed, and my impatience started to wane. While I'm not sure I believe in a God who gets involved in book sales, I wasn't entirely displeased that someone who did was making my case. I quietly echoed Sjogren's "amen" and looked up. As I stood to leave, Sjogren handed me a twenty-dollar bill. Before lunch I'd mentioned that I wanted to take advantage of the time away from my kids to try to catch a movie. "Buy yourself some popcorn too," he offered.

It's Saturday night and the music from the "celebration"—as the worship service here at Vineyard is known—is audible throughout the church building. I make my way down the stairs into a big open area with tables. Some people are helping themselves to free coffee, others are eating pizza they bought at the snack bar. At the far end, Kande Wilson, the church's director of outreach, is trying to organize volunteers. (After a botched surgery about eight years ago during which Sjogren was technically dead for seven minutes, he handed off the day-to-day work of the church.) She lists the choices: doling out hand warmers and hot chocolate at Wal-Mart and a gas station, passing out miniflashlights in front of the movie theater, or distributing single-use breathalyzers at local bars. Dispensing trinkets like this is a classic guerilla marketing tactic, and the baubles are all accompanied by a little greeting card similar to the one the toilet-cleaning crew passed out so recipients will know exactly what the ultimate product is and where to find it. "These are small things, and your job is to do them with great love," Wilson tells the assembled group.

I decide to tag along with the bar team and hitch a ride from a twenty-nine-year-old pharmacist named Alex Machen, a pretty single mother with long, coffee-brown hair and squarish glasses who has been practicing servant evangelism for the past year and a half. She'd already been out cleaning toilets with Sjogren that morning. Machen considers these outreach efforts to be little pushes in God's direction. "You might have to touch somebody a couple of times before they get nudged over," she said. "That is the goal . . . you know you might not bring somebody to Christ that day but you know what? You're nudging them."

We pull up to the first bar on our list. It's in a strip mall, fronted by a glass door with stickers on it. I peek through the glass and see, shrouded in a haze of blue smoke to the right, about six lone figures sitting at the bar and an empty room with pool tables to the left. The other people in our group arrive and Karin, our leader, asks us to join hands and pray. (I will come to find out that this is but the first of many times we will seek God together that evening.) That done, we press our way through the glass door and Karin announces our purpose to the bartender. "I'm not sure . . ." the bartender dubiously replies, but before she can finish her thought a hulking, jean-clad man says, "I'll take one." The ice broken, three other people grab breathalyzers. We turn to leave. "Keep up God's work," the first man says dryly as we make our way out the door.

That was quick and relatively painless, but there are still plenty of yellow breathalyzers to unload so we reconvene to try to decide where to go next, finally settling on Metropolis, part of a local mall. After a few attempts, we all manage to find each other in the parking structure outside the canopied entryway. The parking lot is full but there's no one waiting in line. Karin got here first and already has checked things out: Women over twenty-one get in for free, men have to pay five dollars. Should we pay and enter like regular customers or should we make ourselves known and ask for permission to go inside? It's about nine p.m., and at this point our group has dwindled to four women and one man and could slip in unobtrusively, so the choice seems fairly clear to me, but they decide to pray for guidance, joining hands and closing their eyes once again. We stand holding hands in a circle next to the red velvet ropes. "Lord, tell us what to do," Karin prays. "Amen," they all chorus when she's done. I expect them to have realized the only sensible thing to do is pay our money and walk in the easy way, but apparently that's not what God told everyone else. "I think we're supposed to talk to them," Karin concludes. We walk up to the cashier's desk and Karin makes her case. The cashier heads for the manager's office to ask if we can go in. "Lord, I ask you would grant this favor," I hear Karin pray quietly. The cashier returns and says the manager wants to talk to her.

While the group waits for Karin to come back with an answer, I wander through the club to find the restroom. The place is fairly empty. The only one of the three dance floors getting much use is the one playing country-and-western music, where a smattering of people in ten-gallon hats and cowboy boots are line dancing. I keep walking and see an elevated dance cage with rusted bars and a sign that says Women Only. It's empty. Two teenage girls keep their eyes fixed downward while they bob to a techno beat, alone on the dance floor. When I'm finished in the dilapidated restroom I return to the cashier's desk and find the group has left the building and is standing outside. The manager, it seems, was sympathetic but ultimately unwilling to let them inside. Instead, the volunteers are standing in front of the entrance hoping to talk to people on their way in or out.

As we're waiting I chat with a young volunteer named Neil, who tells me the story of how he came to Christ. He had been an atheist in high school but one day, while he was working at Toys "R" Us a couple came in asking for a Talking Bubba Bear, which they wanted to buy for their son for Christmas. Talking Bubba was such a hot item at the time that Neil had never seen one, and he told them so. The woman was so upset she began to cry, but her husband comforted her by telling her that if God wanted the boy to have one, they'd find one. As they left, Neil turned around to straighten up the shelves and there, just behind another box, was Talking Bubba Bear. "I ran them down and gave them the Talking Bubba," he recounted. "That just kinda got me thinking there and eventually I decided I did believe in God." In the faith of evangelicals, if God wants to tell you something he could use anything—even Talking Bubba—to get his message across.

Our conversation was punctuated by the occasional arrival of a new bargoer and finally all the breathalyzers were handed out. None of the recipients seemed particularly interested in why the volunteers were there, and no one asked to be prayed for. On the face of it the evening did not seem much of a success, but these volunteers are trained not to look for instant results.

The next morning I went back to Vineyard, where I met Lee Taylor, who had been on the receiving end of one of Vineyard's outreaches. She'd become a Christian in August 2003 during a time of particular confusion in her life. Need—or a feeling of brokenness—is a common theme among people who become born-again Christians. Generally speaking, people don't reach out for God or toward church unless there is something in their life that wants fixing. Evangelicals like to talk about a God-shaped hole in all of us that only Christ can fill. For some people there is a perpetual feeling of emptiness or inadequacy that brings them to Christ, for others it's a moment of difficulty. For Taylor it was the latter.

Taylor had been raised Catholic, although it was more of a culture for her than a religion. She started thinking about God, though, when she found out that her ex-husband was using drugs. She felt that she should seek sole custody of their children, but the kids loved their father and she was worried that removing him from their lives might be harmful to them. "I was just so distraught about what to do," she told me. "It was at that point that I started realizing that I needed help beyond what I could find here on earth." She asked her husband, a lapsed Christian, to teach her how to pray. He suggested they find a church, and it was at that moment that Taylor recalled a hot summer day two years earlier when a young volunteer from Vineyard had passed cold drinks to her and her children through her car window as they waited in the left-turn lane of nearby Sharon Road. "I can remember it as though it was yesterday," she said. "I thought, 'Hey, that's kinda cool.'"

She hadn't thought about that day since, but when Taylor's issues with her ex-husband emerged, she found herself in precisely the right state to be receptive to God. "I felt broken. I had a huge problem and I didn't know how to solve it," she said. When the memory of those cold drinks popped into her head she decided she and her new husband needed to go to Vineyard. Her husband's daughter Lindsay already belonged to the church, so they went together. "The songs were so powerful to me, I just started bawling," she remembered. "Lindsay said, 'Do you want to go down and pray?'"

Taylor turned her life over to God then and there—and that's when the pain began in earnest. "I had a lot of questions and doubts," she said. "You say the prayer and you're saved, and your life becomes harder, I think. I had to come to terms with a lot of things I'd done in my life." Suddenly Taylor was looking at her past in an entirely new light, through the lens of biblical morality. She wasn't proud of what she saw: her divorce, abortions, affairs, marriages she'd broken up. She started to question whether she could really be saved—the term evangelicals use for their salvation—with all those sins in her past. "Your standard is all of a sudden different," she explained. People at the church lent their support and helped her sort through the confusion.

It's been two years since Taylor became a Christian and she is solid in her faith, but her family in New England still doesn't know she's been born again. "They know that I go to church, they know I'm very involved, but I don't really push it on them," she said. "I wish I could have called them when I got saved and said, 'Hey, I'm saved!' but they would have thought I'd lost my mind." Taylor regrets that she hasn't told her parents yet but she's afraid of rejection. "It's a struggle," she said.

An experience like Taylor's is exactly what Vineyard volunteers are aiming for. The outreach may appear insignificant at the time, but the volunteers hope that when a person is ready to turn to God, those little touches will be remembered. I asked Taylor what had gone through her mind in the moment she was handed that cold bottle of water. Handing out drinks or other token items seemed to me to be uncomfortably close to what a person wearing a saffron robe and a shaved head might do in the departure lounge of LAX. Taylor told me that back when she lived in Southern California she would probably have had the same reaction, but in the Midwest it seemed almost natural.

Vineyard's approach to evangelism has been adopted by churches in other cities as well. The summer before I went to Cincinnati I twice encountered members of a new church in Manhattan doing similar things, once passing out packets of Big Red chewing gum and on another particularly scorching day handing out cold bottles of water. The tactic is intended to work in much the same way as former New York mayor Rudi Giuliani's broken window approach to fighting crime. The mayor focused on small crimes because he believed clamping down on petty offenses would discourage bigger ones. Similarly, by meeting a person's minor needs, the volunteers hope they are sending the message that they will also be there when the needs are great. And, of course, as people touched by Vineyard's volunteers turn to religion for solace like Taylor did, the congregation grows. A person who has had a powerful transformational experience will want to tell friends about it. "That's where the multiplier is," said church growth expert John Vaughn. "It's the power of the changed lives that those churches understand." Interestingly, statisticians, pollsters, and demographers agree that the overall number of evangelicals is not increasing, despite the efforts to convert people. Some leave the religion once their moment of need is over, others raised in the religion eventually walk away, as I did. The end result is that the numbers, in the long term, are essentially flat.

Sjogren wants to take his outreach concept even further in his next church, Coastland Church, which he plans to plant in Tampa in 2008. There, Sjogren says, servant evangelism won't be a program but a lifestyle. Sjogren recalls the old Robert Schuller maxim, which he plans on resurrecting in the new church: "Find a need and meet it, find a hurt and heal it." His wife Janie offers a description of her own. The church should be a force, not a field. It's not a place they should aim to have people come *to*, it's something that should go out to the community. "We need to give ourselves away," she said.

That kind of thinking about evangelism is relatively new. When I was growing up a popular way of trying to bring people to Christ involved a little yellow pamphlet called "The Four Spiritual Laws." The Christian would guide the target convert through the booklet. Law 1: God loves you and offers a wonderful plan for your life. Law 2: Man is sinful and separated from God. Therefore he cannot know and experience God's love and plan for his life. Law 3: Jesus Christ is God's only provision for man's sin. Through Him you can know and experience God's love and plan for your life. Law 4: We must individually receive Jesus Christ as Savior and Lord, then we can know and experience God's love and plan for our lives. Then, the Christian would offer to seal the deal by praying with the target the prayer that would make him a Christian: "Lord Jesus, I need you. Thank you for dying on the cross for my sins. I open the door of my life and receive you as my savior and Lord. Thank you for forgiving my sins and giving me eternal life. Take control of the throne of my life. Make me the kind of person you want me to be."

That confrontational approach may have made more sense when it was conceived fifty years ago, when the country was more homogenous and you could assume that most people believed in God and that the Bible was basically true. Today it's tough to imagine anyone being particularly receptive to that sort of ambush. (Although I tried using the Four Spiritual Laws once or twice back in my Christian days to convert a guy I had a crush on and it never worked for me; in fact, I never managed to convert anyone.)

"The culture has changed dramatically since then and, because of that, I think evangelism has changed to meet people where they're at," said Mark Ashton, Willow Creek's pastor of spiritual discovery or, in layman's terms, head of outreach.

Churches have realized that becoming a Christian is a monumental decision that is unlikely to be made quickly. "The invitation is such a huge ask, it's like asking someone to marry you," Ashton said. "It happens in the context of a relationship and love and servanthood and trust. That doesn't happen in a short-term encounter." Willow Creek's mode of evangelism is diametrically different from Vineyard's. Instead of planting seeds through brief and random acts of kindness, Willow Creek relies primarily on what they call "relational evangelism." It's a more organic approach: As you build a friendship with someone and get to know them, they are also getting to know you and, by extension, your faith. It then seems normal to share that part of your life with them. Willow Creek talks about the responsibility for evangelism and teaches seminars on it, but Ashton doesn't want it to be a special event. Instead, the church strives to build a culture where it's a routine part of daily life.

On the face of it, the relational method of evangelism is more natural because the encounters take place between people who have a relationship and, presumably, some level of affection or respect for one another. And yet that's exactly the reason these situations can be so awkward for the person on the receiving end: The existing friendship makes it harder to say no. The Christian and the non-Christian see these encounters from two entirely different perspectives. While it may be discomfiting for the non-Christian and feel like an invasion of privacy, to the Christian any discomfort is inconsequential next to the fate of a person's soul. In the evangelical frame of mind, one need feel no more embarrassed by an attempt to share God's grace than one would telling someone her hair was on fire.

Ashton first came up with his approach of relational evangelism when he was a junior in college. A group of guys would regularly gather in his room and eat popcorn while they talked about girls and other things of vital interest to college kids. When he wanted to share Christ with them, he worried they would think he was strange if he whipped out the Four Spiritual Laws, so one evening he came out and just asked them if he could talk about Jesus. To his shock, they said okay. Eventually, three of the ten guys who were regulars at the get-togethers became Christians.

Since then, Ashton has standardized the approach. Usually two Christians each invite two non-Christians to come talk about Jesus once a week for four weeks. It's critical there be more non-Christians than Christians so they don't feel ambushed. If people like the group they bring their friends and it grows. These "seeker groups" start as four-week sessions, but Ashton said there are groups at Willow Creek that have been going on for more than a year. In his experience, the average time it takes a person to come to Christ is between six months and two years from the time they start exploring the idea. "There are basically two kinds of strategies for evangelism: come and see, and go and tell," Ashton explained. "Willow has traditionally built on a come and see strategy . . . Vineyard is go and tell."

About fifty people are sitting on chairs arranged in circles in the basement of an old brick church on Manhattan's Upper East Side and eating fried chicken, salad, and rice pilaf off wicker trays perched on their laps. They're making small talk for the moment, but as soon as they've finished dinner they'll get down to the business they've come for: The Alpha Course, which introduces people to evangelical Christianity.

The current incarnation of the Alpha Course was born in an Anglican church in London when clergyman Nicky Gumbel realized that most of the people who attended a program his congregation offered for new Christians were, in fact, unchurched and had questions about even the most basic aspects of the religion. In each session attendees were broken up into small groups, and the ten people in his had the questions typical of unbelievers, such as what happens to followers of other religions and why does God allow suffering. They talked through those and many others at the weekly sessions. Halfway through the program they went away on a retreat together. While there, all ten announced their conversion to Christianity.

Gumbel realized there was value in creating an inviting environment in which people could pose questions and air misgivings about Christianity without feeling judged. No inquiry or comment would be deemed too trivial, threatening, or illogical, and there would be no pressure to continue if someone wanted to drop out. The program would just be friends bringing friends, a place where one could get a hot meal and have an interesting conversation, if nothing else. That was fifteen years ago. Today, the ten-session Alpha Course is offered in more than twenty countries and is widely used in American churches—including Vineyard in Cincinnati. There are Alpha Courses in prisons and in offices. There is Alpha for the military, for students, for youth, and a special Alpha for Catholics.

I'm attending week four at Trinity Baptist Church. As people finish their desserts and sip the last of their coffees, a man with a guitar stands up and everyone else picks up the lyric sheets that have been placed on the chairs and sings along. Many in the crowd appear to be mildly uncomfortable. Across the room from me is a well-dressed woman wearing brown pants, a beige sweater, and a color-coordinated silk scarf. As the leader asks everyone to bow their heads in prayer, she keeps her eyes open. After the prayer we sit back down in our circles and turn to watch a video of Gumbel delivering a message on how God guides us. With his plummy English accent, Gumbel is charming and nonthreatening, with the slightly milquetoast manner common to Anglican preachers.

When the video is over, Eddie, our group leader, opens the discussion. In addition to Eddie, our group consists of two other Christians who are here to guide us, a young man whose inclinations are not clear to me, and three visiting students from mainland China with lots of questions. "What do you think of the concept of God guiding you?" Eddie throws out to get the conversation rolling. Jian, one of the Chinese students and a philosophy scholar, delivers the first of many stumpers she will issue this evening. "Before he said God is in us," she said, referring to Gumbel. "Now he said that he is with us. Is that compatible?" The three Christians—Eddie, a young woman who works for the outreach group Campus Crusade for Christ, and a young male actor—take turns struggling to respond. They all have different answers, including that God is everywhere, but none seems particularly definitive. Jian has a follow-up: "Is God also in hell?" Somewhat ignoring the Alpha Course's assertion that there are no bad questions, Eddie moves the group along by declaring "This is getting too far away from our subject."

Eddie steers the discussion to safer territory: "How do you feel that God has guided you?" he asks. He shares a personal story. He and his wife had just sold their condo in Hawaii and were driving with their baby across America looking for somewhere to live. They stopped in the New York area to visit family and, out of the blue, an uncle offered them an apartment on Fifth Avenue—clearly God's signal that they should settle in Manhattan. The actor takes his turn, saying he knew God was leading him to New York when he landed a job in a theater production. It occurs to me that in another setting these things would be considered nothing more than plain good luck.

Jian is contemplating a variation of the question at hand. "If you obey, how can you be responsible for all the consequences?" she asks, cocking her head. The three Christians' responses are fairly simplistic and don't seem to satisfy her. (Alpha leaders are trained not to give definitive answers so they don't shut down spiritual exploration.) Even I, a native English speaker, can't quite figure out what they're trying to say. Eddie tells a story about the time his son threw food at a dinner guest and the Campus Crusade woman next to me says something about being in control of the choices we make but not of the outcome. But Jian is unrelenting: "When the disciples were killed, who was responsible?" I start to suspect that perhaps Jian's questions are as much for sport as they are for enlightenment. It's tough to tell, though. She scrunches up her face and ponders every answer she's given, obviously considering the responses.

I'm sure Jian will never be convinced by these arguments, so when the meeting breaks up I stop the woman in beige on her way home to ask her why she came to Alpha. She introduces herself as Sharon and tells me that she's Jewish but has always been drawn to Christianity. She said she hadn't prayed the prayer to accept Christ yet but anticipated she'd become a Christian by the time the course was over.

A few weeks later I called the organizer of the course to see what had happened on the retreat they'd gone on a couple of weeks after my visit. I expected him to tell me about Sharon, but instead he brought up Jian, whom he said had become a Christian. I was amazed, as Jian had seemed so skeptical the night I met her, so I called her to see what had changed her mind. She agreed to meet me for coffee and tell me her story.

When Jian arrived in New York for her year of exchange, she was contacted by an organizatiion called Bridges International, a Christian group that works with international students in the United States. Bridges hosted a welcome party for the Chinese students at Jian's university and invited them to participate in a weekly conversation group so they could practice their English. Later, Bridges started sending Jian e-mails inviting her to church and, eventually, to attend the Alpha Course, which seemed like a bait and switch approach to me, but Jian said she hadn't seen it that way. Initially Jian wasn't interested, but she read the list of weekly Alpha Course topics and saw one of the early lectures was about why Jesus died. Jian was in the process of doing research on the metaphysics of death, so she thought the talk might be interesting in that context. She went to the course and enjoyed Gumbel's homily. When she left, she still had unanswered questions, so she went back. "If he'd answered my questions in the first week, I might not have kept going," she said.

In the first lecture Jian attended, Gumbel addressed the question of who Jesus was and delivered an address that was a variation of the "Lunatic, Liar, or Lord?" theme developed by C. S. Lewis in *Mere Christianity*. The argument goes like this: Jesus said he was God, so he must have either been crazy, a liar, or else he was who he said he was. The accounts of Jesus in the Bible don't indicate instability. On the contrary, his sermons were cogent and coherent. So he wasn't crazy. Could he have been a liar? What liar would be willing to be brutally killed for his untruth? If he wasn't crazy and he wasn't lying, he must have been the son of God, the reasoning goes. This is a great simplification of the case that Gumbel makes in his lecture, presumably, from Jian's reaction, more convincingly. "That gave me a new sense of Christianity," she said. "I could think about the faith in a logical and very vigorous way. At least some Christians welcome challenges from outside. This attitude, this open attitude appealed to me very much because if [Christianity] is the truth it should be and can be and must be tested and challenged in a vigorous, rational, logical way."

Her interest piqued, Jian kept attending the Alpha sessions. After a lecture on prayer, Jian decided to try it for herself. She started out by praying for the ability to love. While she wasn't suddenly overcome by warm feelings, the hatred she had consistently felt faded and she found herself able to treat people nicely, even people she disliked or who she thought hated her. "I try to love them not just by saying it but by concrete actions," she said. "My philosophy of life has been changed little by little. I started to emphasize giving, not receiving." Jian said she used to be extremely critical of the people in her life, but that attitude also changed. "After I experienced God's love I became very tolerant and I started to encourage [my parents] and my friends, even if they made some mistakes," she said. "When they do something wrong they need love and tolerance because that love gives them the power to correct their mistakes."

When she returned home from the lecture on prayer, Jian called her mother, and during the course of their conversation, told her what she had learned. "She was touched immediately, she was moved suddenly," Jian said, explaining that her mother had always been an atheist and thought that any kind of faith was not only meaningless but crazy. Her mother cried, and then prayed. Now she prays daily. Her mother's experience had a profound impact on Jian. "When I talked to her about the Alpha Course I did not intend to persuade her, I just intended to tell her what I do in New York," Jian said. "I was surprised by the spiritual power of the Bible, and I realized just the name of Jesus Christ and the hope to pray for something you need, long for, can change a person."

Ever analytical, Jian began reading the New Testament so she could make up her own mind about what was written there. "I read very carefully, especially the four Gospels," she said. "My conclusion is Jesus Christ is the best person we could expect in this universe and I recognized that many verses in the Gospels are true. Not only ethically right, but true." Jian was most convinced by the passage in I Corinthians 13 about love: "Love is patient, love is kind. It does not envy, it does not boast, it is not proud. It is not rude, it is not self-seeking, it is not easily angered, it keeps no records of wrongs. Love does not delight in evil but rejoices with the truth. It always protects, always trusts, always hopes, always perseveres. Love never fails." Jian had spent a lot of time thinking about the definition of love and had discussed it with her professor the previous semester because she felt that if she could comprehend the meaning of love she could grasp the deepest essence of human nature. When she read the passage in I Corinthians, she felt she had gained understanding. "Those verses are, at first look, superficial," she said. "They tell me nothing, but the mysterious thing is suddenly I accept that those verses on love are truth."

Her exploration led Jian to conclude that she was a sinner because compared with God's unconditional love, her ability to love was limited. In the act of admitting she was a sinner, Jian said she simultaneously and inherently accepted a relationship with Jesus Christ. Jian realizes that she can't use logic to rationalize everything in the Bible. On the contrary, the discrepancies she finds there strengthen her faith. Logic alone wouldn't be enough to make her become a Christian, Jian explained. The power of the spiritual experience she had and the faith she developed are equally crucial to her decision. Her ability to have faith despite the "ridiculous stories" she finds in the Bible is exactly what convinces her Christianity is real.

The final but essential element of Jian's decision was the notion of freedom. "If God forced me to believe in him I would have resisted," Jian said. "I would have rather suffered hell if God only favored people who believed in him blindly. Even if God promised me eternal life but disrespected my choice, I would rather suffer hell forever." Jian dislikes the emphasis that pastors put on the gift of salvation, because it makes it seem as though people strike a deal with God. A person's decision to come to Christ shouldn't arise from a desire to get something in return, Jian said. "It should be, of course, love first of all, and it should be heartwarming and it should satisfy one's heart forever."

Jian reasoned her way to Christianity while Lee Taylor reached out for Jesus during a personal crisis. People come to Christ through different means and for different reasons, but nearly all of them are guided by other well-meaning Christians using the most modern methods available to sell their message of eternal life. Today in America those are the tools of viral and relationship marketing. As casual and as natural as they may seem, these encounters between Christians and potential converts are rarely accidental but rather are thought through and extensively prayed over. Outreach is at the core of evangelical Christianity, and its considerations color every encounter Christians have with the mainstream.

CHAPTER FOUR

How They Keep You: Community

I 'M TRYING TO get my four-year-old son, Theo, dressed and out the door of our Colorado Springs hotel room, but he's completely absorbed by a Woody figurine that my husband bought him the night before. After trying several times—unsuccessfully—to penetrate the imaginary world I've lost him to, I complain to my husband that if we don't get moving soon I'm going to be late for the interview I've scheduled at a nearby church.

"Church?" Theo says, looking up. "I love that church! Can I come, too, Mommy?"

My husband, Oliver, and I look at each other with alarm, but Theo quickly dispels our fears of religious zealotry. "I just love that tunnel thing."

The previous day, while I attended two services at the New Life Church in Colorado Springs, Oliver, Theo, and our infant son Xander amused themselves by wandering around the massive complex. They started out by having coffee and snacks at the World Wide Café, the proceeds of which fund the church's mission programs. They then wandered back to the area where Sunday school classes are held and found a room that contained a warren of tunnels and a ball pit. Theo was in heaven. During the evening service he crawled through the plastic tubes hollering back and forth to some bigger kids, one of whom turned out to be the son of the church's pastor, Ted Haggard. If the weather had been better, he would have been able to use the giant playground outside.

The powers that be at New Life don't mind that people are wandering around at all hours, any day of the week—in fact, it's what Haggard wants. At any given time you can find members hanging out in the lobby or in the café perched on stools sipping coffee. Carts of preschool kids periodically are pushed by with no apparent rhyme or reason. There is the same feeling of happy chaos that you'd find in a busy home. The church's model is the ancient synagogue, which served as community center and gathering place. To encourage this, the café is open much of the day on Sunday and three times a week for lunch. Members often meet there for a meal. If they run low on cash, there's an ATM.

This kind of easy access is how churches keep people coming back. The church today is much more than just a place for spiritual edification; it's a community. At other times in history, and in some places still, community happened naturally in the town square or on the front porch, centers where people could casually bump into each other and catch up with each other's lives. But today those natural meeting places are tougher to find. For suburban teenagers, it might be the local mall. For many adults the big, all-encompassing megachurches have come to occupy that spot in their lives. Rick Warren, for example, did extensive research before deciding where to locate Saddleback, as do many pastors when trying to find a place to plant a church. Warren chose a place where there was rapid growth and sprawl, where people would need some sort of center. When Saddleback first started holding services at the site it now occupies, it was an outpost. Since then new roads have been cut and housing and retail developments have popped up around it. New Life is undergoing a similar process. It is literally the church on the hill, and the area around it is so sparsely built that it is visible from miles away, but there are signs of future construction all around. Not only do churches like these become the central point in their members' lives, they act as a catalyst for exurban growth and physically create communities where once there was just open space. They don't just service communities, they build them.

These churches offer somewhere safe and wholesome to take the family, a place where there is always a friendly face and someone to chat with. It's no coincidence that so many churches use the word *community* in their names, nor that the biggest churches tend to be in the crowded inner cities or in the diffuse exurbs, two places in which people are rootless, having often moved from other parts of the country, and where there is often no obvious place to congregate. In these places the megachurch supplants the local government, offering schooling, sports facilities, child care, and counseling.

Haggard wants New Life to be where people gather not just to get spiritual nourishment but to find the sense of belonging so many people crave. Think the bar in the old sitcom *Cheers,* but substitute a shared love of God for the camaraderie of drinking. In Haggard's vision, there will always be someone at the church. A mother will come and let her children play while she works on her laptop. A couple looking for a night out will pop in to see if anything is happening there; going to a movie would be Plan B. Already Haggard's own kids often drop by the church when they're bored at home and frequently they find something there to amuse them, such as a rehearsal for a play or a youth meeting.

There almost always *is* something going on. At New Life and at other big megachurches, members can indulge in just about any hobby under the auspices of the church, and can do so with other like-minded Christians. The benefit for the people involved is that they are able to feel they are glorifying God in many different areas of their lives, rather than compartmentalizing church. They also are able to spend time with people who understand them and who can encourage them in their Christian walk. What has most struck me in my conversations with evangelicals is how easily they segue from the most banal of conversations into talking about God—his will, guidance he has given them, what the Bible tells us to do. These are subjects that for them are as normal and everyday as talking about the morning commute is for the rest of us, yet for nonbelievers these rapid shifts are jarring and frankly, discomfiting. Those awkward moments don't happen between evangelicals. They find kinship in the centrality of God in their lives.

Churches that provide such a wide array of activity do so for more than just entertainment—although that plays a role. The benefit the church derives is twofold. First, offering an abundant menu of activities helps draw in new members through many different points of entry and second, people who come to church not only on Sunday morning but also organize their extracurricular lives around it will develop strong friendships and be devoted members. The idea is that committed communities are built through fun.

There are more than a thousand special-interest groups at New Life, called "small groups." Some of them are the usual Bible study groups, but many of them are activity based. There are hiking groups, aerobics classes, and weight training. There are groups for scrapbooking, for quilting, and for cooking with kids. Need your taxes done? Need help with your personal investing? Look no further. Want to learn Chinese? Want piano lessons—in Spanish? Learn how to kick a habit? Train your dog? You can do it all here. Looking for someone to ride horses with? Motorcycles? Go fly fishing? You'll want to check out Cowboy Up for Christ, New Life Riders, and Reel Men.

Churches elevate what are essentially recreational events or support functions to something more transcendent by calling them "ministries"—which also lends them an Orwellian air. The woman who guided you to your parking space is a member of the Parking Ministry. The man sitting behind the audio mixer belongs to the Sound Ministry. Even fun has a higher purpose. The weekend volleyball league for fathers is part of the Sports Ministry. By conducting even the most mundane business of their lives under the church umbrella, evangelicals can derive an increased sense of purpose from all that they do. Everyone in your Weight Watchers group or your aerobics class is also there because they love Jesus and want to find a way to somehow lose weight or become fitter or just have fun for the glory of God. But there's something a little Stepford-y about these church communities, where everyone believes the same thing and sees the world in the same way. To Christians it's comforting to be surrounded by people who won't challenge their beliefs. These massive church communities are inherently isolationist, and, in that sense, are reminiscent of the post-Scopes era of retreat. Even the outreach programs have an "us-and-them" mentality. In this world there are the Christians, who are members of the club, and the non-Christians who are not.

While evangelicals are now integrated into the mainstream as never before in terms of culture and politics, they still retreat to a place—the church—where they can renew themselves by spending time with their own kind. Churches of every size are accommodating this tendency by offering services that go beyond the nuts and bolts of worship and becoming places that completely envelop people's lives. The larger the church the more it is able to offer.

There are people at Calvary Chapel in Fort Lauderdale who are so involved in church activities that the staff jokes they should set up cots and sleep there. Lee and Diane Holman are one of those families. The couple met at the church in 1993, when Lee was a church deacon and Diane was the assistant to the senior pastor's wife. Back then, Lee sang in the choir and was involved in a couple of ministries, so he was at the church a minimum of three days a week and often as many as six, and Diane was there every day but Saturday. Their involvement with the church has evolved over the course of their marriage and now ebbs and flows along with the life stages of their four children, and they no longer work at the church. Diane, a youthful brunette who reminded me of Judy Garland in *The Wizard of Oz*, is now a homemaker. Lee, a broad man with sea blue eyes that he's passed on to his baby daughter, works from home as an Internet technology consultant. When I spoke with them the baby was only a few months old so they were slightly less occupied with church activities than they normally would be.

Calvary is a huge suburban church, and a person can spend endless amounts of time on its seventy-five-acre campus, which includes a church, a school, sports fields, and a full-service restaurant called the Daily Grill. The restaurant is open seven days a week, and Diane claims the food is quite good. To get to the restaurant you have to walk through the church grounds, but once inside you feel like you're at a Houston's, only the music is Christian and the TV screens sometimes show excerpts of the pastor's sermons. The church also has a coffee bar called the Daily Grind, a cafeteria called the Calvary Café, and a place that serves snack bar fare in the youth center called the Hub. To get a sense of how embracing a community Calvary can be, I asked the Holmans to walk me through a typical week in their lives.

The Holman's three boys, aged ten, nine and six, go to school at Calvary, and Lee drops them off there most mornings. He typically parks the car and walks in with them and, often, will wind up chatting with someone he bumps into before he returns home to start working. Lee is now an elder in the church, which means people often come to him for guidance.

On Mondays, though, Diane drives the boys to school, because at eight a.m. she has her Moms in Prayer meeting, at which a group of about thirty mothers meet at the church and spend an hour praying for their children, their families, their friends, and their community. It's a mixture of silent prayer and praying out loud. Usually someone shares a prayer request, and they pray for that need, or they'll have some sort of thematic prayer. For example, Diane said once a month they pray for each part of their children's bodies, from head to toe. They start by releasing their children into God's hands. Then they pray for their minds, that they will have knowledge of God. A handout supports each area of focus with Bible verses. They pray that their children's eyes will see things from God's perspective, that their ears will hear God's word, that their noses will be filled with the sweet fragrance of Christ, that their mouths will engage in conversation gracious and wise, that their hearts will repent their sins, that their waists will wear the belt of truth, that their arms will take up shields of faith, that the work of their hands will be diligent, that their legs will walk by faith, and that their feet will be shod with the preparation of the gospel of peace. It's a long and detailed prayer only touched on in this description, but it shows the degree to which Christians seek God's guidance in everything they do. There truly is no area of their lives they find too trivial or too insignificant for divine consideration.

When I first spoke to her, Diane hadn't been able to attend Moms in Prayer meetings for a while because the baby was still too little to be left for that long, but she was looking forward to going back. She wasn't out of the loop, though, because she'd been receiving e-mails with prayer requests and had been praying all week long for her kids, her friends' kids, their school community, and their church community. And she knew the women were praying for her, too. Before she had the baby they all laid hands on her and prayed very specific prayers. They prayed for the surgeons' hands and that Diane would have no complications. They prayed she wouldn't be afraid, but would have a calm spirit and would enjoy the experience. Diane said that she felt her friends' prayers all through her delivery.

After school on Mondays the boys have soccer practice, as they also do on Wednesdays and Fridays. They play in Calvary's league, which is comprised of teams from the church that compete against one another. Before the baby was born, Lee used to teach a class for new Christians at the church on Monday nights called Deep Faith. It ran from seven p.m. to nine p.m., but typically Lee would get to Calvary about forty-five minutes early and spend another forty-five minutes after the class talking to people.

Tuesday used to be a busy night because it is small group night. Lee and Diane have each led many small groups in their home, although they've both taken a break from teaching since the arrival of child number four. In the past, when they were teaching at the same time they would alternate weeks; Lee led the men one week while the women stayed at home with the kids, and Diane would teach the following week while Lee and the other husbands took care of things at home. Lee has taught small group studies on a single book of the Bible, including in-depth courses on First Peter and Revelation, among others, "going in and digging real deep into God's word," he said. He's also led a program called Crown Financial, which teaches people to manage their finances and how to get out of debt and start saving. Even when it's just Lee teaching, Diane is busy with her role as hostess. While there's a serious study element to these evenings they are also social events, like a book club. People start turning up with food at about six fifteen, and they eat dinner and chat while people trickle in. The teaching starts at seven thirty p.m. and goes for an hour and a half, but people stick around afterward to talk. It's not unheard of for an evening to run past midnight, particularly if someone wants to discuss a serious issue in his or her life. Lee and Diane often serve informally as counselors to other couples who may be having marital troubles or anyone else who has an issue that needs to be dealt with, something Lee sees as his obligation not just as an elder in the church but as a Christian. "The folks that are in the classes we teach, the people that we counsel with, the people we run into—they're all part of our lives," he said, explaining that in the aggregate Christians make up the body of Christ. "God's word says that when one part of the body suffers, we all suffer."

About every other Wednesday Diane volunteers at the school. She helps out in all three of her sons' classrooms and is there for about four hours, sometimes longer. She brings the boys home from school herself that day because Lee has a busy night at the church, which holds two services Wednesday evenings. Usually he'll attend the first service at six thirty, stick around to talk to people during the break, and attend part of the eight thirty service before he slips out to go home. There are youth programs for kids of all ages on Wednesday nights, but during the school year his kids go to bed shortly after eight so it's too late for them. Diane looks forward to the summers when the whole family can attend because Wednesday night services are her favorite. She says they're more like a Bible study than a Sunday sermon. The pastor will often spend a year on a single book of the Bible and go through it slowly, verse by verse.

Diane normally attends the women's Bible study at the church from nine to eleven on Thursday mornings. Before the new baby, she was the leader for table eight, which meant that she'd usually turn up after dropping the boys off and start getting things ready. She was responsible for all the women who sat at her table. She'd call them to make sure they were coming, send a note when needed, and answer any questions they had. "I was there to help them grow in their walk with the Lord," she said. The group started with a worship session and the study followed. Then each table would break into its own discussion, for which Diane was her table's facilitator. When that was over she'd pop over to the school cafeteria and have lunch with her boys. Meanwhile, Lee tries to attend the weekly department-head meeting at the church that takes place every Thursday, to which he has a standing invitation due to his position as a church elder. About every other week he gets called to go visit a person in the hospital or otherwise minister to someone.

On Fridays at five p.m. when the church staff leaves for the week-end an emergency line switches over to an answering service and Lee is in the rotation to be on call for any urgent situation that might arise with a church member. Saturday is the big day for the Holman family. Depending on what time of year it is, the kids are involved in various sports leagues. During soccer season, the whole family was out on the fields at the church by nine fifteen every Saturday morning. Last year both Diane and Lee coached a team; this year only Lee is coaching. He also fills in as the person in charge of the whole shebang if that person can't make it. They've been involved in youth soccer at Calvary for six years and Lee said the vibe is very different from that at city soccer leagues. For one thing, he can count on one hand the number of times they've had an incident with an over-zealous parent. Lee points out that not everyone involved in the league is from Calvary. "There's also an outreach aspect to it," he explained.

Calvary has a raft of sports ministries and back when he had time Lee played softball. But Calvary's team didn't play in the church league, they played in the bar league against teams with names like "The Elbo Room." They weren't bad, either, and even won the league a few times, which surprised some of the bar guys. He and his teammates would often ask the players from the other side if they wanted to pray with them after the game. Usually their opponents declined. Lee vividly remembers one guy, though, who came up to the Calvary team after a game and asked them to pray for his eighteen-month-old son who was in the hospital. The doctors didn't know what was wrong, he said, but had little hope the baby would get better. The Calvary guys spent some time praying with him and went on their way. Lee said he had forgotten about it by the next week, when he pulled up to the game and found the man there waiting for him with tears running down his cheeks. "I'm thinking, 'Oh, no,' but then he's got this huge smile on his face," Lee remembered. The morning after the Calvary team prayed for the child, the doctors said they didn't know what had happened but the boy was okay and could go home. The potential for encounters like that is the reason the Calvary team chooses not to play in a church league.

The Holmans attend Calvary's Saturday night service, sometimes bringing a child who has been playing with the boys since the game back to his parents. They leave the house shortly after five to get the kids settled into their respective children's classes so that they can be in the sanctuary by six for the adult service. Saturday night is what pastor Bob Coy calls the "lab service" because the topic is usually the same as Sunday morning's and he can work out the kinks. The kids' services follow a similar format. They start with a lesson and, if the children are old enough, they have a little word puzzle to go with it. Then they go down to Disciple Planet, a big room where they worship. They sing contemporary songs and make little hand motions to go along with the music. One of the pastors gives them a practical application of the lesson or they watch a prerecorded video about the subject of the month. In March the subject was courage; in February it was purity. Then the kids will have a snack and get picked up by their parents. After church the family goes out to dinner, if they haven't eaten beforehand, often to Moe's Southwest Grill. If they managed to grab a bite before church they'll take the boys to the playground so they can run around with their friends while Diane and Lee chat with the other parents.

As much time as the family spends at the church, they don't generally go on Sundays. They prefer to keep Sundays free for kids' birthday parties or family time. Occasionally, though, they'll go to the eight o'clock service on Sunday morning and go out to brunch afterward. The notion of attending church on the Sabbath is one the evangelical community has largely abandoned. In many churches Sunday is the day committed Christians *don't* go to church because the services are intended for seekers. Pastors still preach sermons about the importance of using the Sabbath as a day of rest, but it no longer retains its place as a sacred day of worship.

There is a downside to all this activity, one that I know well from my days inside the church—it's exhausting, not just in a physical sense but in an emotional sense as well. There is considerable pressure to be a "good Christian" and, while always affirming that we are all sinners, to put forth a countenance as close to perfection as possible. In an environment where the talk is constantly on redemption from sin, imperfection and, even more so, real problems are concealed to a remarkable degree. The more frowned upon (i.e., the more sexual) the transgression, such as use of pornography or adultery, the more hidden it will be, which is ironic given the persistent reminders that we are all sinners, and that there is no hierarchy of sin. There is an inherent dichotomy in the church: On the one hand there is the emphasis on the sinful nature of man; on the other is the charge to be Christlike. The two dictums are irreconcilable.

Surrounding yourself with people who expect you to behave in a certain way and have specific opinions is tiring and can leave little room for individuality. What's more, sheltering children in this environment may put parents' minds at ease, but creates a potentially volatile situation when the kids eventually leave the nest. A teenager who decides to sample a "sinful" activity has a hard time knowing where to draw the line. I know I did, and an astonishing number of the girls in my Christian school got pregnant because sex was treated as taboo and birth control never discussed.

But, understandably, evangelical parents want their children to be raised in an atmosphere where their primary influences are Christian, and a robust church youth program helps them do that. With so much to do, kids need never be confronted with worldly temptations such as drinking or doing drugs. Most of the Holman boys' friends are from school or from church, and they've managed to find all the Christian kids in their neighborhood. Not that they're forbidden to play with non-Christian kids. There are a couple they like to skateboard with in front of the house and, while Diane feels she has to keep a slightly closer eye on them when they're with their unsaved friends, her three boys are usually there together and Diane trusts that they know what's right. "Do you know Jesus?" she overheard her nine-year-old ask a playmate once. "Why don't you know him? He's God, he's really, really good."

It's important to evangelical Christians like the Holmans that their closest friends share their faith because it so completely infuses their lives. "Everything we do is filtered through God," Diane told me. "In God's word it tells us to fellowship, and the reason why is to encourage one another in the body of Christ, to help someone out. Life is hard, wouldn't it be nice to have someone to encourage you?"

Last summer the Holmans decided to have a pool built in their backyard. They asked friends for recommendations and the same company's name kept coming up. Lee called them and eventually found out the guys also attended Calvary. They all sat down together and prayed for God's guidance on the project. They broke ground on the last day of school and were swimming by August 1. The workers came in on time and on budget, and the kids could sit outside and watch them work. "I didn't have any concerns about language or disorderly conduct," Lee said.

Evangelicals' belief that God must be glorified in everything they do—even building a pool—leads them to stick together and means that their networks spread far beyond their local church. There are Christian dating services (eHarmony, for one), Christian Yellow Pages to help them find one another, and many churches now offer classifieds on their Web sites through which church members can advertise services. In some towns there are Christian coffee shops and nightclubs. And even without specific listings, evangelicals find each other through the grapevine and through subtle symbols such as the hollow dove or the two-line fish. Most evangelicals will know which local—and national—businesses are owned or run by other Christians. Any evangelical will be able to tell you that the Chick-fil-A fast-food chain is owned by a fellow believer; that Carl Karcher, founder of Carl's Jr., is a person of deep faith; that Tom Monaghan, the man who started Domino's Pizza, is a devout Catholic who funds pro-life groups, and that the shopping bags at Forever 21 (which sells provocative clothing that no good Christian girl should be caught dead in) have "John 3:16" printed on the bottom. (This is the most important verse in the evangelical canon, which every Christian can recite from memory: "For God so loved the world that he gave his only begotten son that whosoever believed in him should not perish but have eternal life.") When Robert Schuller spoke of the retailing of religion, he likely never imagined the state of things today. The evangelical community has become an economy of its own. The pages of Christian magazines are filled with advertisements for Christian cruises, Christian book-of-the-month clubs, Christian software, chairs, and furniture. Even the children's television channel my son likes to watch, Discovery Kids, routinely airs a commercial for a CD called "Worship Jamz," a pop version of church songs released by the same people who put out "Kidz Bop." In America everything is commoditized, and with the mainstreaming of evangelicals, faith is no exception.

* * *

It's Saturday morning and about two dozen adolescent girls are sitting in a classroom at the Thurgood Marshall Academy, a public school in Harlem, engaged in an animated discussion about interracial dating. From there they segue into what attracts boys and girls to each other at this age and whether or not money plays into the equation. Many of the girls don't really want to be here and are being forced to turn up each Saturday by their parents, but their reluctance doesn't prevent them from getting involved in the conversation and voicing strong opinions. In a room a few doors away the boys are having a similarly frank conversation. These are the sons and daughters of the Blue Nile Passage, a program designed to develop the spiritual, cultural, and moral character of its participants. Blue Nile has a mentoring element and an educational component for parents and children that teaches them about personal growth, health and wellness, spiritual grounding, community consciousness, historical black experience, economic awareness, and politics. It's an intense, demanding, nine-month rite-of-passage course that not all of them will finish successfully. Blue Nile is part tough love, part black power, and part Christianity. It's also an offshoot of Harlem's famous Abyssinian Baptist Church.

I'm visiting Blue Nile at the invitation of its executive director, Cliff Simmons. Cliff and his wife, Diane, are the urban, African American counterparts to Lee and Diane Holman in their involvement with Abyssinian. Diane is at the church several days a week for choir practices and performances, working for the tape ministry (which distributes tapes of the sermon to members) and helping out with one of the special luncheons that seem always to be taking place. Their daughter attends youth group on Friday nights and church with her parents on Sunday morning, and their youngest son is a mentor in Blue Nile. Cliff works nights doing desktop publishing for an investment bank, so his days—or what's left of them once he's come home and slept for a while—are free for Blue Nile. He's there all day Saturday but organizing things takes up a lot of his time during the week as well.

Whereas churches like New Life and Calvary invite people in to live their lives under their big tents, African American churches reach out into the communities around them. The church is an integral part of people's lives in both cases, but in profoundly different ways. White churches, particularly those that evolved out of the tradition that rejected the social gospel, tend to the spiritual and emotional first and the physical second. In a nod to Calvary founder Chuck Smith and the social gospel proponents before him, there are programs in nearly all of them to provide food and clothing for the needy, but these outreaches are not particularly emphasized in middle-class suburban churches that tend to be predominantly populated by baby boomers. In black churches, on the other hand, spiritual and physical needs are generally dealt with equally. White megachurches tend to be suburban while black megachurches tend to be urban, so the congregations have different lifestyles and socio-economic profiles. More than that, though, the history of the African American church in America is entirely different from that of the white church.

African Americans in America began to convert to Christianity in the mid-1700s when evangelists such as George Whitefield started sharing the gospel with them. These preachers brought the message that all people were equal in the eyes of God, one that had obvious appeal and inherent hope for enslaved blacks. If any group of people in America needed to find solace from their lives, it was slaves, and, indeed, African Americans became Christians in large numbers between the War for Independence and the Civil War. For the most part, slaves were only allowed to attend white churches, sitting in separate sections, but many slave communities also held clandestine church meetings. African Americans already were developing their own style of worship through the spirituals they sang, with their message of emancipation from bondage both spiritual and physical.

The church became exponentially more important for blacks after abolition because it provided a critical center where African Americans could gather, and offered structure to newly forming communities.

African American churches sprouted up at an astounding rate and quickly became the most important institution in Southern black society, providing literacy programs and mutual aid societies that helped pay for burials, care for the sick, and support widows and their children. The church was often the only wholly black institution in town and the only place African Americans could attain positions of leadership.

At the time of the Emancipation Proclamation in 1863 there were already established black churches in the North, and these congregations opened missions in the South for their newly freed brothers. Membership in these black denominations soon numbered in the hundreds of thousands. The northern Christians helped finance the building of churches and the social services offered there, which grew to include better-developed educational programs and schools, clinics, and hospitals. Efforts to meet community needs have changed and expanded over time. More recently, as the government's attempts at welfare have proved insufficient, the church has stepped into the breach.

While the beliefs of black Protestant churches are in line with the definition of evangelical that I have used in this book, African Americans tend not to use the term because of their discrete history. When they were free to start their own churches, African Americans understandably wanted to distance themselves from the white churches they had attended as slaves. Until recently, segregation within the church body was almost complete. Today there are escalating numbers of churches, particularly megachurches, that have some integration in their congregations, but in most cases blacks and whites continue to worship separately. One of the biggest sources of division between the two groups has been politics, despite similar attitudes about morality. For the most part, black Christians still tend to be Democrats while white Christians are generally Republican. There are signs of change, however. In the 2004 election many African American pastors spoke out against gay marriage, for example, and some openly supported President Bush.

From the beginning, the focus of black churches has been both social and political. Many of the freed slaves who became clergymen capitalized on the platform and prestige their positions as church leaders afforded them to run for office. The church soon turned to the task of overcoming racism and the injustices it wrought, and played a key role in the civil rights movement. Not only were many of the movement's leaders drawn from the clergy, but churches were an organizing force rivaled only by black trade unions. Today African American religious institutions continue that legacy, reaching deep into their surrounding communities to offer a wide array of services, including schooling, housing, and job training.

In addition to its many ministries, Abyssinian Baptist Church has a development corporation as part of the church's stated mission "to win more souls for Christ through evangelism, pastoral care, Christian education, social service delivery, and community development." It's a calling that has been at the forefront of Abyssinian's activities since its earliest days in Harlem, where it moved from downtown Manhattan in the 1920s. By the end of that decade the church had already purchased a home for the aged; by the end of the next decade it also operated a community center and had a membership of more than seven thousand. During the Depression, the church clothed and fed thousands of people and provided work for many. By the 1950s Abyssinian offered daily activities for its members. The day I visited Blue Nile, Cliff Simmons spoke to a group of parents and recounted the story of Abyssinian's history. The church and its members are rightfully proud of the contributions it has made to its community and congregants are encouraged to aspire to such deeds as well. By sharing in the church's history they share in its accomplishments.

Today Abyssinian is a virtual town center, with a federal credit union and a job bank. It also has a slew of enrichment initiatives, including a cotillion, an adolescent development program, SAT preparation, a college and career fair, an athletic league, a tutoring program, an AIDS awareness course for youth, a food buying club, and financial literacy classes. Its Web site has a searchable database of scholarships, membership profiles, and classified ads. Abyssinian also offers some of the same fare you'd find in a suburban white megachurch, with exercise classes for seniors, a physical challenge series, counseling services, Weight Watchers, a mentoring program, and fellowship groups for men and women. And then there's the music, which has always been an integral part of the African American religious experience. Abyssinian does music in its usual expansive way: In addition to seven choirs, the church has arranged world-class performances by musicians and groups such as Andre Watts and the New York Philharmonic Orchestra.

On top of all this is the not-for-profit development corporation, which has been responsible for more than $500 million in housing and commercial development in Harlem. The Abyssinian Development Corporation was started in response to Abyssinian's pastor, Rev. Calvin Butts's urging that the church rebuild the community brick by brick, block by block. Since its founding in 1989 it has created more than a thousand units of affordable housing in eighty-two buildings, with another three hundred units in the pipeline. The Abyssinian Development Corporation has overseen the renovation of apartments for the homeless, the construction of a one hundred-unit residential building for seniors and, in conjunction with the city, has renovated condominiums for families with moderate incomes. Also, in conjunction with the city, the ADC established the Thurgood Marshall Academy for Learning and Social Change, a public school. The corporation's reach is demonstrably broad, as per its stated mission to "increase the availability of quality housing to people with diverse incomes; enhance the delivery of social services, particularly to the homeless, elderly, families, and children; foster economic revitalization; enhance educational and developmental opportunities for youth; and build community capacity through civic engagement." Through ADC, Abyssinian's scope goes well beyond that of the traditional church.

Politics goes hand in glove at Abyssinian just as it does in the black church as a whole. Adam Clayton Powell Jr., who succeeded his father as pastor of ABC in 1937, was one of the century's best-known politicians. The church, which grew to ten thousand members under his leadership, served as his political base. Powell began his political career as a city councilman and in 1944 was elected to serve in the U.S. House of Representatives, where he stayed for fourteen terms. Powell was an ardent civil rights activist and presided over a stack of legislation to benefit blacks and other minorities. Butts has upheld Powell's legacy, having coordinated voter registration drives and led campaigns against racist hiring practices, negative billboard advertising in Harlem, rap lyrics that degrade women, and police brutality. The church continues to fund the NAACP, the Legal Defense Fund, and the United Negro College Fund.

Even Butts's sermons are politicized. I attended Abyssinian on one of the Sundays Diane Simmons was performing with the choir. Butts was preaching from Luke 16, which tells the story of Lazarus, a beggar who longed for crumbs from the rich man's table. "Why accept crumbs when we baked the bread?" Butts demanded of his congregation. He used the story as a message of empowerment, which he said would come from self-worth not money. Self-esteem is derived not from taking handouts, he said, but by supporting oneself and one's community. He used the current fiscal state of his institution as an example. The church had undergone a multimillion-dollar renovation, and Butts was calling upon the members to help pay for it. He didn't go looking for rich donors, he said, because the congregation needed to be able to hold their heads high. "How could you black men and women take pride in an institution that you won't support yourselves?" he demanded of them.

The message of Abyssinian and Blue Nile is that black people need to work hard and take care of their own. Sermons about one's physical needs and God's promise to attend to them are common at African American churches, partly due to an ethos that lingers from the days of hardship during which the black church was born, and partly because so many of those churches are still located in the inner city where their congregations struggle financially. Bishop T. D. Jakes, of the Potter's House in Dallas, is America's most famous

African American pastor and has a broad view of the role the church should play in its members' lives. The Potter's House works with prison inmates and with those who are affected by or infected with the AIDS virus. It has a huge counseling department and myriad support groups and holds job fairs and voter registration drives. Its reach is enormous—and still Jakes would like to be doing more. "Wherever there's a need, we want to supply service," said Jakes, an imposing figure with a gravelly voice and a penchant for white suits.

The clearest picture of what Jakes would like his church to be is Megafest, the massive four-day event he stages each summer in Atlanta when he takes over the Georgia Dome, the Georgia World Congress Center, and the Philips Arena. Part festival, part revival and part conference, Megafest is attended by more than 100,000 people each year. They go to fashion shows and concerts, where last year they were entertained by the likes of Gladys Knight, Chaka Kahn, CeCe Winans, and Steve Harvey. Suze Orman spoke about managing money because Jakes is concerned that many in his congregation need to improve their skills in that area. He points to the growing number of single mothers and of seniors who run out of funds at the end of their lives. "We have to deal with that by educating our people how to effectively deal with money," he said. Jakes also brings in business incubators and motivational speakers. There are separate events for youth and children and there is, of course, plenty of preaching. He'd like to offer the same scope of services at the Potter's House someday.

Black churches and white churches share a desire to care for their communities, but they differ on what that means. The African American church was born not out of material might but out of a need for support both spiritual and temporal. Community is the physical area around the church and the people who live there—regardless of faith—and the black church believes its job is to care for all their needs. In white churches the community is one of faith and the imperative is, as Calvary's Lee Holman put it, to build disciples. While suburban white megachurches all provide turkeys for the needy on

Thanksgiving and gifts for underprivileged children at Christmas, ever since the divvying up that left mainline denominations (inheritors of the social gospel) tending to bodies and evangelical churches focusing on the souls within them, these programs have been little more than an afterthought. The activities these churches offer mirror those available in secular America, enabling them to grant respite from the outside world. For some of its members, the church is a place they can cloister themselves and their families, away from the influences of a godless society. For most, though, the church provides a sanctuary to which believers can retreat and gain strength for further engagement.

II

Culture

CHAPTER FIVE

Spreading the Word

A SMATTERING OF Manhattan's media elite have gathered on top of Rockefeller Plaza at the luxurious Rainbow Room on a clear September evening to honor one of the most successful writers the book industry has ever seen. Bellinis flow freely as black-and-white clad waiters circulate with caviar-topped new potatoes. A veritable who's who of evangelical Christianity has flown in for the event and makes small talk while half distracted by the urban panorama visible through the floor-to-ceiling windows. HarperCollins CEO Jane Friedman wraps up her remarks and steps aside to let her boss, media mogul Rupert Murdoch, take the podium. "When one of our authors sells a million books, people think he's a genius. But when one of our authors sells nearly 20 million books, people think we're geniuses," Murdoch tells a chuckling crowd.

It's not Sidney Sheldon or Arundhati Roy whom the glitterati have come to celebrate, but a more unlikely publishing superstar—Southern Baptist pastor Rick Warren. Warren is the author of *The Purpose-Driven Life,* the best-selling hardcover book in publishing history. It has sold more than 25 million copies and is a cash cow for its Christian publisher, Zondervan, and parent company Harper-Collins, which in turn is owned by Murdoch's News Corporation. *The Purpose-Driven Life* was the best-selling book in America in both 2003 and 2004.

Surprising as it may be, Warren's is not the first religious book to take the publishing world by storm. While *The Purpose-Driven Life* sold nearly a million copies a month for the first nine months after it was published, the sales record it breezed through had been set by another Christian book in 2001, *The Prayer of Jabez.* Christian publisher Tyndale's Left Behind franchise of apocalyptic thrillers has sold more than 63 million books and audiotapes, and the release of the twelfth book in the series landed its authors a spot on the cover of *Newsweek.* More recently *Your Best Life Now,* a book written by Texas's smiling pastor Joel Osteen, sold millions of copies and overtook Warren's on best-seller lists.

All of these books are God-heavy and loaded with scripture. Their messages are overtly evangelical. None of them is likely to win a Pulitzer. It's difficult to imagine they would hold any appeal for people outside of the faith. Yet the sales figures tell a different story. Since 2001, a Christian book has been one of the top seven best-selling hardcover books each year in both the fiction and nonfiction categories. Since then, a Christian book has been the number one seller in the nonfiction category every year except 2002, when Bruce Wilkinson's *A Life God Rewards* came in at number two, and 2005, when *Your Best Life Now* took the second slot. So what gives? How do these formulaic, evangelistic books wind up at the top of best-seller lists time and time again?

The Christian publishing industry has always been the most sophisticated outpost of evangelical culture, but Christian books have now knocked down the fences that once separated them from the mainstream. The incursion started with *Left Behind,* coauthored by pastor Tim LaHaye and writer Jerry Jenkins. But while readers may have flocked to the Left Behind books for their thrilling end-of-days plots and not for their spiritual content, *The Purpose-Driven Life* is little more than a forty-day devotional that sets out to answer the question "Why are we here?" and helps readers find God's purpose for their lives. It's accessible and, to its critics' chagrin, reduces the Bible to digestible little nuggets. Frothy though it may be, the book's spiritual content makes up its bulk.

Some of the book's staggering success can be explained simply by the sheer size of the Christian book market and the rate at which it is expanding. "Religious books have emerged as the most impressive growth category in the book publishing industry over the past four years," the Book Industry Study Group wrote in its "Trends 2005" report. "We predict that over the next five years total book industry revenues will increase 18.3 percent, paced by religious books with a 50 percent rise."

There may be even more expansion in the realm of Christian fiction, particularly Christian chick-lit, which has been growing in leaps and bounds over the past several years, in part because these titles are getting shelf space at the big-box retailers such as Costco and Sam's Club. But chiefly, sales of Christian novels are picking up for the simple reason that they are getting better. Christian fiction is going through the same kind of transition that Christian music began in the 1980s: it's mostly poor with a few exceptions breaking through—although the caliber is improving and some authors can hold their own in the secular market. (Karen Kingsbury, for example, was dubbed by *Time* magazine "The Queen of Christian Fiction" and has more than 4 million books in print.) The industry is working to create better fiction and, in 1999, launched the Christy Awards as part of an effort to raise standards. It seems to be paying off: *Publishers Weekly* has started taking Christian fiction more seriously and now includes Christian novels in its general fiction review pages instead of relegating them to the religion section. Even *People* magazine now runs reviews of Christian novels. Part of the improvement has come about from authors and publishers realizing that good Christian fiction doesn't have to be evangelistic. Authors are beginning to deal with real-life issues such as rape and divorce and are now writing in all kinds of Christian subgenres, from romance to sci-fi.

I went to the 2005 Book Expo America at the Jacob Javits Convention Center in New York City to see how Christian publishing houses presented themselves to the secular marketplace. I looked at the floor plan, found the section set aside for religious publishers on the level below the main exhibition hall, and made my way down the escalators. I wandered back and forth through the aisles looking for Zondervan, Thomas Nelson, or any of the other big Christian companies I had become familiar with, but couldn't find any of them. I finally bumped into a publicist I knew from Thomas Nelson who was loading posters at the Thomas Nelson Bargain Books booth. "Oh, we're upstairs," she told me. "Right between Time Warner and HarperCollins."

I rode the escalator upstairs and there they were—in a booth in the middle of the exhibition floor, decorated with plush cream-colored carpeting and as impressive as that of any other publisher there. Walking through the Thomas Nelson displays, you would have to look closely before realizing they were a religious company. Sure, there were books about God, but many secular publishers put out religion books. Zondervan also had a deluxe display, in a corner of the long HarperCollins booth next to Harper's many other imprints.

Not surprisingly, secular houses are now realizing that a good Christian yarn can be spun into gold. As Murdoch said in reference to *The Purpose-Driven Life*: "The reception accorded this book—whose phenomenal sales seem to have come in completely under the mainstream radar—tells us that this is an underserved market." Many publishers have put programs in place to capture those readers. HarperCollins—home to Michael Crichton and Michael Chabon, and publisher of such titles as *Confessions of a Video Vixen* and, to the extreme dismay of many Christians, *The Satanic Bible*—owns Zondervan, a Christian company that Murdoch bought in 1988, as well as Harper San Francisco, a religious publisher Murdoch acquired in 1987 when he bought Harper & Row. Time Warner, which published Kim Cattrall's *Sexual Intelligence* and Jon Stewart and his Daily Show writers' *America: A Citizen's Guide to Democracy Inaction,* started the Warner Faith imprint in 2001. Bill Clinton's publisher Random House has WaterBrook, an autonomous religious publishing division launched in 1996. In 2006 Simon & Schuster bought inspirational publisher Howard. Maureen Dowd and John Berendt's publisher, Penguin Putnam, is also home to megachurch pastor Bishop T. D. Jakes and recently started Penguin Praise. When Christian authors get really big, secular houses try to steal them away from their Christian publishers or faith imprints. Jan Karon moved to Viking after her first three Mitford books were published by Lion; LaHaye and Jenkins jumped from Tyndale to Putnam; and, in what may be the most lucrative deal in publishing history, Osteen jumped from Warner Faith to Simon & Schuster's Free Press imprint for an undisclosed sum that has been reported to be as high as $13 million.

The increasingly permeable barrier between mainstream and Christian publishing is being breached from both sides. Christian publisher Thomas Nelson, the ninth biggest publisher in the world, has had considerable success in the arena of non-Christian publishing, although it puts out secular books under different imprints to avoid confusion. For example, its Nelson Current imprint is home to bestselling conservative shock jock Michael Savage; chef Wolfgang Puck's cookbook *Wolfgang Puck Makes It Easy* and Ed McMahon's memoir *Here's Johnny!* were issued under its Rutledge Hill imprint; and gardening books come out under the Cool Springs label. But even with all the secular publishing endeavors, Nelson's spiritual commitment remains firm. Executives there frequently ask authors for a statement of faith, which they provide to Christian retailers to help them understand where a specific author is coming from spiritually. All the authors published under the religious imprints must write from the Christian perspective; Nelson will publish a non-Christian author under a secular imprint as long as the book honors the Christian worldview and is wholesome entertainment.

Warren's publisher, Zondervan, is owned by a secular media giant but it hews closely to its well-established religious underpinnings. One of the first questions its editors ask themselves when considering proposals for new books is "Does this conform to our mission statement?" which Zondervan's sales force recites with such frequency that even its secular distributors know it by heart: "To be the leading Christian communications company meeting the needs of people with resources that glorify Jesus Christ and promote biblical principles."

Still, the company keeps an eye trained on its bottom line as closely as any secular publisher and runs its business with the same precision, something that hasn't always been true of the Christian publishing business. "Standards are higher," said Zondervan's vice-president of marketing John Topliff, pointing out that most of the editorial staff has master's degrees, many in areas such as marketing, sales, and design. "I think that's new in the last fifteen to twenty years. It's just a higher level of education and sophistication."

Incursions into the Christian market by major New York houses keep Christian publishers on their toes. I attended several days of publishing board meetings at Thomas Nelson's headquarters in Nashville, in which editorial staff get together with marketing and sales staff. About two dozen executives sat around several long tables arranged in a big square to listen to a presentation from the team at Tommy Nelson, the children's imprint. Before they started, they bowed their heads in prayer. "As we do business today I pray . . . you would give us creativity," someone prayed. "We want to do this because you called us to do it. We want to do it well." After the prayer, talk turned to the increasing competition they're getting from secular publishers for space on the shelves of Christian bookstores. "Simon & Schuster is ramping up CBA," someone said, referring to the Christian Booksellers Association, the trade group that represents Christian bookstores, which have historically bought the bulk of their books from Christian publishers. "So are Scholastic and Golden Books." Another person added: "They're offering multi-book deals," mentioning Naomi Judd, who had done a children's book for Thomas Nelson but has also been published by Simon & Schuster, which was fighting to publish her children's books as well. Thomas Nelson had worked out a deal with her, but Simon & Schuster offered double the money. Despite that, it seemed that Judd, herself an evangelical, was leaning toward staying with Thomas Nelson. "She says that we get it and they don't get it," an editor explained. "She doesn't want to continue because they keep editing the faith out," Thomas Nelson's chief publishing officer, Tamara Heim, told me later.

Nelson also managed to snag Robin McGraw, Dr. Phil McGraw's wife (both are evangelicals), to do a book for women. With Dr. Phil's show as a built-in platform, the potential for sales is considerable. Heim is herself a prime example of one of the reasons Christian publishers are able to compete. Before coming to Thomas Nelson she served as the president of Borders Books, the second-largest chain of bookstores in the country. She'd left Borders to spend more time with her family, she said, and was offered other jobs but didn't feel God was leading her to any of them. When the call from Nelson came, though, she agreed to move her family to Nashville from their home in Detroit so she could take a less prestigious job at a smaller company for a reduced salary because she believes that was what God was calling her to do. "The way I see it, it's like I stepped up because the purpose is so much higher," she told me. When she pulls out of the parking lot each night and sees the trucks being loaded with books, she thinks about the lives those volumes might change and is thankful to be at Nelson.

There are tangible reasons for Heim and the publishers of Christian books to be happy, too. For starters, studies show that evangelicals buy more books than adherents to other religions. More than that, Americans of all religious backgrounds seem to be in a seeking mode, an attitude most likely bolstered by the September 11 terrorist attacks. The search for spirituality is, in large part, fueled by baby boomers who, now that they've made their money and raised their children, are looking back on the first half of their lives and trying to figure out what it all means. They're at the age where they are losing spouses and friends and confronting questions about life and death. They're looking to the spiritual realm for answers. In the individualistic world of evangelical Christianity the road to growth is a personal one. While a good pastor can give advice and guidance along the way, so can a good friend or a good author. Christians often supplement church with personal study and rely on books to help them in their endeavors to lead more Christlike lives.

While Christian writers and editors vociferously refute this characterization, it's impossible to overlook the therapeutic aspect of these books. *Breaking Through to the Blessed Life,* the subtitle of Bruce Wilkinson's *The Prayer of Jabez,* puts the responsibility for that leap forward in the hands of the reader. "The little book you're holding is about what happens when ordinary Christians decide to reach for an extraordinary life—which, as it turns out, is exactly the kind God promises," the book begins. Wilkinson urges people to transform their lives by reciting daily the prayer of an obscure character from the Bible named Jabez. "And Jabez called on the God of Israel, saying 'Oh, that You would bless me indeed, and enlarge my territory, that Your hand would be with me, and that You would keep me from evil, that I may not cause pain'" (1 Chronicles 4:10). Just as Jabez's prayer was granted, so, too, will ours be. Wilkinson advises his readers to keep a journal of the changes that occur in their lives as a result not of the prayer itself but of their deeds. "It's only what you believe will happen *and therefore do next* that will release God's power for you and bring about a life change," Wilkinson writes. The fusing of the self-help movement with religion that has informed evangelical Christianity for centuries is evident here.

Osteen's *Your Best Life Now* is similarly focused on an individual's responsibility to take control of his own life. The book's chapters are divided into seven sections, all of which emphasize action: "Enlarge Your Vision," "Develop a Healthy Self-Image," "Discover the Power of Your Thoughts and Words," "Let Go of the Past," "Find Strength Through Adversity," "Live to Give!" and "Choose to Be Happy." While God is on virtually every page of the book, there's nothing particularly biblical—or even spiritual—in any of those concepts. They're the same sorts of ideas that could be found in any number of secular self-help volumes.

Warren's *The Purpose-Driven Life* is intended as a user's manual for humans. It starts out by asking readers to make a covenant with

God and promise that they will—with God's help—commit the next forty days of their lives to discovering God's purpose for them. The covenant is written out and there is a place where the reader can sign his name. Warren has already cosigned. The book is divided into forty chapters and the program calls for readers to finish one each day. The chapters are grouped into five sections, each one of which identifies one of the purposes that God has for our lives— worship, community, discipleship, ministry, and evangelism—and argues that by pursuing those we can find fulfillment. More instructive than most of its competitors and, at the same time, more conceptual, the book is full of suggestions for living a fulfilled life and achieving positive self-worth. "What I'm able to do God wants me to do," reads one paragraph heading. "You have dozens, probably hundreds, of untapped, unrecognized, and unused abilities that are lying dormant inside you," Warren writes. "Many studies have revealed that the average person possesses from 500 to 700 different skills and abilities—far more than you realize." Warren quotes hundreds of Bible verses to make his points—although purists are uncomfortable with the way he uses them, taking them out of context and using many different translations to bolster his arguments.

In a sense, these books are self-help made easy. Where traditional self-help books try to empower readers and help them find the strength within themselves to change their lives, Christian books tell readers that God can change their lives for them if they just cede control to him. Then, if your life isn't getting better, it's because you're not "letting go and letting God," as the mantra goes. In this world, you don't have to figure out what you want and how to get it, you have to figure out what God wants for you and let him take care of the rest. Many of these books promise riches and other fulfillment for readers who manage to get themselves onto God's path. They're self-help from a different perspective: The self is about divining one's purpose in life, and the help comes from God.

So while Warren expressly says his book is not a self-help book and begins it with the sentence "It's not about you," his book—just like

the bulk of Christian books that have crossed into the mainstream—
is, in many ways, exactly that. The massive audience for Warren's
book extends well beyond Christian circles to nonbelievers. "They're
buying it and they're reading it and frankly we hear reports all the
time of people being converted to Christianity as a result of reading
it," Stanley Gundry, editor-in-chief of Zondervan's book group told
me. "Then they become evangelists for the book and buy them by
the scores and give them to their friends."

But even with a receptive audience, successes like *The Purpose-
Driven Life* don't come out of the blue. While Zondervan executives
and Rick Warren like to say that the book's success is "all God"—
and perhaps that's as plausible an explanation as any for how a simple devotional could become the best-selling book of all time—they
gave it quite a helping hand themselves. Warren doggedly pushed for
media coverage and, under the banner of his ministry, orchestrated a
brilliant, ongoing promotional program.

When Warren wrote *The Purpose-Driven Life* in 2002, Zondervan
had already sold more than a million copies of his book *The Purpose-
Driven Church,* which equipped pastors with tactics to expand their
churches. At that point, more than 115,000 pastors subscribed to his
pastors.com, which provided them with tools for their ministries, including ideas for sermons. These churches and pastors served as a
natural sales base for Warren's second book. Similarly, Osteen,
whose Lakewood Church in Houston draws more than thirty-eight
thousand people each weekend, had a built-in market not only
through his immense congregation but through his widely disseminated television broadcasts as well.

Warren realized the potential his book had to spread to other
churches, writing the forty-chapter volume with his now widely used
"40 Days of Purpose" program in mind. In "40 Days of Purpose,"
entire church congregations simultaneously read a chapter of his

book a day and have weekly discussions in groups of eight to ten people. Pastors in participating churches deliver sermons during those six weeks drawing from materials provided by Warren's ministry. Across the country, entire churches read the book simultaneously. Warren estimates that more than 10 percent of the country's congregations have gone through the program, as have companies and professional athletic teams. Warren's organization has even started coordinating citywide Purpose-Driven campaigns.

Zondervan didn't immediately see the possibilities, according to officials at Saddleback, and objected to a forty-chapter book, but Warren insisted, and, in the end, rightly so. The "40 Days of Purpose" program was launched in October 2002 with a simulcast or video message from Warren to fifteen hundred churches. Warren's organization made copies of *The Purpose-Driven Life* available to those congregations for seven dollars, little more than a third of the twenty-dollar suggested retail price. In the first round of "40 Days of Purpose," Zondervan sold nearly half a million discounted copies of the book. To date, more than thirty thousand American churches have gone through the program and books have been made available to all of them at a reduced cost.

While Zondervan was initially reluctant to offer so many books at such a deep price cut and effectively neutralize its profit margin, an astounding thing happened when they did. Of those who went through the forty-day program, 83 percent actively recommended the book to someone else and 46 percent bought copies—in many cases multiple copies—at retail outlets for friends and family. Zondervan also put out supporting products—all of which are plugged in the book—including "The Purpose-Driven Life Journal," "The Purpose-Driven Life Scripture Keeper Plus," and a twelve-song CD. With the "40 Days of Purpose" campaign continuing to be offered at churches several times a year, there is a perpetual stream of sales. "It is a marketing approach that nobody can compete with," said Bob Wenz, former vice president of national ministries at the National Association of Evangelicals. "We've got 340,000 churches in this country and when 10 percent of them say, 'Buy this book,' you're going to sell millions of copies."

The book got another boost when Ashley Smith was taken hostage by a gunman who had escaped from an Atlanta courtroom. Her captor, who had already allegedly killed four people during his attempt to break free from police custody, turned himself in after she read to him from *The Purpose-Driven Life* and cooked pancakes for him. It was a lucky turn of events—or one divinely orchestrated, depending on your perspective—that sparked a new round of sales of the book and on which Warren shrewdly capitalized with a flurry of media appearances, including a profile in the *New Yorker* magazine and even a surprise visit to the Oprah Winfrey show to sit at Smith's side.

Warren, who describes his tactics as a "stealth strategy," has been very sophisticated and deliberate in controlling his message, and he is willing to go to great lengths to protect it and his public image. He and his staff closely monitor what is written about him and, on more than one occasion, have sent aggressive e-mails, almost obsessive in their attention to detail, to quash portrayals of himself with which he disagrees. In one particularly messy incident, Warren managed to delay the publication of a book by Greg Stielstra, a senior marketing executive at Zondervan who had directed the marketing campaign for *The Purpose-Driven Life*. Stielstra wrote a book for another HarperCollins imprint, HarperBusiness, called *Pyromarketing: The Four-Step Strategy to Ignite Consumer Evangelists and Keep Them for Life*, that used *The Purpose-Driven Life* as a case study. After Stielstra entered into his deal to publish the book, Zondervan's editor-in-chief suggested he make Warren aware of the book. Stielstra complied and met with Warren's agent at the time, Bucky Rosenbaum, who had three requests: He asked that *The Purpose-Driven Life* not be the only case study in the book, that Stielstra approach the book as an outside observer and that Rosenbaum be shown the manuscript before publication. Stielstra acceded to all three demands.

Shortly after that meeting, Stielstra e-mailed Warren and outlined the three points of the agreement. He included a portion of the book to show how *The Purpose-Driven Life* was being handled. Within hours he received an e-mail from Rosenbaum that said "This is fine and consistent with our agreement."

But a few months after HarperBusiness had accepted Stielstra's manuscript, he received a call from a member of Warren's team, Doug Slaybaugh, who told him he would use "every ounce of influence" he had to see that any reference to *The Purpose-Driven Life* was removed from the book. Shortly after that, Warren's new agent, Jeff Slipp, asked to see a copy of the manuscript with the expectation that he would be allowed to make changes. Warren's representatives also went to Zondervan president Doug Lockhart and made the same request. Stielstra sent Slipp a copy because he couldn't imagine that anyone on Warren's team would object to the way *The Purpose-Driven Life* was handled.

He couldn't have been more wrong. Slipp and Lockhart went back and forth with Stielstra, who agreed to amend anything that was inaccurate or harmful to Warren. He ended up making two rounds of changes to the manuscript. At Saddleback's request, Harper typeset and resubmitted the revised manuscript to Slipp, who deemed it acceptable. But shortly after that, Warren called Lockhart directly and told him he wanted all references to *The Purpose-Driven Life* deleted from the book.

Harper's editorial team came to Stielstra and suggested he use the previous presidential election as a case study instead. Stielstra declined and asked HarperBusiness to publish his book as it was or give the rights back to him so he could take the manuscript to another publisher. "Except for casting my vote, I had no involvement in the 2004 presidential election. By contrast, I was the marketing director for *The Purpose-Driven Life*," Stielstra told *Publishers Weekly*. Eventually, HarperBusiness relented and published *Pyromarketing*.

Warren issued a statement that ran in *Christian Retailing* magazine and was also sent to *Publishers Weekly*, which had been following the story. "My only concern was that no one, neither Zondervan Publishing nor myself, claim credit for the astounding success of *The Purpose-Driven Life* (*PDL*) book. The worldwide spread of the purpose-driven message had nothing to do with marketing or merchandising. Instead it was the result of God's supernatural and sovereign plan, which no one anticipated," the statement read in part.

Stielstra has since left Zondervan and gone to work for its competitor Thomas Nelson.

There's little doubt that Warren cares deeply about his ministry, but he has also created a formidable marketing model that other publishers and even other industries will look to copy. It's one that has already been put to good use by Paul Lauer of Motive Entertainment, who tapped into the church network to promote *The Passion of the Christ, The Polar Express,* and *The Chronicles of Narnia.* Evangelicals make up a community with massive purchasing power and because they're so centralized around megachurches it's one that can be easily reached. What's more, aside from their religion, evangelicals don't have anything else in common. They are male and female, young and old, rich and poor, black, white, Hispanic, Asian, Arab, and anything else. They are a buying bloc millions strong who can't all be reached at the same time *except* through their churches. Perhaps the biggest lesson of the success of *The Passion of the Christ* and *The Purpose-Driven Life* is that there are millions of individuals out there who, given the right stimulus, will coalesce to form a formidable, coherent marketplace.

Warren may feel that shining a spotlight on the decidedly temporal concern of marketing may dilute his message, but evangelical Christianity is inherently entrepreneurial and, particularly in America, always has been. Evangelicals were early innovators in both radio and television, with televangelists employing the same techniques as direct retailers selling their wares on TV. One promises that Jesus will change your life, the other that the latest ab machine or acne medicine will. The products are different but the techniques and assurances are remarkably similar.

The Purpose-Driven Life also illustrates the power of books to propel a pastor to celebrity status and of that status, in turn, to sell books. It's a dynamic of which publishers are well aware. Zondervan, conscious that the success of *The Purpose-Driven Life* can't continue indefinitely, is particularly sensitive to that cycle. I attended an editorial meeting at Zondervan's headquarters in a leafy area of Grand Rapids, Michigan, in which a group of editors discussed book proposals that had come their way. They lingered in debate over the merits of one in particular, submitted by a young but promising pastor. "Is there as much potential as I think in this young man or do you think we ought to pass?" one asked. They unanimously agreed that it was the wrong book at the wrong time but were reluctant to let an up-and-comer slip through their fingers. "Let's explore with him whether this proposal or another is the first step in his publishing career," an editor concluded. No one needed to be reminded to be on the lookout for the next Rick Warren.

Even without a television or radio ministry, Warren is now one of the best-known and most influential pastors in America. He has been invited the White House, the Council on Foreign Relations, the United Nations, the Kennedy School of Government at Harvard, and the World Economic Forum in Davos. He has been on television countless times, including appearances on *Oprah*, *Larry King Live*, *Today*, *Good Morning America*, *The Early Show*, and many, many others. Once a tubby guy in a Hawaiian-print shirt, these days Warren sports a slicker haircut, snazzier suits, and whiter teeth. In his recent publicity shots he abandoned West Coast pastels for an edgy goatee and East Coast black, which he wears from top to toe. He moves in elevated circles and has surrounded himself with a cadre of advisers. He doesn't preach at Saddleback nearly as often as he used to, but on one of the last occasions I managed to see him there he had even shed the aloha-print shirt. Warren is now much more than just a pastor, or even an author. Like his church, Warren is himself now a franchise, and Purpose-Driven is his brand. In addition to the many Purpose-Driven products, including scripture cards, an audio edition for commuters, and a special edition for graduates, Warren now writes a column in *Ladies Home Journal* called "Purpose," Hallmark has released a line of greeting cards, and a snippet from the book is featured on Starbucks coffee cups.

The huge sales of Christian books have changed the retail marketplace. Books like *Left Behind* and *The Purpose-Driven Life* were such massive hits that they were carried by general retailers like Costco, Sam's Club, and Wal-Mart. Chain bookstores, such as Borders and Barnes & Noble, which already had growing religion sections, continued their expansion. The sales forces from Christian houses are selling their wares to mainstream booksellers, and New York publishers are asking Christian bookstores to stock their titles. It can be trickier for secular publishers to sell to Christian booksellers, many of whom remain suspicious of outsiders. It's a lesson that Harper & Row (HarperCollins's predecessor and the company that acquired Zondervan) had to learn the hard way. "Initially Harper sales reps sold our books into those markets but, in the final analysis, those men and women weren't real successful," Zondervan's Gundry told me. "They didn't believe in them, nor did they understand them." There's a clear advantage to having Christians market to Christians—they know how to mobilize the network and speak in a language to which evangelicals respond. Part of the reason evangelical Christians can be so easily activated into a single voting or purchasing bloc, despite crossing nearly every other demographic line, is that they generally trust insiders and distrust outsiders. If someone at church is telling them to see a movie, buy a book, or support a candidate, they're going to assume the product in question is okay.

The message may be spiritual but the fruits of all this are decidedly material. With its celebrity pastors, multimillion-dollar advances, and sales figures that rival those of such literary giants as Tom

Clancy, Patricia Cornwell, and Stephen King, religious publishing has become a business like any other. In the face of the crass commercialism apparent at places such as the CBA convention and in church-lobby bookstores it is hard not to be reminded of the story of Jesus angrily overturning the tables of the money changers doing business in the temple. Mission statement or not, the survival of Christian publishing companies is dependent on earnings, just as at secular houses. That impels publishers to constantly manipulate the Christian message into new and marketable forms that will produce a continual stream of profitable products. These books may, in fact, teach people to live more godly and fulfilled lives. At the same time, they help their authors gain in wealth, power, and prestige—leaving their teachings sullied in the wash of lucre.

CHAPTER SIX

Make a Joyful Noise

What a beautiful smile, can I stay for a while?
On this beautiful night, we'll make everything right,
my beautiful love, my beautiful love . . .

A YOUNG BLOND woman is cradling a glass of wine as she sings along with the Afters, who are performing the single from their debut album at Star 102.5 FM's Starry Night in the Garden at the Buffalo and Erie County Botanical Garden. The event has just begun and most people are still waiting in lines at the various food and wine booths that surround the massive front lawn. The sparse crowd clustered in front of the stage that has been erected off to one side of the grass grows as people carrying plates piled high with samplings from local restaurants make their way down to listen to the music. A young man in a gray and black striped shirt standing in front of me clinks his beer bottle with a blond girl in a beaded top and short black skirt. Dotted around now are people bobbing their heads and bouncing to the beat as they sing along—a couple of girls to my right in camisole tops and tiered miniskirts, a single guy up front. Across the lawn a tall woman holds up a camera and shouts "I love you!"

I make my way over to her. "I love them," forty-six-year-old Brigid McDonald repeats to me. But when I ask her if she knows that the Afters are a Christian band she takes a sudden step back and is stunned into silence for a moment. It doesn't matter, she says, recovering herself and after a beat proffers: "The older I get the more I like Christian bands." She doesn't have to worry about whether or not their music is inappropriate for her ten-year-old, she explains.

Lead singer Josh Havens tells the audience that "with all the horrible things in the world, our love will lead us on," and launches into the band's final song of the evening, "Love Lead Me On." The group leaves the stage with the audience shouting for more and begins to load the sound gear back into their van as fans come up and ask them to pose for pictures or to sign CDs.

There aren't many groups who proudly wear the Christian label and perform for beer-drinking audiences, but the Afters hope to break down a lot of barriers. Their first manager told them they couldn't be a Christian band and a pop band at the same time, that they'd have to choose. "We said, 'You know what? This is what God called us to do and we're going to play the music we're going to play for whoever will listen,'" Havens tells me after the performance.

It turns out all kinds of people will listen. In the week preceding this show in Buffalo, the Afters performed at another radio-station show with Vertical Horizon in Akron, Ohio; in a bar in San Jose, California, also with Vertical Horizon; at a stadium show with Everclear in Modesto, California; in a small church in Medford, Wisconsin; at a county fair in Greenville, Texas, and for a church in Columbus, Ohio. They adapt their sets for each audience, but all the songs they sing come from their only album, which was released on two labels, Simple, a Christian label, and Epic, a secular one, an increasingly common arrangement. They released the "Beautiful Love" single into the secular radio market, where it spent sixteen weeks in the Top 30; it hit the top of the Christian chart. The album had only been out for about four months at the time of the Buffalo show, but there were already plenty of fans in the audience who had memorized the lyrics. After the Modesto gig the band was in such demand that they spent three hours signing autographs.

The Afters clearly have a secular following. Their single "Beautiful

Love" was chosen as the theme song for the MTV reality show *8th & Ocean*, which made it one of the twenty most downloaded songs on iTunes and propelled it onto the Billboard Hot 100 list. The catchy tune was also in the Lindsay Lohan movie *Just My Luck* and the band was featured on MTV's *Advance Warning*, a show that spotlights up-and-coming artists. Other musicians who have appeared on the show include Brie Larson and James Blunt.

Still, the better part of their fan base seems to be drawn from the Christian world, if a perusal of the blogosphere is any indication. Trey Orman, a fifteen-year-old from Garland, Texas, describes himself as a huge admirer. A typical high school freshman, when he's not in school or doing homework he spends his time playing basketball, dabbling on the computer, talking on the phone, or hanging out with his friends. He listens to music on his iPod in school (even though they're technically not allowed there) and in his room while he's doing his homework. In addition to the Afters, he listens to a mix of things, including Green Day, the All-American Rejects, Blink-182, Blindside, Thousand Foot Krutch, Relient K, and Switchfoot—but mostly Christian music. "I believe in the message that's in it, and I just enjoy it more," he explained.

Orman has a mix of friends, Christian and non-Christian, and almost everyone he's played the Afters for has really liked them—including his parents. Even more than the message, though, Orman likes the band's music. "I love Josh's voice," Orman said. "The songs lift me up if I feel bad. If I'm in a horrible mood, I get in a better mood after I listen to them."

The Afters' ability to appeal to both secular and Christian crowds is an indication of how good Christian music has become, and of the degree to which evangelicals have adapted to mainstream culture. Stylistically, the best Christian music sounds like the pop or rock you hear on radio stations everywhere. Where it differs is in the lyrics. In music as in so much of the evangelical world, Christians are adopting the look and feel of secular American culture while changing its substance. In that sense, the music is an effective evangelistic tool.

People listen to it because it's good. Then they listen to it closer and are exposed to the Christian message. Music has long been used to communicate ideas; in the sixties it was the antiwar agenda, in the eighties it was famine relief, and, most recently, it was the Live 8 concerts that aimed to raise awareness about global poverty. Listening to music is an emotional experience as much as a cerebral one. Kids at concerts have their guard down and are open to the message of the musicians, whom they often idolize. Ideas cloaked in music may penetrate where words alone may not.

The Afters' willingness to play for an alcohol-consuming crowd further illustrates how integrated into the mainstream Christian bands now are and how much evangelical attitudes about secular lifestyles have changed. The organizer of the Buffalo event told me the Afters were different from the other bands playing there in that they didn't ask that their trailer be stocked with beer—although at least some members of the group don't take issue with drinking. The band members were comfortable performing for an alcohol-imbibing crowd and weren't worried that their Christian fans would be upset at their doing so, which would likely have been the case a decade ago. The old prohibition against alcohol, while still held by some, is rapidly fading in evangelical circles, and many of those who choose not to drink themselves no longer regard it as a sin.

Havens said he resisted being classified as Christian or secular because he thought those labels are unnecessary. "If I were a dentist, I wouldn't only fix the teeth of other Christians, and it's the same for music as well," he told me. "My faith is just an embedded part of who I am. Whatever my vocation would be, my faith would be integrated into it somehow. When I was at Starbucks, I still would try to live out my faith."

Starbucks, of course, is where it all started. Havens and guitarist Matt Fuqua were both working there and belonged to other bands. One slow night they pulled out their guitars and started playing for the customers, who loved it. "We instantly clicked," said Havens, a blond twenty-something who has the brooding look of an indie rock star in publicity photos but who, in truth, seems to be unable to suppress a boyish grin much of the time. "It seems like as soon as we started playing together the buzz started." While they weren't old friends, they knew of each other from high school and each was aware that the other was a Christian. They began playing acoustic sets together, and the response was overwhelming.

Eventually Havens and Fuqua moved from acoustic to electric guitars, at which point they realized they needed more band members. Luckily, Brad Wigg had just moved to Dallas and started working at Starbucks, as had Marc Dodd. Soon the duo was a foursome, with Wigg on bass and Dodd playing the drums. "I believe in divine appointments in some respects, so in that regard I believe that it's not a mistake that we ended up together," Havens told me. With their catchy music, chiseled faces, and onstage charisma, the band quickly developed a devoted local following. Before long they were in the studio and released an album on an independent label as Blisse, the band's first name, that became a staple on Dallas radio stations. Two years and a name change later, they were picked up by Simple/INO records and released simultaneously into the Christian and secular markets. The dual approach wasn't new for them. They'd been playing a mix of churches, bars, and clubs for years. The music was the same, but they'd tailor their approach to their audience. "You've got to be sensitive to the people that you're playing for and obviously you don't lead worship for people who don't know what worship is," Havens said.

The Afters follow in the footsteps of several other bands that managed to parlay success in the Christian world to a career in the big leagues. Switchfoot, P.O.D., Lifehouse, and Sixpence None the Richer are just a few that managed to cross over. But many of the bands that start out on the Christian music circuit stop broadcasting their religious roots once they make it in the mainstream—sometimes at the urging of record execs who don't want to limit their potential sales by pigeonholing them. Lifehouse, Sixpence None the Richer, and Evanescence all fit into that category to varying degrees.

"There's concern that if they're tagged a Christian band, that will alienate consumers," says Deborah Evans Price, who covers Christian music for *Billboard* magazine. "Mainstream record companies are no longer shying away from signing these artists. However, they're still pretty wary about being completely open about the fact that they're Christian bands."

The God in their music has been an issue for the Afters on occasion. There have been times when the song was under consideration for use on a television show or movie soundtrack, but eventually was passed over because of the religious content. "I think there are walls, still, that make it harder for per se a Christian band to succeed in the mainstream industry but I think those walls are being torn down," Havens said. The band even encountered a bit of that uneasiness from their secular label at first. They were signed by Epic Records on the strength of "Beautiful Love," but when the label's president, Steve Barnett, heard how much "Jesus" was on the album, he reportedly had second thoughts. Eventually he relented and let the album go out with all its Christian content intact.

There were shrewd business reasons to do so. While Christian music is perceived by many as the poor stepchild of the mainstream music industry, the numbers tell a different tale. Religious music posted sales of more than $700 million in 2004, more than jazz, classical, and soundtracks combined. Throw in gospel and Christian music represents more than $1 billion in sales each year. Those numbers are only going to get bigger—in recent years Christian music has been the fastest-growing segment of the music industry, and Christian albums are increasingly available outside of religious bookstores. Today one can buy Christian music in places like Borders, Wal-Mart, Target, and Best Buy. A decade ago a Christian band was lucky if 20 percent of its sales came from secular retail outlets. Today some musicians sell as many as 50 percent of their records outside of the Christian retail stream.

In general terms, listeners are looking for music with a positive, uplifting message, especially after 9/11, and even much of the secular music industry has abandoned the sex and drugs that rock and roll used to embody. Evangelical kids in particular are homing in on Christian music because it makes them feel good about their faith. When I was a kid there was no cool Christian stuff, so in the rough-and-tumble world of teenagers it could take a bit of backbone to talk about one's beliefs. Now there are hip Christian bands and Christian rock stars (Bono, for one), allowing image-conscious teens to wear their faith with pride and to feel they're part of something that even non-Christians admire. They have a kinship with Christian artists that non-Christian kids don't. It's one they don't share with secular artists, making them feel even more invested in Christian music. And there's such a wide variety of Christian music now that teens can find a band to suit their every taste. I listened to the ballads of one Christian singer-songwriter quite frequently as a teen but when I wanted something harder or more pop I had to tune to secular radio. That's no longer the case. Some of the music is so edgy it borders on subversive, which makes it appealing to teens, and palatable even to non-Christians.

A handful of Christian bands have had hits in the mainstream marketplace with blatantly religious songs. The MercyMe album *Almost There*, which featured the hit single "I Can Only Imagine" went platinum in 2003 and double platinum in 2004—despite its overtly spiritual lyrics. The song, written by lead singer Bart Millard as a teenager when his father was dying of cancer, ponders what heaven is like. I'd heard that the song had been a huge hit but was unfamiliar with it. When I listened to it for the first time, it was so religious that I was sure I was listening to the wrong song and spent days trying to find the *other* "I Can Only Imagine." Surely, I reasoned, a song with lyrics like this could never have met with mainstream success: "Surrounded by Your glory, what will my heart feel / Will I dance for You Jesus or in awe of You be still / Will I stand in Your presence or to my knees will I fall / Will I sing hallelujah, will I be able to speak at all / I can only imagine."

The tune had already run its course in the Christian marketplace when, a year after its release, Dallas's Wild FM 100 morning show played it during an all-request hour. For the rest of the day the phones were jammed with listeners who wanted to know what it was. Radio audiences had similar reactions in other cities where it was played. Program directors in many markets, including Phoenix, Denver, Minneapolis, Monterey, Atlanta, Orlando, and Columbus said they'd never seen such a big response to a song. Some stations said they got hundreds of e-mails the first day they played it. At one station where the lines were busy because so many people had called in about the song a listener drove to the station to find out what it was. At WXXL in Orlando "I Can Only Imagine" beat out a 50 Cent song in a listeners' call-in battle and went on to win five nights in a row with 100 percent or nearly 100 percent of the vote each night. After a DJ from WZNY in Augusta played the song once, the station's lines were busy for the next twenty minutes with people calling to thank him. WSTR in Atlanta received more than a hundred supportive e-mails after putting the song on the radio. People loved it so much that they began demanding it get airtime. But despite that burst of mainstream success, MercyMe's fan base remains primarily Christian.

Even without secular distribution, Christian bands are able to sell plenty of records. Casting Crowns, a seven-member worship band who had never toured or even played outside of their home area sold more than a million copies of their debut album without any mainstream airplay. Christian rock kings Third Day have sold 5 million albums, including one record that went platinum, and are sponsored by General Motors. Jars of Clay have sold a similar number of albums.

While one can get a glimpse of the magnitude of the Christian music market by looking at things such as record sales and airplay, its enormity is even clearer from inside the Christian world. It was that vantage point I was seeking when I spent half a day driving to a place called the Agape Farm in the middle of Pennsylvania during a sticky week in June. Each year, church groups, families, and bus-loads of teenagers drive thousands of miles to attend Creation East, the country's biggest Christian music festival, kind of a Christian Woodstock.

About seventy-five thousand people make the long trek to listen to the sixty-odd bands that play the three-day event, one of dozens of similar festivals held each year. As soon as I arrive, it's obvious that Creation is no Woodstock. Before I had listened to a single note of music I could feel just from walking through the crowd that this was palpably different from any other music festival I had been to. It wasn't so much the way the kids were dressed—although the occasional T-shirt saying, "I mosh for Jesus," "I Love Christian boys," or "Jesus Surfs Without a Board" were dead giveaways—but something more subtle. A smell, or lack of smell, for starters: no beer, no alcohol, no marijuana smoke wafting through the air. When we sat down to eat at a picnic table in the makeshift food court, the people next to us bowed their heads in prayer before they tucked in to their barbe-cued ribs. And then there was the chasteness of the whole thing. I hardly saw anyone holding hands, let alone kissing in public. When my husband let out a four-letter expletive because a bug nearly the size of a field mouse landed on our son's face, it seemed as if a thousand aghast faces turned in his direction.

For the most part, the music at these festivals is just good enough to do what it needs to. To fulfill its purpose, that is to give Christian teens a place to go that isn't filling their heads with secular, sexual messages, this music only needs to seem hip enough to make these kids feel like they're not missing out on something better. When I was a teenager, my friends and I would occasionally go to a local club that had an underage night, where we would dance to the likes of Madonna and Wham! But going there always involved a tussle with someone's parents, or a flat-out lie. Sometimes, though, the Calvary Chapel church up the road would invite Christian bands and host Friday night dances. Our parents were happy to let us spend an evening at church, and the music, while not as cool as the club tunes, was good enough to draw even my non-Christian friends. We'd spend the night doing the Pogo to wannabe Devo music, then go home to parents who didn't hassle us about where we'd been.

The Christian music industry has obviously evolved since then. A handful of the bands that play these festivals have met with commercial success, and some of them are downright good. Switchfoot, whose "Meant to Live" hit number five on mainstream charts, continues to play them despite a recent reluctance to talk about their Christian roots, presumably because it's a safe way to show solidarity with their Christian base without alienating their secular fans. Other crossover acts that perform at Creation include the Newsboys and Stacey Errico. The teens that attend these Christian festivals today have the same fervor as fans anywhere. The girls rush the stage and scream in delight when their favorite band members take the stage. The musicians swagger for the swooning crowds. But there's a different tone to the exchange. Although there are, naturally, sexual undertones, they exist on a more subconscious level than at a secular concert. Here the zeal is fueled by a sense that all of this is serving a divine purpose, that it is all done for the glorification of God.

The worship element is embraced even more openly on some of the smaller stages at Creation. The tent that is the home to programs for young kids throughout the morning (many attend the festival *en famille*) is used in the afternoons for praise and worship music. On the afternoon I attended, a band called Rock 'N' Roll Worship Circus was playing. The music was loud—no soft rock here—but the tent was filled with a cross-generational crowd and parents were singing along with their teenage children. There was a crush of people up at the stage with their hands raised in praise. The people in the back of the tent were a bit less fervent, but also seemed to know all the words to the songs.

The separation of acts here at Creation mirrors one in the industry as a whole. Bands naturally fall into one of two categories: "worship bands," whose music is intended primarily to praise God, and bands with Christian members who play music that happens to be about God because that's what they care about and what they write about. MercyMe considers themselves a worship band. ("I don't play music to entertain, I play music to change lives," lead singer Bart Millard told me.) Switchfoot does not. The members of Lifehouse are Christians, and the spiritual content in their lyrics is evident. They started out performing in churches and they get extensive coverage in Christian magazines, but, while open about their faith, they stop short of calling themselves a Christian band. Some of these bands see their role as a "light in the world," to use the biblical term. They don't necessarily sing songs that are overtly Christian but sing about things that everyone experiences and use that commonality to connect with people.

As the number and the passion of the kids at Creation testify, Christian acts that cross into the mainstream do so with a built-in fan base. Mainstream labels have begun looking at the Christian music industry as a kind of farm team. Bands that are picked up from Christian labels come with a following and with recording and touring know-how. They've worked out the kinks on somebody else's dime. Signing Christian bands that are already tried and tested has become common practice among labels. Switchfoot recorded with Christian label Sparrow Records before being picked up by Columbia. Grammy-nominated rock band Skillet was on Ardent, a Christian label, before being brought on board by Lava. "Instead of a label signing a brand-new band, investing all this potential upstart money . . . and having zero fan base, these artists are coming with some established level of base," said Skillet's manager Zachary Kelm. "Typically that is from touring and the records they've sold. Skillet had been around for six years, they'd sold more than 100,000 units, they know how to tour, and they know how to do an interview."

One of the latest bands to make the transition into the mainstream was the pop-punk group Relient K, which recorded on Gotee Records before signing with Capitol Records. Their first record with Capitol, *Mmhmm*, has since gone gold. Capitol's head of A & R, Jamie Feldman, said he picked up the band because their last album sold 400,000 copies without any mainstream airplay, which is almost unheard of, and they have an Internet fan base of nearly 100,000. Feldman saw those numbers and wasn't put off by the band's Christianity. "The material itself I wasn't afraid of," Feldman said, pointing specifically to the group's hit single "Be My Escape." "If you want to, you can say it's a song about faith and written to a higher power . . . but it could be about a significant other or a family member." In crossing over, Relient K was careful to guard their appeal in both markets. "They know where their bread has been buttered in the past and don't want to alienate anyone," Feldman said. "They are also able to present their material to a fan base that didn't know them. They really played both sides of the fence very, very well." When I spoke to Feldman "Be My Escape" had gone gold. It has since been certified platinum.

While increasing in frequency, the crossover trend isn't a new one. The path from the Christian to the secular marketplace was first trod in the late 1980s by Amy Grant, who was followed by Michael W. Smith. What's different now is the kind of music that penetrates the mainstream. Back then it was sweet, somewhat saccharine; today most crossover acts are alternative bands, edgier and harder. Many of these bands had been performing and recording in Christian circles for years before they broke out. In many cases, bands retain their relationship with their Christian labels, which continue to distribute them to religious retailers while the secular labels handle the mainstream market. Such partnering arrangements are easier to manage in a consolidated marketplace where most of the Christian labels are now owned by secular media conglomerates. The three big labels, EMI, Sony BMG, and the Warner Music Group, all own smaller Christian labels.

That kind of overlap, while relatively new to the rock market, has long been an inherent part of the country market, whose Southern, Bible-belt roots predetermine that many artists grow up in churches and that religious and gospel music informs their craft. But even there the interplay of Christian and secular music is becoming more pronounced. Country star Randy Travis moved to a Christian label after giving up drugs and alcohol and recorded three gospel albums. He hadn't had a country radio hit in years when he released "Three Wooden Crosses" on Word, which took off. It reached number one on the mainstream country charts, a first for a Christian label. Now the five-time Grammy winner leads praise and worship at churches when he's on the road and often kicks off a concert by giving his testimony. In addition to Travis, country musicians Billy Ray Cyrus and George Jones have also released religious records.

And then, of course, there is Johnny Cash. For all his drinking and philandering, faith was an integral part of Cash's life from the time he answered an altar call as a boy. It was important enough to him that he left Sun Records when they refused to allow him to record an album of hymns, which he later did on another label. He played at Campus Crusade for Christ concerts and at Billy Graham crusades, and counted the iconic evangelist among his closest friends. He made a recording of the entire New Testament and wrote a historical novel based on the life of the apostle Paul. The book was titled *Man in White,* in direct contrast with his 1975 autobiography, *Man in Black,* in which Cash promises to tell "how I've fallen and how I've turned around again to feel (God's) love and His forgiveness." According to Patrick Carr, who cowrote Cash's 1997 autobiography, the country-music legend was a committed Christian throughout his life and viewed his years of drug addiction as wilderness years in which he lived without God.

Of course, not everyone in the evangelical world thinks that leatherclad rock stars are good for Christianity. When rock and roll first came on the scene, Christians widely denounced it, which is not at all surprising given that their isolationist, antimodernist stance at the time led them to be suspicious of anything new and worldly, and rock music surely was that. The term *rock and roll* was coined in 1951 by a Cleveland disc jockey named Alan Freed, who took it from the song "My Baby Rocks Me with a Steady Roll." Rock, or rock and roll, was a euphemism for intercourse, and there was certainly a lot of sexual energy in this new form of music, giving Christians something of which they could immediately disapprove. The genre moved on from singing about sex to singing about hallucinogenic drugs and eventually threw in references to the devil as well. It's easy to understand why Christians, who have a penchant for reading things literally, thought rock music was something to be avoided at all costs.

In the fundamentalist world, the old proscriptions about rock music and dancing are still in place. Bob Jones University, for example, prohibits students from playing not only the music of crossover bands like the Afters but even the tame tones of Christian stars such as Michael W. Smith and Stephen Curtis Chapman. That, though, is an extreme position, and the vast majority of evangelicals are comfortable with at least some Christian rock. Part of the reason the community was able to dispel its suspicions about contemporary music so much more quickly than it was about movies, for instance, is that the origins of Christian rock music are in the church itself. The first contemporary Christian label was Maranatha! Music, which came out of Chuck Smith's Calvary Chapel in Costa Mesa. Smith was known as a teacher whose Bible-based teaching hewed to a literal reading of scripture. Twenty or thirty years ago when the industry was in its nascent phases and fundamentalists were still dominant, many people thought Christian rock music was inherently bad; today that is a minority view.

That doesn't mean that every sector of Christian music is embraced by everyone. What has widely been accepted is what is known as Christian Contemporary Music (CCM), most of which is produced in Nashville and the content of which is largely religious. MercyMe counts as CCM; Switchfoot, Lifehouse, the Afters, and other bands in the mainstream, less clearly so, if at all. (There is, of course, always debate about this. The Christian music industry tries to claim them as their own; the bands and their secular labels often resist the classification.) CCM includes artists who believe music should be used as a means of spreading the Gospel or as a creative form of worship. Artists such as the members of Creed who think their faith is a personal issue, as their ethnicity might be, and largely separate from their music, take heat from conservative Christian quarters. For the most part, though, the new, culture-friendly mainstreamed evangelical supports Christian artists with secular careers and is happy to have cool, God-friendly music to listen to that isn't merely part of a subculture.

The intersection of Christian music and secular music can be downright disorienting. When I visit my family in Southern California, I often can't figure out if I'm listening to Christian radio or mainstream radio. There are several Christian stations in the area, and I have a tendency to let my radio scan the dial. Many times I have stopped at what I thought was an alternative music station only to find out it was Christian. Or, when on occasion I've tried to find a Christian station, I've stopped at a song with spiritual lyrics only to realize I'm listening to Lifehouse or Switchfoot on an adult contemporary station. I'm not the only one who is confused. "There are, I'm sure, a lot of rock fans who have no idea that P.O.D. was a Christian act," said Geoff Mayfield, director of charts and senior analyst at *Billboard* magazine. Many people who liked the band's hit song "Alive" thought the lead singer was singing to a girlfriend, instead of to God.

That indistinctness is perhaps the most salient factor of Christian music today. Particularly for young people, music is the sharp end of the sword of evangelical Christianity. By becoming culturally relevant, music is now able to pierce a veneer of atheism or agnosticism or indifference. People not remotely interested in Christianity will pick up an album, often unwittingly, that is Christian to one degree or another simply because it's good. Music is helping change perceptions about evangelicals—it's putting hip, mainstream Christians in the public spotlight and eroding the stereotype of the ultra-conservative right-winger. It's tough to equate Switchfoot, Lifehouse,

Evanescence, and other alternative Christian bands with the Religious Right. Christian music allows the evangelical lifestyle to be seen as countercultural, in much the way that the Grateful Dead's music once legitimized the deadhead lifestyle. Particularly among teens and young adults, the music gives Christianity cachet.

CHAPTER SEVEN

Jesus Goes to Hollywood

"W HAT ARE YOUR favorite movies? How many of them were Christian movies?" screenwriter Lauri Evans Deason asks the eighty-odd people who are spending this Friday night on the second floor of the Lamb's Theater in Times Square seated somewhat uncomfortably around circular banquet tables. "Stories don't have to be overtly Christian to be great."

This is the kind of nugget these men and women have come to the Act One screenwriting weekend to hear, some from as far as Ohio. Tomorrow this crowd will be instructed in the nuts and bolts of screenwriting, down to what font to use for their screenplays, but tonight's themes are much loftier and include "redemptive story-telling" and "haunting moments."

Thomas Parham, who teaches theater, film, and television at Azusa Pacific University and who has written for the television shows *JAG* and *Touched by an Angel*, is explaining what redemption means in the context of good film. Not surprisingly, his definition is infused with Christian values—Act One, which was started by Barbara Nicolosi in 1999 for Christians who aspire to careers in Hollywood, aims to teach people how to be relevant and effective in Hollywood and how to do so with their faith intact. Redemption is a concept Hollywood doesn't fully grasp, Parham explains. It is not vengeance, nor is it euthanasia, he says, referring to *Million Dollar Baby*. But while his definition of redemption may be biblical,

Parham is not advocating using films for evangelism. On the contrary: Good movies are parables, not propaganda, he says.

That is an important lesson at Act One, and a big reason Nicolosi started the program in the first place. While the program has the potential to cultivate talented Christians who can put their mark on the big film studios and television networks, that wasn't Nicolosi's initial intention. "We started it not to fix Hollywood but to fix the church," she told me. "We were seeing real dreck coming into town from people of faith. The kinds of projects people were willing to make were embarrassing." Today Act One has in-depth training programs for writers and executives, but it started out as a kind of reputation saver for Christians.

There are plenty of reasons why evangelicals might need an image adjustment in America's entertainment capital. While their community has become savvy, sophisticated, and influential in other areas of culture and in politics, they still haven't cracked the nut of Hollywood—and it drives them crazy. They complain that on the rare occasions when there are evangelical characters in films or on TV shows, they are always portrayed as dolts or zealots, and that the entertainment industry is out of touch with the mores of flyover country. "Hollywood doesn't reflect my values" is the mantra Christians recite as they point to the extramarital sex and nudity that have become mainstays of both film and television. Mothers say they can't watch television with their teenage sons anymore because prime time is just too racy. (Somehow, violence doesn't seem to bother them as much.) And don't even bring up homosexuality. *Brokeback Mountain* is the film that dare not speak its name in Christian circles.

After the massive—and unexpected—success of Mel Gibson's *The Passion of the Christ*, Christians seemed poised to take Hollywood by storm, much as they had other industries. The Left Behind books had been followed by the phenomenon of Rick Warren's *The Purpose-Driven Life*. The succession of Christian bands marching their way to secular Top 40 charts has yet to end. Yet evangelicals haven't made the same kinds of gains in the entertainment industry—at least not the way many of them hoped they would. Christian filmmakers are, indeed, alive and well in Hollywood, but they're not crafting movies with overtly religious content. Instead, they are making films with good wholesome values and broad appeal.

To be fair, the gripers are right. Hollywood *doesn't* reflect their values and there *are* very few sympathetic portrayals of Christians in the entertainment produced there. But, to a large degree, Christians have only themselves to blame. They have learned to play nicely with secular America in almost every other cultural sandbox, but when it comes to the entertainment industry the evangelical community forgot the old adage about catching more flies with honey. The Southern Baptist Convention organized an eight-year boycott against Disney because of "antifamily" and "anti-Christian" practices at the entertainment giant that included allowing gay days in the theme parks and producing films such as *Pulp Fiction*. Pointing to management changes at Disney and saying the company had become more family friendly, the SBC finally voted to lift the boycott in 2005, but one wonders if Disney's then-upcoming release of the film adaptation of *The Chronicles of Narnia*—one of the evangelical community's most beloved books— had anything to do with it. It would have been tough to persuade Christians to shun such a rare treat. And, of course, the years of protest didn't make the evangelical community any friends in Hollywood. "The weirdest thing about the past seventy-five years is that Christian leaders yelled at power centers as they trained people not to go there . . . yet they wanted people they were hostile to, to make their stuff," said Mark Joseph, a media strategist and film consultant. "It's a bizarre set of expectations."

Getting a film made is a much more difficult proposition than getting a book published or an album recorded. There are myriad components that go into a movie, including a screenplay, a director, actors, producers, and camera operators. And even when a project has been approved, or greenlighted, getting it from paper to the silver screen can take years, sometimes decades. That is true for people with storied careers in the industry. The process is even more arduous for outsiders; without the cooperation of the people in charge it's next to impossible to get a movie into general release.

Hollywood is not a democracy, nor is it a meritocracy. Power in Hollywood is concentrated in the hands of relatively few. By alienating those people, the evangelical community virtually ensured that its concerns wouldn't be heard. If the tables were turned, would it be any different? If Christians controlled the entertainment industry would they suddenly start greenlighting projects with strong gay or sexual themes, even if they were great art? Unlikely.

The distrust of modernism and the desire to withdraw from culture that is the legacy of fundamentalism has been most visible in its relationship with the film industry. There are still plenty of evangelicals who have never in their lives been to a movie theater. But evangelicals' complaints about content will almost always fall on deaf ears in Hollywood. The tactics that the Christian community relied upon until recently—either sticking their heads in the sand and avoiding secular entertainment or confronting Hollywood through boycotts—simply haven't worked. Hollywood operates by its own rules and if evangelicals want to have a voice there, they have to learn how to play the game.

In every other industry, Christians earned themselves a place at the table by honing their craft within the confines of their own subculture and proving that there was an audience for it. Evangelical publishers put out better and better books until eventually even nonbelievers wanted to read them. Christian music got so good that it started being played on mainstream radio stations. But Christian movies have not yet reached the production levels that are standard in Hollywood, and having a good project, or a good idea for a project isn't enough.

Film, like any art, is deeply subjective. If an executive is approached with a script that he doesn't get or just doesn't want to make, he is likely to pass on it, even if it has moneymaking potential. Given the disconnect between Hollywood and Christian values, it's more than likely that a movie industry executive won't like a Christian film. Potential profits do come into play, of course, but so do a number of other factors. "Money runs this business, but that discounts the importance of perception, high profile, being respected by your peers, stuff like that," said Jonathan Bock, president of Grace Hill Media, a public relations company that helps studios promote films to Christian audiences.

Now Christians across the country are trying to figure out how to get traction in the entertainment industry. *Christianity Today* columnist Andy Crouch said that if you take a group of evangelicals who are baby boomers or younger and talk to them about politics, you kill the room. Music gets a more positive response, but talk about film and they come alive. "There's a tremendous passion about how to crack the code of Hollywood," he said. "That's where all the energy is."

Last year, the Vanderbilt Center for Better Health in Nashville, Tennessee, convened a gathering of more than a hundred people who represented a cross section of the entertainment, business, media, religious, and political fields to put their heads together to try to find ways to mitigate the negative influences coming from entertainment and media. The atmosphere, according to participants, was not one of anger with Hollywood but rather one of self-recrimination for what the evangelical community hasn't done mixed with enthusiasm for the task ahead. The participants realized that if they want their values to be represented in entertainment they need to fund more projects of their own.

The inroads evangelicals have made into every other area of culture are big enough to accommodate a tank division, but the road to Hollywood is still a rocky one for them. In fact, Hollywood is so foreign to most evangelicals in America that they have taken to talking about it as a mission field. (There are even online prayer networks that give people specific projects or people in Hollywood to pray for; they believe prayer is a powerful tool in their efforts to change the industry.)

Evangelicals consume so much secular film now that *Christianity Today* has a Web site devoted to reviewing films from an evangelical perspective, one of many publications and Web sites that now do so. Smart evangelicals have figured out that they can influence Hollywood by spending money there. Instead of boycotts, they're encouraging other Christians to see movies of which they approve. Researcher George Barna now works with studios to organize preview nights, on which he holds special screenings for faith audiences the evening before an official release. By turning out in large numbers on opening weekend—the most important time in determining the fate of a film—they can influence the Hollywood powers that be.

Interestingly, the frustrations about the film industry don't extend to Christians who have successful careers there, partly because they see their roles—and the role of Hollywood—very differently. While many Christians outside Hollywood would like the studios to produce message movies and believe film should be used to promote their faith the way that books and radio are, Christian filmmakers say they are trying to make art, not propaganda, and that film doesn't lend itself to preaching. On a strictly pragmatic level, movies that try to sell you something are rarely entertaining, said Ralph Winter, the producer of *X-Men* and *The Fantastic Four*. Instead, films are at their best when they ask questions.

That's not to say that evangelicals in Hollywood don't want their beliefs reflected in their work. But Christian culture and biblical values are not the same thing, and the principles evangelicals cherish can be conveyed in different ways. As Winter put it: "In the context of a story, the values I want to espouse about redemption or salvation might be inside an R-rated movie about the mafia." Terry Botwick, an executive and producer who has worked both in Christian and in secular entertainment, points out that even the Bible isn't particularly wholesome. Spiritual ideals are one thing, morality is another, more relative, construct that reflects the standards of a community at a particular moment.

Christians outside Hollywood sometimes fail to grasp how difficult it is to make a movie that is good. "It's complicated because there are a lot of moving parts—although it looks easy and seemingly everyone on Southern California and New York is writing a screenplay," producer Ralph Winter said. "Just because video cameras are easy to use doesn't mean everybody should be doing it. There's an art form to it. When done well, it's transcendent."

Craft is important to Christians in the entertainment industry, who stress that they are, first and foremost, filmmakers. It's not that their faith isn't a priority, it's just that, at least in the professional arena, they don't want it to be defining. Strategist Mark Joseph uses the analogy of male nurses. When men first started becoming nurses in noticeable numbers, it was a *thing*. People talked about it. They were "male nurses." Eventually, though, they didn't want to be male nurses; they didn't want to be defined by their gender. And it had become so common that people didn't feel the need to anymore. They simply became men who were nurses. Just nurses. A similar thing is happening with Christians in Hollywood. There was a generation of them, Joseph said, who didn't mind being called "Christian filmmakers" because they were just happy to be there, "not realizing in the process that they were acknowledging their own weirdness and the fact that they didn't belong there." Now, though, as they move into positions of strength, they don't want to be known as the "Christian director" or "Christian actor" but rather as professionals who happen to have faith. In film, as in music, evangelicals are rejecting segmentation.

Many Christians will decline a project if it too obviously offends their sense of morality, but to be effective in Hollywood they have to be willing to work within the system rather than against it—in spite of accusations of selling out. "Those who work within Hollywood know that it's better to light a candle rather than curse the darkness," said Paul Lauer, founder of Motive Marketing, which masterminded the marketing of *The Passion of the Christ* to Christian audiences and is credited in large part for the film's success. "If you're trying to work with people, you certainly can't go to work and say 'You suck.

You're destroying America.' You have to somehow be more diplo-
matic and work alongside people."

Hollywood is a club whose membership rules differ wildly from
those that govern believers, and though it is not impossible to adhere
to both, it can be difficult to do so without any compromise. It's similar to the conflict that plagues any minority group trying to become
part of the mainstream. "What finally happens is that we lose some
of our color," Act One's Nicolosi said. The staff and students at Act
One have "huge discussions" about what it means to be a Christian
in Hollywood and whether they can tell the stories Hollywood wants
them to and still honor God. "Is it right to subvert the agenda of the
people who are paying you?" Nicolosi asked. "You're constantly having to tout your own values in terms that the prevailing values of this
town will countenance. You have to make yourself sound like a secular materialist if you're going to work in this town. It's a problem,
because we don't run this town and we have to find a way to work
here."

Christians may have to work within the rules, but that doesn't
mean they can't try to change them a little, too. Programs like Act
One and people like Ken Wales, a veteran television and film producer who urges his students at the USC School of Cinema and
Television to explore their own spirituality in their art, are putting
the pieces in place for a quiet Christian revolution. Winter said that
if evangelicals want to make their mark on Hollywood they need to
place themselves everywhere. They need to be not just actors, directors, and producers but also agents, lawyers, and executives.

But training Christians to operate in the world of Hollywood is a
slow process. Nicolosi said the thing she didn't count on when she
started Act One was how long it takes people to mature in their
craft. It takes years for a screenwriter to fully develop, and years
again for a film to get made even after the screenplay has been
bought. But there are signs that the program is beginning to reap its
reward. Act One just had its second graduate in three years win a

coveted and highly competitive Walt Disney Studios/ABC Entertainment Writing Fellowship. Another Act One alum was a writer on the movie *Curious George* and recently sold an idea for a children's film to Paramount Pictures. Her projects aren't openly religious but they are family friendly. "She's probably never going to write about God in her life and that's okay," Nicolosi said.

One of the most fundamental changes in Hollywood, insiders say, is that Christians have started "coming out," much in the same way members of the gay community did. They are feeling free to voice their opinions and increasingly are being asked to weigh in with their perspective. Open Christians in Hollywood include Patricia Heaton of *Everybody Loves Raymond*; Denzel Washington; Dean Batali, a writer on *That 70s Show* and *Buffy the Vampire Slayer*; Dave Alan Johnson, producer of *Bruce Almighty* and *Patch Adams*; and Todd Komarnicki, who was a producer on *Elf*.

The Passion of the Christ was a watershed for Christians in Hollywood because it opened the eyes of many studio executives to the potential in the Christian marketplace, but the process was already well under way. Over the course of the previous several years during which, largely due to Bush's presidency, evangelicals had moved into the spotlight, Christians in all walks of life had become emboldened about their faith. The number of people in the entertainment industry who are open Christians has grown by leaps and bounds, said Larry Poland, CEO of consulting firm Mastermedia International, who started working in Hollywood twenty years ago. Today there are Christians in executive positions at most of the major film studios and television networks.

Evangelicals who work in Hollywood are on the front lines of cultural engagement—and that's a tough place to be. They take heat from co-workers who think their beliefs are nothing short of weird, but some of the harshest treatment of evangelicals in Hollywood comes from other Christians. When a prominent person in the entertainment industry comes out publicly as an evangelical, other

Christians suddenly feel justified in weighing in on every decision that person makes. Say a bad word in a movie? Do a sex scene or a nude scene? Christian filmgoers are likely to start writing letters of criticism. "You set yourself up as a target for either side and, oddly, it's the friendly fire that hurts you the most," Winter said.

While evangelicals say they want to see more faith-based programming, they generally aren't willing to help make it happen. Winter said he's tried to raise money for religious film projects and has found it very difficult. When Christians are willing to ante up, they often want their money to go to making an evangelistic movie. "I'm actually kind of cynical about it," said Terry Botwick. "A lot of the Christians confuse evangelism with good storytelling. Some of these people have reached into their own pockets and funded a film, but they're not professionals. Then they scratch their heads and wonder why it can't work. A lot of money has been spent by well-meaning, sincere people, and if they'd put all of that money into getting professional management, they could have built their own studio by now." His advice to them: Enroll in a program to learn the business, then come to Hollywood and pay your dues.

There have been efforts by Christians to make films with religious themes, and they have met with varying levels of success. Bishop T. D. Jakes's 2004 film *Woman Thou Art Loosed* was the story of a woman struggling to overcome abuse, addiction, and poverty, and featured scenes of Jakes preaching. Jakes didn't disclose the production budget, other than to say it was done on a shoestring; the film grossed almost $7 million. In 2005 *The Gospel*, a modern-day prodigal son story, did even better, making nearly $16 million and costing only $4 million to produce. That same year *Diary of a Mad Black Woman*, the story of a woman whose husband leaves her for her best friend on the eve of their twentieth anniversary and who finds the strength to go on in Christianity, showed there is real life in faith films for the African American audience. Made for a mere $5.5 million, it has grossed more than $50 million to date.

Even Christians outside Hollywood are learning that they can be more effective by maintaining their Christian mission but dropping the label. Every Tribe Entertainment was started by Texan Mart Green, who made his fortune in Christian bookstores. Green was approached by the Forum of Bible Agencies to make a commercial to promote Bible use. Around the same time, though, Green heard a speech by Steve Saint, whose father was one of five missionaries murdered by the Waodani Indians in Ecuador in 1956. The tribe eventually converted to Christianity and now Saint and Mincaye, one of his father's killers, are close friends. Green thought the story, which was told at the time in *Life* magazine, would make a great movie. A friend challenged him to do it himself although Green had never set foot in a movie theater. Green responded by founding a production company that, instead of the thirty-second commercial he'd set out to do, made a documentary about the story and a feature film called *The End of the Spear*. The movie was produced and written by Bill Ewing, who had spent years as a production executive at Columbia Pictures until he felt led by God to leave that job and, eventually, join Green in his venture.

Green and the people who work with him at Every Tribe are evangelicals. The company was born out of a desire to promote Bible reading. The two projects the company have finished deal with explicitly Christian material, but Green didn't give the company that label because he didn't want to limit his audience. "I use the name Christian bookstore because I'm serving Christians," he explained. "In the film industry I'm not just talking to Christians. To put 'Christian' on it says it's only for Christians." It's a tack many people of faith in Hollywood are taking, rejecting being categorized as evangelical—no matter how much their faith influences what they do—in favor of a more mainstream image.

Even when a company isn't labeled Christian, if the public knows the principals are evangelicals the faith community holds them to a higher standard. "You're harder on your brother or sister than you would be on a total stranger," Joseph said. Green can attest to that. The lead actor in *The End of the Spear* is Chad Allen, a gay activist, and

Green took a lot of heat from some quarters of the evangelical community for casting him in the role. The film still did okay, opening at number eight at the box office, but ticket sales soon slipped. Every Tribe executives can't help but wonder if some Christians who would have gone to see the movie stayed home because of the controversy.

Meanwhile, Terry Botwick is putting together a large film fund that, in partnership with one of the major studios, will finance about twenty films over five years. His company is not going to be a Christian company, but because he is a Christian his faith will influence how he conducts his business and what he chooses to produce, just as any Hollywood executive's personal inclinations affect his decision making. "There are tensions between business and personal interests," Botwick said.

The most successful of the new group of Christians putting money into film is Denver-based Phil Anschutz, the billionaire founder of Qwest who's had remarkable success in Hollywood—although he's done a clunker or two as well. His companies have produced *Ray*, for which Jamie Foxx won an Academy Award; *Around the World in 80 Days* (the clunker); *Holes*, and *Because of Winn-Dixie*. His biggest film so far, though, has been the blockbuster *The Chronicles of Narnia*, which Anschutz's Walden Media released in partnership with Disney. The film grossed more than $744 million worldwide and is one of the twenty top-grossing films of all time. Anschutz's entertainment holdings and Walden's handling of *Narnia* are compelling examples of Christians recognizing the need to be perceived as mainstream in order to play in the Hollywood big leagues. While Anschutz is a Christian, the company is not one where evangelical culture prevails. Many of the people working at Walden and, indeed, some of its most senior executives, are not Christians, although Anschutz has pledged never to make an R-rated film, and Walden's mission to make family-friendly movies that "demonstrate the rewards of knowledge and virtue" makes it unlikely the company will ever produce something deeply offensive to the evangelical community. For the moment, Walden is a shining star in the evangelical universe, Christian company or not.

Disney had to tread a very fine line in its promotion of *Narnia*. They knew that if convinced the film was faithful to the book, evangelical audiences would rush to see it. At the same time, they didn't want it pigeonholed as a Christian movie. Paul Lauer relied on the same blueprint he used in the marketing of *The Passion of the Christ* to take the film straight to the faithful, organizing special screenings for religious groups. The tensions between the Christian and secular communities that studio executives faced in marketing the movie were the same ones that had always surrounded the book. *Narnia*'s author, C. S. Lewis, is one of the most beloved and respected in the evangelical world, but the fiction fantasy series transcends religion and is popular with children everywhere. Devout as Lewis may have been, Christians don't have a monopoly on affection for his novels.

The imagery in *Narnia* is, for Christians, very clearly that of Christ, of his crucifixion, and his resurrection. And yet, many people who read the books and see the movie are entirely unaware of the allegory. Lauer said that when he first read the books as a child he had no idea there was anything religious about them, but he still benefited from their lessons on morality. Later he came to see a more profound meaning in them. *Narnia* is a template that could serve other Christians in the film industry well, a story so resonant that it transcends its religious themes. Lauer notes that even Jesus used parables to get his message across.

Disney's challenge was to make a film that evangelicals could access on that deeper level without turning off other viewers. They needed to speak to divergent audiences simultaneously, in much the same way that President Bush does when he infuses his speeches with words that have specific meaning for evangelicals but seem innocuous to other listeners. Disney's head of publicity, Dennis Rice, went to great lengths to explain that the studio did not consider *Narnia* a Christian film. They marketed it to faith audiences just as they would market a movie to any special-interest group that might be interested in a particular movie. It's just good business.

Although film companies aren't yet ready to make a lot of big movies specifically for the evangelical audience, they have realized that getting Christians to see a film can make a big difference to the bottom line. While there are some movies Christians will never like, when there's a chance they will, studios make efforts to get them to the theater. In *Yours, Mine & Ours* the band playing at a party is a Christian group called Hawke Nelson—a secret nod to evangelicals. When it became clear that Steve Martin had become popular with evangelicals who enjoyed the Cheaper by the Dozen movies, Sony's Amy Pascal held up the release of *The Pink Panther* by seven months and spent $5 million to tone down some racy scenes so the film would get a PG rating. Studios have also begun engaging marketing firms that specialize in the faith audience. Bock's Grace Hill Media has been hired to market such films as *A Walk to Remember*, *Lord of the Rings*, *Cinderella Man*, and *Kingdom of Heaven*, among others, sometimes staging special screenings of the films at churches. After years of feeling abused by Hollywood, Christians respond well to the extra attention—as long as they don't feel they're being exploited. The dual-track approach is akin to the one seen in publishing and music, when a book or record is marketed to the Christian and secular audiences separately. It also draws inspiration from Rick Warren's use of the church as a marketing base for *The Purpose-Driven Life*.

Even when openly Christian companies manage to get a movie made, they've only taken one step on a long path to success. They still have to put it where people can see it and must somehow make them want to see it. There aren't Christian movie theaters the way there are Christian bookstores and the lines of distribution are controlled by the very people evangelicals who aren't part of the Hollywood machinery tend to dislike and distrust. "It's complicated," Barbara Nicolosi said. "So what do you do? You disdain the people who can do it so well, so you're not open to learning from them." Anschutz also owns the Regal Entertainment Group, the country's largest chain of movie theaters, yet Walden still relied on Disney to help distribute *Narnia*. Marketing a film is similarly tricky, and expensive. Bock said that studios generally spend the same amount promoting a film as they did making it.

Of course, Mel Gibson's *The Passion* is the eight-hundred-pound gorilla that studio executives can't ignore. If nothing else, it showed that there are Christians out there who will spend good money—a lot of it—to see a film that strongly appeals to them and to their faith. For many evangelicals, *The Passion* broke down the invisible barrier that stood between them and their local movie theater, enticing many of them to occupy those velvet seats for the first time in their lives. "That's where all these extra numbers came from," Joseph said. Critics expected the film to make about $25 million. Instead, it made more than $100 million in the first five days and went on to become the highest-grossing R-rated movie in history.

The evangelical turnout for *The Passion* was as much about politics as it was about entertainment, said Craig Detweiler, chair of mass communications at Biola University. Christians felt that Mel Gibson was being singled out for attack by pockets of the traditional media, and they took the assault personally. "*The Passion* became a must-see event for the Christian community, a chance to vote with their feet and send Hollywood a message," he said.

Since then studios have been dipping their toes into the water to see if there's more money in that pool and if they can figure out how to tap into it. Bock said that four of the six big studios are "deeply committed" to making small films for Christians, and are putting them straight into video—which is a start. Fox, which distributed *The Passion of the Christ* on video, has begun releasing movies directly to the Christian audience under its Fox Faith banner. Warner Brothers issued a remastered version of *Ben Hur* and included a Bible study on the DVD version that was headed for the CBA marketplace. Studios are also starting to gamble on smaller-budget general release films that they think will appeal to evangelicals. *The Exorcism of Emily Rose* was written and directed by a Christian, Scott Derrickson. It cost Sony $19 million to produce the film, which starred Laura Linney and went on to gross $138 million worldwide, making it one of the studio's best performers in 2005.

The process that Christians are now facing is not all that different from the one African American filmmakers went through. Studios started out making small films for exclusively black audiences but, little by little, they began investing in projects with crossover appeal, such as *Big Momma's House*. Bock said studios are taking a similar tack and making "godsploitation" films for the Christian audience. More and more of those will cross over, he said. In addition to the next installment of *Narnia*, Christians are looking forward to *Nativity*, the story of Mary and Joseph in the year before the birth of Christ, which is set to be released by New Line in December 2006 and is expected to draw a broad audience. Walden is also working on a movie called *Amazing Grace*, the story of William Wilberforce, who was instrumental in the fight to abolish slavery in the United Kingdom, and is developing a project called *Manhunt*, to which Harrison Ford is attached.

The television response to Christians has been somewhat different from that of the film industry and has involved a series of God-friendly programs. *Touched by an Angel* was followed by *7th Heaven*, which in turn was followed by *Joan of Arcadia*. ABC spent $20 million on a *Ten Commandments* miniseries. The medium is more reactive because television projects don't take as long to get on the air, so attempts to reach out to the faith audience came earlier. Also, television is more segmented so Christians have been able to rely on cable channels such as ABC Family (once Pat Robertson's Family Channel) and PAX to provide shows that don't offend their moral standards. In many markets there is also Christian television, although those shows don't make much of an impact on the culture at large.

The evangelical audience is extremely sensitive to attempts to exploit it and can spot a faker a mile away—they just don't talk right. NBC has a particularly dubious track record when it comes to trying to entice Christians, first with its 2005 miniseries *Revelations*, which scored big in its first week but saw its viewer numbers fall off a cliff in subsequent episodes. Evangelicals hated it because it bore little resemblance to the biblical book to which its title refers. The network followed that with *The Book of Daniel*. It's tough to imagine that NBC executives ever thought the series—with its pill-popping priest who had a wife a little too prone to pour herself another martini, a gay son, a drug-dealing daughter, and another son who in religious terms could only be labeled a fornicator—would pass muster with evangelicals, but they did. The show's creators thought Christians were ready to see an honest, warts-and-all portrayal of a family of faith. They thought wrong. The American Family Association quickly activated its e-mail chain and urged people to call their local affiliates and request that they stop carrying the show and, more important, to call the show's sponsors and ask them to pull their advertising. *Daniel* was dead within a matter of weeks. Those kinds of campaigns leave television studios loath to try to appeal to Christian audiences, for fear of getting it wrong. Evangelicals are not yet ready to publicly acknowledge their flaws. To wit, the movie *Saved*, a satire of born-again teenagers that evangelicals just didn't find funny.

At the same time, an evangelical doesn't even have to mention Jesus in order to make something that preaches to the choir—or at least entertains it. There's nothing explicitly evangelical about *Touched by an Angel*, but the show hits all the right notes with that crowd—largely because its executive producer and chief writer, Martha Williamson, is herself one of the faithful. The series broke the God barrier in the same way that the girl-girl kiss on *Roseanne* broke the lesbian barrier. The strategist Mark Joseph thinks a show that successfully takes on Jesus is only a short time away.

Just as evangelicals are trying to learn how to talk to Hollywood on its own terms, film executives are doing the same with evangelicals. Sony's handling of *The Da Vinci Code* is a prime example. It's impossible to overstate how much Christians disliked *The Da Vinci Code*, with its assertion that Jesus had a wife and children. There is an entire cottage industry devoted to debunking the novel's claims, and evangelical publishers alone have put out dozens of books detailing where *The Da Vinci Code* goes wrong. When it came time to start thinking about promoting the film version, the studio began looking for ways to avoid the public-relations fiasco that accompanied the 1988 release of *The Last Temptation of Christ*, another movie seen as sacrilegious. People involved in that film received death threats and hate mail.

This time, instead of ignoring the community's sure disgruntlement, the studio found a way to make evangelicals part of the discussion by giving them a forum to air their criticisms. At the suggestion of Grace Hill's Bock, Sony put up a Web site at www.thedavincichallenge.com, on which scholars posted essays debunking the book's claims. The site presents the writings of some of the heavy hitters in the evangelical intelligentsia, many of whom figure that the film is coming out anyway so they might as well use it as an opportunity to tell people about the Jesus *they* believe in. Pastors have been urging their congregations to go see the movie so they'll know what's in it and can then address it. But that approach hasn't been universally welcomed. Nicolosi, for one, thinks the campaign is a sham just intended to generate more buzz. She's not a fan of boycotts, but thinks Christians should ignore this and other films they find offensive.

Hollywood has realized it doesn't have to produce movies with Christian themes, it just has to infuse as many as possible with a message that evangelicals can live with—and it is doing exactly that. Ted Baehr, who founded the Christian Film and Television Commission in the early 1980s, said the number of films with strong spiritual content has increased dramatically since he started the organization. And for all their griping, the viewing habits of middle-of-the-road evangelicals aren't dramatically different from those of the rest of the country. They embraced movies such as *Wallace and Gromit: The Curse of the Were-Rabbit, Ice Age: The Meltdown, The Incredibles, Polar Express, Spider-Man 2, The Terminal, Collateral, Hotel Rwanda,* and *Raising Helen*—many of the films the rest of America loved. They don't need religion to make them shell out their ten dollars, they just want good clean fun, which Hollywood is giving them more and more of. They haven't had to take over Hollywood because the industry has, to a large degree, come around to them. Studios may not be ready to make religious films, but they have shown a willingness to make wholesome pictures that appeal simultaneously to Christians *and* to a broader audience. Ironically, in the area of culture where evangelicals feel most stymied, their values are becoming those of the mainstream.

III
Power

CHAPTER EIGHT

Onward Christian Soldiers

T HE LINES IN front of the X-ray machines and metal detectors at the base of the Empire State Building are moving slowly, and after I clear security I will still have to figure out which elevator bank will take me to the correct floor. I wait impatiently to ascend to the floor occupied by The King's College, one of the country's most outward-looking evangelical institutes of higher learning. King's location here in the most famous building in New York City seems unlikely, but then its ambition and approach are not that of your average Christian college. The stated mission of King's is to "prepare students for careers in which they will help to shape and eventually lead strategic public and private institutions." In other words, the college was founded with the express purpose of training young Christians to wield influence in America.

After decades of working at secular colleges for Campus Crusade for Christ, an evangelical outreach group, King's president, Stan Oakes, came to the realization that the soft sciences at most secular colleges and universities are taught primarily by non-Christians and that those are the very areas that, in fact, shape policy and culture. He concluded that Christians needed an institution devoted to preparing them to work in secular society, a school that would teach them the other side of the humanities, the conservative side. And so The King's College was born—or reborn, really, since the school had been around in one form or another since 1938.

Before it moved to Manhattan, King's was in Briarcliff Manor, a leafy town up the Hudson River, so its current position in the center of what many consider to be the most Godless city in the country is no accident. "We are all about engagement—preparing students to be leaders in one of the strategic national institutions of our society," the school's promotional material announces. That's an approach decidedly different from that of most other Christian colleges, where parents send their children to be cloistered, both from the temptations of college life and from the influence of humanistic thought.

At King's students are encouraged to tangle with secular thought on a daily basis. To see this in action, I stopped in on a statesmanship class, taught by professor David Tubbs, a former lecturer at Princeton University. The students sat at long desks arranged in an angular semicircle and sipped sodas. They were in the middle of a discussion of Shakespeare's *Measure for Measure* and the analyses of literary critics Allan Bloom and Harry Jaffa, two esteemed secular professors. They had read Jaffa's essay "Chastity as a Political Principle" and another by Bloom.

In *Measure for Measure*, Angelo, a man of strict morality, is temporarily ruling Vienna and has reinstituted an old law against fornication that condemns to death those who break it. A young man named Claudio had slept with his fiancée, and his virtuous sister Isabella pleads with Angelo to spare Claudio's life. Angelo is taken with Isabella and her purity, and tells her he will spare her brother in exchange for her virtue. The students are talking about Angelo's reasons for wanting to have sex with Isabella and thus destroy the very attribute that most attracts him to her.

A conversation about sex in a roomful of young evangelical students, most of whom are likely to have little firsthand knowledge of the subject, is a fairly unusual occurrence, unless the discussion is about why premarital sex is bad. I expect the dialogue today to be judgmental and naïve. In fact, the students are remarkably free and frank and their discussion doesn't revolve around biblical principles; instead, they consider the play in the context of the morality of the day. While there are mentions of sin and the mercy of the Christian tradition, the students talk about Christianity and Christian ideals from a detached perspective. When God comes up, he is referred to as "the Christian God." They go off on a tangent about the historical use of the terms *punk* and *whore* and their relationship to the words *ho* and *pimp*, then launch into a debate about why Angelo wants to sleep with Isabella and whether or not she seduced him. To want to have sex with someone he's attracted to is "a man's instinct," one student says. These are conversations I can't imagine taking place at any other Christian college I have seen. The professor teaches from a secular perspective. At one point he even says: "Most people would say there's nothing morally questionable about fornication—it's just consensual sex between adults."

I spoke to Tubbs later by phone and he told me that he approaches the class at King's in the same way he did classes at Princeton or Notre Dame, where he also worked. "I don't think there would be big differences in either the syllabus or what's going on in the classroom," he said. Professors at King's couldn't shelter their students even if they wanted to because the minute students walk out of the Empire State Building they're in the middle of one of the city's seedier neighborhoods and immediately confronted with the worldliness of New York. Regardless of their own personal experience, the students in Tubbs's classroom aren't likely to be shy about sex because they encounter it on a daily basis. The discrepancy between the traditional morals the students hold and the overt sexuality of the city provokes, at the very least, awareness and reflection. Also, the students who come to King's are likely drawn from a somewhat different pool than those at other Christian colleges. The young woman I sat next to in Tubbs's class had planned on attending New York University before she was recruited by King's.

Oakes sees King's as an academically and intellectually demanding place where students are offered a "better" way of thinking. A secular liberal arts education is all about learning to think and about exploring new perspectives. At King's students also study opposing positions, but the college is grounded in the belief that there is a "true view," as Oakes put it. The school's brochure says King's competes with the "pervasive but false ideas" taught at secular colleges. Certainly this agenda conflicts with that of a traditional liberal arts education, which aims to give students an intellectual agility that will enable them to consider the merits of many different schools of thought and perspectives. Indeed, exposure to new and challenging points of view and a broad array of subjects—stretching the student as a human being—is the primary aim of liberal arts schools.

King's core curriculum centers on the idea that there are three freedoms that need to be protected: spiritual freedom, political freedom, and economic freedom, described here as "the freedom to create wealth and use it as you see fit in benefiting society. This includes a commitment to free markets and wealth creation for the poor." The school identifies a series of "defining questions" to which students will develop answers over the course of their enrollment. They include: When is it right for a nation to go to war? What is the natural condition of man—wealth or poverty? Upon what basis do leaders make difficult decisions: Polls or principles? What causes crime— poverty or man's nature? What kinds of problems should government solve and which ones should be solved by private initiative? How do we encourage wealth creation in a society?

Christianity is important at King's but it isn't pushed in the same way it is at most evangelical colleges. The students are given a remarkable level of autonomy, and not just when it comes to their spiritual lives. There are no obligatory chapel services. There are no specific prohibitions against drinking, dancing, or smoking, other than those mandated by law. The residential policy prohibits students from entering student housing while intoxicated, which seems to imply that students may, at times, reach such a state. Students live in apartments and while none of them is coed, some of the women and men are housed in the same building. There are no rules prohibiting them from going into each other's apartments, only a ban against guests of any gender after one a.m. on weeknights and two a.m. on weekends. The spirituality of the students at King's—and it is quite apparent—is not forced upon them. Rather, for many of the students who went to public schools, it's a relief to be somewhere where the majority of their classmates share their beliefs. The students I spoke to told me that most of their classmates attend church every Sunday and the student body organizes Bible studies and worship sessions. "The more things you do that are mandatory, the less students want to do for themselves," Oakes said.

Oakes openly acknowledges that because King's doesn't provide the protective environment other Christian schools do, due both to its location and to its philosophy, it is not for everyone. He says they have students who are not Christians and might well have some who are gay. The school's aim is not to try to make students behave in a certain way, but to teach them to think for themselves and to think well—by which he means conservatively.

The curriculum, modeled after Oxford University's famous Philosophy, Politics and Economics course, may not be deeply infused with Christianity, but it is painstakingly conceived. Similarly, King's professors, while not all evangelicals, are carefully selected. Faith is an important factor but even more critical is the philosophical background; at King's, intellectual and social conservatism reign. In its economics curriculum, King's teaches Austrian Economics, a school of thought often favored by libertarians.

The young men and women at King's are relatively worldly: It's easy to imagine them blending in with their eventual co-workers in New York and elsewhere. They are being groomed for positions of influence, but not to go forth and proselytize, at least not openly. "If you go into Goldman Sachs and talk about Jesus, you're going to get fired," Oakes said. As new as the school is—it graduated its first class in 2005—students have had internships at New Line Cinema, Fox, and the Foundation of Economic Education, and on Michael Bloomberg's mayoral campaign and *The Sean Hannity Show.*

As the students from King's and similarly oriented evangelical institutions start to get jobs within influential organizations in the media, in government, in law, in the arts, and in business—some of the fields King's specifically targets—they will be able not only to continue the advancement of the evangelical agenda but also to stage a quiet revolution by bringing their Christian and conservative ideals to bear. Instead of the media and other elite institutions being out of touch with the evangelical mainstream, as they are now, evangelicals will be pulling the levers of power and influence in these and, indeed, all areas of society. The better educated evangelicals are, the reasoning goes, the more clout they will wield.

King's location in the power center of New York helps its students gain savvy about the media, law, business, and the arts—not to mention access to jobs in those fields—but the machinations of politics are difficult to fully understand without spending time in Washington. Michael Farris, a longtime political organizer and president of the Home School Legal Defense Fund, was well aware of that when in 2000 he founded Patrick Henry College in Purcellville, Virginia—less than an hour outside of Washington, D.C.—to train young Christians, specifically homeschooled students, to work in politics and other spheres of influence.

For years Farris had, on one side, parents peppering him with questions about what colleges would best suit their homeschooled children and, on the other, members of Congress asking where they could find homeschooled students to staff their offices (*home school* being shorthand for students who shared their conservative values). Eventually Farris realized that he could, in one move, meet the needs of both groups by starting a college primarily for homeschoolers that would prepare them to take their conservative values into the world at large and, more specifically, into the political arena. He knew that an institution like that would have incredible potential to further the ideals and values he deemed so important. "If our ideas are not in the public square, public policy and the social fabric of America goes in a direction that we believe is not best for the nation," Farris told me in the offices he now occupies as president of Patrick Henry College. "We have a moral duty to get our ideas out."

Patrick Henry, then, is a school of contrasts. It aims to build the next generation of America's leaders from the pool of students that has commingled least with that society. It is the most biblically infused of the schools that I visited, but its raison d'etre is clearly and expressly to train students to influence the secular world.

The school's stated mission is "to prepare Christian men and women who will lead our nation and shape our culture with timeless biblical values and fidelity to the spirit of the American founding." As such, there are, at this point, only a handful of majors open to the 320 students at Patrick Henry: history, classical liberal arts, literature, and government—by far the most popular. The college draws a remarkably qualified student body. The 2005 freshman class had a median combined SAT of 1340. According to Faith Brobst, an alumnus who hails from Columbus, Ohio, and, until she heard about Patrick Henry, planned on going to school close to home so she could keep her part-time job in a library there, the emphasis on leadership begins as early as the initial recruitment process when the school is looking for students who are personally dedicated to excellence, not simply those whose parents want them to go there. Indeed, not every student survives four years at Patrick Henry. The message, stated and unstated, is: "Don't come here to play around, come here if you really want to make a difference," Brobst said. "The academic rigor of the school is really very intense."

Competitive as they may be academically, the students at Patrick Henry look different from those at other colleges, even other Christian colleges. I first encountered them when I attended one of the required daily chapel services. The dress code at Patrick Henry is business casual, so there were no jeans to be seen anywhere, but what struck me was how many of the girls were wearing long skirts and had long hair. They dressed in a manner that probably grows out of fundamentalist sensibilities but recalls conservative elements of the Holiness Movement, which began in the 1880s and taught that Christians could perfect their sinful natures. At the time of its inception, the Holiness Movement was closely associated with Methodism;

eventually it provided a base for Pentecostalism. Conservative factions within the movement eschewed many of the trappings of modern life, including television and film. Adherents to these factions also favored conservative dress styles (think Amish in color), little to no makeup, and long hair for women.

Chapel attendance may be compulsory, but the students showed nothing but willingness to be here. As in most places, the service began with some singing. By the third song students had their arms in the air and their eyes closed. One young woman had her hands clenched together over her heart and her brow furrowed in earnestness. A few students spontaneously broke into harmony. Then, after a prayer, Farris took the podium and delivered the morning message. The topic was "Builders Versus Snipers," and from the examples he used (for example, the press criticizing Bush over his handling of the war in Iraq are snipers, not builders), the school's political leanings were crystal clear.

I filed out with the students and into a class called Freedom's Foundations. Students brought in bottles of water and cups of coffee, but they were careful to be seated with their computers open before the class began. This is not the kind of place where tardiness is overlooked. The class was studying Rousseau, and the professor, Dr. Robert Stacey, asked questions that gently led the students to a foregone conclusion about the difference for Christians between being good men in God's eyes and good citizens in the estimation of society. Here at Patrick Henry students study the secular classics, but with a biblical frame of reference. The approach is one that reinforces already held beliefs, rather than one of exploration.

"Why do we work?" Stacey questioned. "Ladies, why do you want to marry men who work?"

A young woman answered: "So we can make a profit."

"And what is your husband going to do with those profits?" Stacey parried back.

"Buy me jewelry," the student responded as the class—and the professor—broke out in laughter.

That exchange illustrates the general assumption about gender roles at Patrick Henry but also betrays a certain glib tone I noticed in the classroom, as though implicit in the social contract of the place was the understanding that what happens there is just a means to an end. In liberal arts college, "preprofessional" is a bad word; the four years of college are supposed to be about intellectual growth for the sake of intellectual growth. Not so at Patrick Henry. The education students receive here is important, but only as an undergirding to the real work they are being prepared to do: to go out and lead or, in the case of most of the women, to be supportive of men who do and to raise the next generation of leaders. "I'm speaking to a roomful of potential government servants," Stacey stated at one point.

I recognized myself during my years at my Christian high school in the students at Patrick Henry. There's a security that comes from being in a room full of your peers who all believe as you do and who interpret the world in the same way, and even more affirmation with an authority figure who concurs. These kinds of classroom interactions will fill the students with certainty and confidence and buoy them up for their encounters with secular America. These young adults are enthusiastic and keen to set out and do the work that they believe they were predestined to do. There are few things more exhilarating than the feeling that you have divine power on your side. These young men and women are on a mission—a mission from God.

Once the laughter in the classroom subsided, the students returned to the subject of the necessity of work, their outlook clearly influenced by the Bible. "Human nature prevents us from being anything but selfish," one young woman said. "As Christians we do believe in working hard but we do it for the glory of God," another added. The class moved on to a discussion of the Declaration of the Rights of Man. Together, the class established that at the root of the document was an understanding of liberty as the freedom to do anything that doesn't hurt someone—and then they immediately started to poke holes in that theory. "This is the definition of liberty that is the basis of a lot of the skewed decisions that come down from the Supreme Court," Stacey told the class. Stacey's class will wind up at a common point at the end of their discussion, in large part because they all share comparable worldviews and therefore make similar assumptions. The big philosophical questions about things such as human nature have already been decided by Patrick Henry students.

That self-assuredness, though, may not be a gift. A similar educational background left me with few doubts about my beliefs—until I went off to college and met with well-reasoned arguments that countered them. This buttressing approach can only take one so far; unless you are able to fully grasp an opposing point of view you can't truly know you disagree with it. If you are only told what's wrong with a position, it can be disorienting if you eventually find that there is, in fact, some merit in it. Young men and women who are truly solid in their faith only come to be that way if they are allowed to look at opposing viewpoints head on, weigh the positive and the negative, and then draw their own conclusions.

But a Christian education such as the one offered at Patrick Henry is not about exploration but about fortification. Students here are being trained to take their ideas and influence the world with them, not to go out and learn what the world has to teach. That imperative elevates the importance of debate and moot court in conservative Christian schools—life is about convincing those who disagree with you and about defeating your opponents. Almost a third of the students at Patrick Henry are involved in debate and the school has a formidable team that routinely wins national tournaments. In evangelical politics the courts are seen as the key to turning the country around, so it is critical that the Christian community be armed with talented lawyers. Training students to be skilled debaters and orators is the first step.

But the real strength of Patrick Henry lies in the practical experience it gives its students. A significant portion of graduating credits come from internships or from a "directed research and writing" project on an issue or problem one might be asked to tackle in a real job. In the days before the 2004 presidential election the school stopped holding classes since so many students were working on campaigns or on get-out-the-vote efforts. During her time at the school, which is close enough to Washington, D.C., to get in on a daily basis, Faith Brobst had internships on Capitol Hill, in the Department of Labor, and at the White House. She was offered a permanent job in the White House but she turned it down because she felt she could have more of an impact in the private sector. She's now working at Charles Colson's Prison Fellowship Ministry. She is committed to going wherever God leads her, but her aspiration has always been to be a wife and mother. She hopes that the husband God brings her someday will be a government official or a lawyer so she can use the skills she developed at Patrick Henry to support him.

In the evangelical community the man is the head of the household, as stated in the New Testament epistle of Ephesians, and women submit to their husbands. Surprisingly, you'll find few evangelical women who find that dictum sexist. While there are differing interpretations of the command to "submit," the evangelical women I have met have seemed comfortable with it. While many evangelical women work outside of the home, their primary role is that of helpmate. The education young women receive at Patrick Henry will serve them in the workplace, but it will also equip them to better educate their own children. Furthermore, a school such as Patrick Henry is an excellent place to find a like-minded mate, something that the students and their parents hope will happen during their time there. The wife's role in the home is somewhat exalted, and evangelical women everywhere take it seriously, but nowhere more so than in the homeschool population. I was intrigued by the duality of these homeschooled students, at once profoundly ambitious and deeply traditional. I decided to take a closer look at the world they came from.

* * *

As I make my way up the stairs past the white columns in front of Purcellville Baptist Church, I hear the sounds of young children talking and laughing. I pull open the double doors to enter the red brick building and see the pews filled with squirming children of varying ages. After being reminded to take off their hats, they stand up, face the two students who are standing on the stage, and, holding either side of an unfurled American flag, recite the Pledge of Allegiance. They then bow their heads in prayer. "Father God, we thank you for this day and for the privilege to homeschool," begins Dona DeGree, coordinator of the Covenant Learning Co-op, which provides weekly science and geography classes for about 250 homeschooled students here in Purcellville. The youngest children use the basement classrooms in this church and the older students meet across the road in the white clapboard skating rink, using screens to partition the rink's wooden oval floor into separate spaces. My guide is Kristin Brodowski, who holds a Ph.D. in mechanical engineering and used to be an associate director at the NASA research center. Brodowski, who has two daughters in the group, is one of the science teachers. Others include a mother who worked as a scientist at the Jet Propulsion Laboratory in Pasadena, California, and a former public school teacher. Mothers are the force behind the homeschool movement, which gives them tremendous power in the home and in the community.

The classes look like those at any school, with children sitting around tables writing on worksheets, cutting things out of paper, taking quizzes, and reading aloud. What's different are the big, white, three-ring binders that sit next to each child. Every binder has an opening page with a Bible verse and the child's name, followed by lists of all the weekly assignments. The parent (usually the mother) who supervises the child at home places a checkmark next to each completed task, and once a week a volunteer at the co-op assigns point values and tallies up the total score. The volunteer is not grading the work—that is for the parents at home to do—just making sure each child is up to speed. For some students, this Wednesday science class is just one event in a busy week. In addition to this co-op, Brodowski's two daughters are part of a history group and a physical education group.

As engaged as the evangelical community has become, the familiar old pull toward isolationism still exists, particularly in education where traditional, biblical roles about gender and family are at the forefront. Evangelicals are fiercely independent, in part because their religion's emphasis on an individual's accountability before God demands them to be, and partly because they are organized around the family unit. This, combined with a general sense that society, culture, and, by extension, the public schools are becoming increasingly dissolute, makes evangelicals want to protect their children from outside influences. Christian parents are fed a steady diet of stories about schools in which children can't mention the Bible, Christmas, or pledge allegiance to the country "under God" and in which students are taught how to use condoms and that it's okay that Heather has two mommies. Rather than let their untarnished offspring be subject to these abhorrent messages, they educate their children themselves. Indeed, homeschooling is still on the rise, to the tune of a 7- to 15-percent increase each year over the roughly 2 million students already being taught at home. While a portion of these new families have made their decision for reasons that have nothing to do with religion, the vast majority of home-schooled students, about two out of three, identify themselves as evangelical Christians. And there seems to be some academic advantage for the children. The Home School Legal Defense Association points to a 1988 study that indicated that students who were taught at home scored twenty to thirty percentile points higher on standardized tests than students who were taught in schools.

And yet, even the homeschooled population shows signs of engagement. While there are certainly some families for whom the stereotype of children sitting around the kitchen table being taught by a religiously overcharged mother inculcating them into the family's extreme brand of Christianity is apt, many of these children are perfectly well adjusted and socialized through extensive networks of homeschooled students who meet regularly for social events, sports leagues, and classes, such as the one I observed. Homeschooled students are now regarded by many conservatives as the unpolished diamonds of the evangelical community, the group of youth with the most potential for future leadership (about 75 percent of Patrick Henry's students are homeschooled). They are disciplined (no pretending to Mom you've done your homework when she's the one you have to turn it in to) and ideologically untainted by outside influences. They are likely to hold very strong views, having had few challenges from peers, and many are quite self-confident, a by-product of one-on-one attention. I first realized the possibilities of homeschooling when I visited Wheaton College outside Chicago.

What struck me when I sat down for the nine a.m. political theory class at Wheaton College on a chilly Monday in November was how lively and fresh-faced the fifteen students looked so early in the morning. Listless bodies and oversized cups of coffee were the stuff of my college days. I suddenly realized that the students' alertness must, at least in part, be due to the college's no drinking policy. None of these students was likely to be hung over, and they are "encouraged" to be back in their dorms by midnight on school nights, although there is no curfew.

Interestingly, Shakespeare was on the docket once again. The class was finishing up a study of *Henry IV, Part 1* and was poised to launch into *Part 2*. "Would anyone like to suggest that Falstaff was a Dionysian figure?" the professor, Ashley Woodiwiss, asked. "In the Nietzschean sense?" queried Angela McClain, a homeschooled senior from Ashville, North Carolina. McClain had a remarkable grasp of Shakespeare, in part because her parents took her to London to see it performed by the actors who understand it best. I realized then that careful, diligent parents may well be able to provide a homeschool education to rival that of any public or private school—even without trips abroad.

Woodiwiss asked the class to consider the scene through the prism of Nietzsche's concepts of the Apollonian and Dionysian, with Hotspur symbolizing the former and Falstaff the latter. It's a discussion that could just have easily taken place at a secular college. I noticed differences, though. Not all of the students had McClain's mental agility, and many of them showed a tendency to think in two-dimensional terms, an unfortunate by-product of some forms of Christian education. Students who attended schools that emphasize the spiritual over the academic often paint the world in black and white—a natural inclination given that they have been educated in an environment that portrays everything in terms of an epic struggle between good and evil.

Wheaton is known as the Harvard of the Christian world and draws from an applicant pool of the same quality as that of some of the nation's best universities and liberal arts colleges, with an average combined SAT score of 1336, and an average high school GPA of 3.72. It mimics secular schools by educating its students—at least outside of the Bible classes—through a liberal arts curriculum that broadens their frames of reference and, just as in secular colleges, encouraging them to test their beliefs. It is the most visible and most influential of all the Christian colleges and, while it is not as self-conscious as King's or Patrick Henry about turning out future leaders, it has in fact produced more of the country's evangelical elite than any other school. Billy Graham, President Bush's adviser and former speechwriter Michael Gerson, and Speaker of the House of Representatives Dennis Hastert are but a few of the school's illustrious alumni. Wheaton put Christian scholarship on the map.

Woodiwiss says that while the material he covers at Wheaton is similar to what he used as a teaching assistant at the University of North Carolina in Chapel Hill, he looks at it differently with his students here. "We come at it from a particular point of view that raises specific kinds of questions . . . questions of causality." What they don't do, he said, is read through a Christian filter. Students first consider things in the same way their secular counterparts would, but then put them in the context of a Christian worldview. Woodi-wiss acknowledges that when his students arrive at Wheaton many of them see things in absolute terms, but he says most of them have changed by the time they graduate. "What a good liberal arts education does is complicate reality for them," he said. "I want them to leave here being theologically reflective of why they're conservative or liberal."

Wheaton aims to be equal parts spiritual incubator and imparter of knowledge. The school's goal is to develop Christian students who can fulfill the biblical imperative to be the salt and light in the world or, in other words, to impart Christian values and show the rest of the world a better way to live. Its educational purpose, it says, is "to relate Christian liberal arts education to the needs of contemporary society. The curricular approach is designed to combine faith and learning in order to produce a biblical perspective needed to relate Christian experience to the demands of those needs." It's a dual-track approach that, when both ends are pursued vigorously, as they are at Wheaton, ultimately leads to a certain level of schizophrenia. Inevitably, there are points at which the imperative to pursue academic excellence pulls in a different direction from the mission to develop students as Christians.

While a suspicion of intellectual thought and higher education is an unfortunate legacy of fundamentalism, that attitude is slowly changing, a shift due in no small part to historian Mark Noll's elucidation of the problem in his 1994 book *The Scandal of the Evangelical Mind*, which has been described as an "epistle from a wounded lover." "The scandal of the evangelical mind is that there is not much of an evangelical mind," reads the book's opening line. Noll goes on to show that the rise of anti-intellectualism was an outgrowth of the modern fundamentalist and Pentecostal movements, which stressed spiritual revelation. He points out that at earlier moments in Christian history, scholarship was valued. Noll possesses a first-rate intellect; he is also a devoted Christian. From any other source such a criticism might have been met with defensiveness, but

Noll, who was until recently a professor at Wheaton, is widely respected in evangelical circles. His spiritual credentials are unassailable, forcing the community to accept the appraisal as constructive.

Still, Wheaton's fundamentalist history has not entirely been put to rest, nor do many affiliated with the school want it to be. On the one hand are the professors, many of whom, like their secular counterparts, want to engage in true intellectual inquiry and, also like professors in non-Christian institutions, often tend to be (relatively) liberal. On the other hand is the more conservative administration, and the alumni who studied at a much more fundamentalist Wheaton and who would like to see it stay that way.

That tension is felt not just by the faculty and administration, but by the students as well. Senior Esther Lee, a smart and serious young woman from Lexington, Massachusetts, told me there is a lot of pent-up intellect at Wheaton that is not unleashed because intellectual pursuits are viewed as too secular. Instead, much of that vibrance is channeled into missions and other more Christian activities. But Woodiwiss told me the suspicion of secular scholarship is a vestige of Wheaton's fundamentalist heritage that is fast fading. "Increasingly, as an institution we are engaging the academic project full-throttle," he said. What that means in real terms is that Wheaton doesn't shy away from teaching things that other Christian colleges may find too worldly. Woodiwiss, for instance, teaches Nietzsche, Kant, Foucault, and Marx.

Some, however, think this intellectual engagement comes with a spiritual cost. Just as I had a crisis of faith when I went away to college, many Wheaton students find themselves testing the religious beliefs they grew up with, albeit in a setting where evangelical tenets are reinforced. At Wheaton the students may all be self-identified evangelicals, but they come from many points on the religious spectrum. Students here are more likely than at most other Christian colleges to be confronted with challenging views they've never encountered before. One area in which that is manifest is students' beliefs about the beginning of the world. According to the October

28, 2005, edition of the *Wheaton Record*, the student paper, 47 percent of students entered the college believing that the earth is less than ten thousand years old (a young earth view consistent with seven-day creationism). When students were asked about their current views, the young earth group had dwindled to 27 percent, the poll found. The largest group of enrolled students—34 percent—held that the earth is at least 4.5 billion years old, which is in line with findings of the scientific community.

Wheaton's science professors in particular live at the nexus of the conflict between reason and religion. They pride themselves on teaching a curriculum that stands up to the scrutiny of the scientific community, but many of their colleagues in other departments—and, indeed, in other Christian institutions—disagree with their point of view. Wheaton is one of only two Christian colleges in America that places enough of an emphasis on science to have a significant geology department. While a student in a Bible class may be told that God created the earth in seven days, Dr. Stephen Moshier, associate professor of geology, tells his classes that scientific observation indicates the earth is more than 4.5 billion years old. But that doesn't mean God didn't have a hand in the process, Moshier said. "It would be my view that God created in that way," he explained. That belief can be called intelligent design in a general sense, Moshier said, but he drew a line between his views and the brand of intelligent design that has been introduced into school curricula around the country, which is largely a political construct designed to inject God and creationism into the public schools.

On both a spiritual and a social level, life at Wheaton is what one might imagine. Chapel is mandatory and students are required to take four Bible classes during the four years at the college: New Testament, Old Testament, Theology of Culture, and Christian Thought. Drinking is prohibited. Dancing has recently been deemed permissible, but only at school-sponsored functions and even then only "teachable" dances are allowed, such as square dancing or the tango. At night students play board games and have theological discussions. For the most part, parents can rest assured that their children are sheltered from the temptations that face young adults on secular college campuses, which are portrayed in the Christian media as centers of debauchery and apostasy. In contrast, students at Wheaton call it "the bubble." Parents clearly are convinced, as enrollment at Christian colleges is soaring, up more than 70 percent between 1990 and 2004 at schools that belong to the Council for Christian Colleges and Universities.

Like other Christian colleges, Wheaton prohibits premarital sex and there are no coed dorms, so there is a certain level of pressure (both societal and hormonal) to marry young. Wheaton shares an unofficial motto with other Christian colleges: "A ring by spring or your money back." The students I met told me they have friends who got engaged as early as freshman year and some of them even got married and lived together off campus.

Still, there are things about the college that might surprise an outsider. Even in this sequestered environment, students have the impulse to put their mark on society through political activism—and not only the Young Republican variety. The Wheaton campus was galvanized when Bono chose the school as a stop on his Heart of America tour in 2003, which was intended to raise awareness about the AIDS epidemic. After the Christian rock star's visit, the students founded the Student Global AIDS Campaign. They dove in with passion, flooding congressmen and senators with calls asking them to support the Global Fund to Fight AIDS, Tuberculosis and Malaria and the Jubilee Campaign, which calls on governments to forgive the debt of poor countries. The following year Esther Lee became vice-president of SGAC and was one of five students who went to Zambia on a humanitarian mission. The year after that she was elected president of the group and helped organize the first-ever conference on AIDS for students of Christian colleges. In the beginning of the AIDS epidemic in the 1980s, Christians turned their back on the issue because they associated it with homosexuality and immorality. Now that it's become clear that not everyone who has HIV or AIDS committed some sort of sin to contract it, the Christian community has taken it upon itself to tackle the issue. "Orphans, widows, sex-traffic victims—these are all victims of structural violence that even the most politically conservative Christian college student can't blame," Lee wrote me in an e-mail.

While the students at Wheaton are involved with a traditionally liberal cause, they diverge from other AIDS organizations when necessary to keep their Christian worldview intact. During my visit I saw fliers for a lecture on abstinence and AIDS, the means favored by evangelicals to combat the pandemic. The Wheaton chapter of SGAC considered changing its name to distinguish itself from the national organization, a secular group that has views that most Wheaton students don't share. Ultimately, though, the Wheaton group kept the name, deciding that as Christians they could work alongside non-Christians for a cause and still retain their own perspective. Some students work with a Chicago-based Christian ministry for gay prostitutes—although at least one student had to contend with parents who were unhappy that she was spending so much time with homosexuals.

The student's AIDS activism may have a conservative tinge to it, but as at colleges everywhere, students at Wheaton leave more liberal than they arrived. While 72 percent of the students who responded to a September 2004 survey conducted by the student paper supported George Bush, only half of the students agreed with the decision to go to war with Iraq. The issues that kept the students in the Bush camp were abortion and gay marriage. Interestingly, of the students who reported that their political views had changed during their years at Wheaton, 77 percent of them said they had become more liberal—in contrast to only 23 percent who said they had grown more conservative. And while Wheaton students were never going to be the voting bloc to tip the 2004 presidential election in Kerry's favor, 17 percent of seniors said they planned to vote for him, as opposed to only 5 percent of the freshman class. The freshmen in the poll were highly concerned with national security and gay marriage, while the seniors were focused on poverty, education, and health care.

As good as Christian education may be, the country's most esteemed schools are still secular and offer a prestige that rising numbers of evangelicals are deciding they want. There is a vibrant—and growing—evangelical scene at colleges across the country, including the Ivy League universities where students are proudly reclaiming their schools' religious heritages. (A good number of the Ivies were started as training grounds for the clergy.) While many Christian students arrive at college and, like me, abandon their faith, others find ways to engage with people who share it and leave with their beliefs intact or even strengthened. At Harvard alone, the evangelical group Christian Impact has more than doubled its membership to 150, from 70 in the fall of 1999. In addition to Christian Impact, there are several other Christian groups at Harvard, including the Harvard-Radcliff Christian Fellowship, the Asian-American Christian Fellowship, Athletes in Action, the Reformed Christian Fellowship, and the Asian Baptist Student Koinonia. Andy Crouch, who used to run the Harvard-Radcliffe Christian Fellowship, which is sponsored by the international missions group Intervarsity, said when he started with the group in 1991 there were about 50 members; now there are easily 180, including the spin-off groups Asian-American Christian Fellowship and the black group Soul Food.

Crouch thinks the growth can be attributed to two factors, which he puts in economic terms: an increase in demand and a simultaneous increase in supply. On the demand side, he said, is a change in Harvard's admission policies. Up until the 1980s Harvard and, indeed, many of the Ivies, were predominantly populated with students from the Northeast and particularly from the private schools there. In the eighties, Harvard embraced the notion of being a national institution and increased the number of students it admitted from other parts of the country, such as the West and the heartland, where there are higher concentrations of evangelicals. It's not that these elite institutions specifically wanted born-again students, but the class president of a public school in Iowa is more likely to be a Christian than the class president of a private school in Massachusetts. At the same time, the Ivies and other elite schools began looking for ethnic diversity and admitted an escalating percentage of Asian Americans and African Americans, two groups with high proportions of evangelicals.

All this was happening just as the social status of evangelicals was changing, and mounting numbers of them were preparing their children to attend the nation's top universities—the increase in supply. Many of these students came out of public high schools, which have well-developed networks of religious clubs that attract kids to Christianity and help keep them there. These students are accustomed to being part of a minority culture and cleaving together, so it's the most natural thing in the world for them to find each other at a place like Harvard.

Evangelical students at Harvard guess it's easier to be openly born-again today than it was fifteen years ago because there are so many Christian role models that students of all—or no—faiths look up to, such as Bono. While "it's certainly not the norm," senior Jordan Hylden, a sandy-haired senior at Harvard who is co-coordinator of the Christian Impact group there, told me, "I wouldn't say my being a Christian, in and of itself, is looked down on. Certainly not in a social way."

Life for Christians at Harvard is very different from that of their Wheaton counterparts. For starters, many professors at Harvard are overtly hostile to the evangelical faith. At Wheaton, science and religion are seen as compatible. Not a view widely held at Harvard. Hylden recounted a scene from his evolution and human behavior course, in which his professor gave a PowerPoint presentation contrasting creationism and Darwinism. On one side he had a picture of a priest to represent religion. He then superimposed a circle with a red line through it over the priest. Not that Hylden is a hardcore creationist. Like most of his counterparts at Wheaton, Hylden holds that a belief in evolutionary theory is not incompatible with his faith. "I believe that God is responsible for creating the world, and yet I believe that God used evolution as a tool," he said.

If evangelical students feel that many of their professors disdain their religion, socially it's another story. Hylden thinks evangelicals are seen, at least by some, as doing something countercultural. They're so uncool, they're cool again. "Almost everybody has at least one Christian friend at this point in their lives," Hylden said. "Sometimes, it's very appealing—now you have a different lifestyle option with friendly, affirming kids."

Like the students at Wheaton, evangelicals at Harvard try to remain chaste (although only one of the students in Hylden's fellowship group wears a purity ring, a trend among evangelical teens to indicate that they are saving themselves for marriage). While they don't get engaged or married in the same numbers as the students at Wheaton, Hylden said there is a running joke about joining Christian Impact and finding a wife or husband. He has several friends who got married right after graduating from college—something his non-Christian friends plan to put off until their late twenties. On the other hand, Hylden said that many of the Christians at Harvard don't see a problem with drinking—once they've turned twenty-one and aren't breaking any laws in doing so. In fact, Hylden and some of his buddies have started a club called the 21-plus JLDC, or twenty-one-plus Jesus Lovers' Drinking Club. "No one is getting hammered," Hylden assured me.

When I visited, Hylden shepherded me to a dorm called Quincy House, where Christian Impact was holding its weekly Bible study. We walked into the junior common room and found a few dozen students milling about. A smiling young woman in jeans and a pink sweatshirt wrote out name tags for people as they entered the room. Most of the students here were Christians when they arrived at Harvard, Hylden later told me, although some—about one in ten, he guessed—were led to Christ through evangelical friends at the college.

The students were clean-cut and casually clad, and a few came carrying Bibles. They took their places in chairs and on the floor, then bowed their heads as one of them led the group in prayer. Three more students, one with a guitar, one with a violin, and one on piano, started playing folksy music and the assembled crowd joined in, singing. They started out slowly but once they warmed up, eyes closed, hands poked up into the air, and bodies began to sway. There were about forty students here now reading the lyrics off a screen hanging behind the piano. The last song was the classic hymn "How Great Thou Art." These students were an earnest bunch who, as the young man leading the prayer put it, were "committed to seeking God together, learning what that means and applying it to our lives."

The speaker of the evening was a candidate for ordination in the Episcopal Diocese of Massachusetts who was exercising his nascent preaching skills. He talked quickly as he inelegantly made his way through his outline points, but his audience listened attentively— despite some scattered yawns that, judging by the pallor of the students' faces and the bags under their eyes, seemed more indicative of a lack of sleep than of boredom. The speaker started by referring to a series of articles that had recently run in the *Boston Globe* about evangelical leaders. He began with Rick Warren and the influence Warren wields. "Is it a Christian impact? Some would say yes, some would say no. Can you spoon feed it?" Like many evangelicals of their generation, this group at Harvard is looking for a more immediate, more transcendent experience than that found in most megachurches, which are largely run by baby boomers—their parents' generation. Today's youth are rebelling against the church of their fathers and searching for authenticity and transcendence, a trend that may signal the beginning of the end of the megachurch. The speaker played to that, telling the gathering that the real doctrine of Christianity is a lived doctrine, a transformational doctrine. Aside from the friendly laughter that greeted his boilerplate jokes, the room was completely still. The students didn't even glance over at each other. When he was finished, they applauded.

At Wheaton, faith is a given and the thought goes into engagement. Is it permissible to pursue intellectual endeavors? A strictly secular career? Or is ministry the preferred path? At Harvard students have the opposite concern. They have attained the secular world's brass ring of academic achievement by gaining admission to the storied school. No one will dispute their scholarly credentials; it's their spiritual lives that come into question. The struggle at scholarly secular schools like Harvard is to allow intellectual exploration and at the same time stay true to spiritual principles. It's a delicate balance that I, at college, was unable—and, in truth, unwilling—to strike.

An undergraduate degree, even one from an institution like Harvard, is still just a launching pad; in many fields graduate school is what really matters. There are those in the evangelical world who think that, even with the best intentions of schools such as Patrick Henry and King's, it's important for evangelicals to have credentials that are unassailable by the secular world, which is where the Harvey Fellows Program comes in. The program provides funds for, as it says in its literature, "Christian graduate students to integrate their faith and vocation and pursue leadership positions in strategic fields where Christians tend to be underrepresented."

The Harvey Fellowship administrators are particularly interested in students who want to pursue careers in media, government, scientific research, and higher education and who have been admitted to one of the top five programs in their field. By enabling them to graduate with no debt, the fellowship makes it possible for students to take jobs they might not otherwise be able to afford to take, such as those in the public sector. There are currently 191 fellows and the program has spent more than $4 million since its inception.

The Harvey Fellowship was founded in 1992 by Dennis and Eileen Harvey, and grew out of Dennis Harvey's own experiences at Harvard, where he saw that pedigree matters. He also heard his father-in-law, an attorney, lament that Christians whom he believed would be gifted lawyers would often apply for jobs at his firm but he was unable to convince the other partners to hire them because they didn't have competitive credentials. Now, thanks to Harvey's fellowship, more evangelicals do—fellows have studied at the California Institute of Technology, Cambridge, Oxford, Princeton, and MIT, but Harvard, Stanford, and Yale are by far the most popular choices. Graduates include a member of the National Security Council, a senior advisor in the U.S. Treasury Department, and a Guggenheim Fellowship finalist.

While Christian education may sometimes look like retreat, in many cases, such as those of Patrick Henry and King's, it is more accurately seen as a regrouping before the incursion into society. Even those schools that completely shelter students are contributing to the overall strategy of engagement by helping create a community that is better educated and better qualified for important jobs. One has to wonder, though, how many of these young people will eventually be lost to secular thought when they come to encounter it on a daily basis. While the students at Harvard are tackling American society on its own terms, the students at Wheaton, Patrick Henry, and King's all are thinking about how to make sure their existing values are reflected in the country at large, albeit in very different ways. Regardless of approach, each of these institutions seems well on the way to grooming leaders who will carry the torch of evangelical Christianity into the public square and further the transformation of mainstream culture.

CHAPTER NINE

From the Ground Up

I<small>T'S SEVEN FIFTEEN A.M.</small> and with the president due to arrive in half an hour the driveways into the Washington Hilton are already blocked off by black cars. I make my way across Connecticut Avenue, along the edge of the circular driveway, and into the hotel, where I am directed down the escalators and toward a long line of people waiting to go through the metal detectors and take their seats in the huge banquet hall, along with the four thousand other foreign dignitaries, politicians, religious leaders, and assorted people who have assembled here for the fifty-fourth annual national prayer breakfast.

The breakfast is always a big event—it's an opportunity for Christians from around the country to see the president and for him to demonstrate how faithful he is—but this year is especially exciting because word has leaked out that the speaker, whose identity is supposed to have been kept under wraps—is none other than the rock star Bono. Indeed, in the center of each round table in the banquet hall is a pile of the white plastic wristbands that are the signature of Bono's ONE campaign to eliminate poverty. If ever there was an illustration of the intersection of politics, culture, and religion, this is it.

Of course, by now everyone is well aware of the potent partnership between evangelical Christians and President Bush's administration, and how the community's loyalty propelled the president to a second term in office. Evangelicals were a force to be reckoned with, and the 2004 presidential election was their perfect storm. The Christian base was energized by what it saw as an assault on traditional marriage. Gay marriage bans on the ballots in eleven states motivated people to go to the polls, and the promise of a federal marriage amendment helped add African American votes to the GOP ledger, particularly in the critical state of Ohio. Catholics and evangelicals banded together on morality issues. While each one of those factors was small, in the aggregate they pushed the president to victory by a razor-thin margin and marked a historic level of Republican voting for the Christian community.

Evangelicals had ample reason to be enthusiastic about Bush in 2004. When he took office four years earlier, he immediately set upon a course that let them know that he had their interests at heart. A self-proclaimed born-again Christian, he surrounded himself with people of like mind. He appointed Wheaton alum Michael Gerson as his chief speechwriter. He made John Ashcroft, a staunch Pentecostal, attorney general. Then–national security advisor Condoleezza Rice identifies herself as an evangelical, and his first secretary of commerce, Donald Evans, was in a Bible study group with Bush in the mid-1980s.

Bush seemed more than willing to blur the lines between church and state, evidenced by his support of faith-based initiatives, his proposal to classify the fetus as a child, his legislation prohibiting late-term abortions, and his stance on both stem-cell research and federal guidelines that require school districts to allow greater religious freedom or lose funding. During his tenure the National Park Service gift stores began stocking a book that claims the Grand Canyon was formed during Noah's flood. The Bush administration also overruled the superintendent of the Grand Canyon National Park when he wanted to remove three plaques with biblical quotations that suggested the Grand Canyon was created by God.

More visible proof of the degree to which the Bush administration was in sync with evangelicals was evident in the front row of the audience on the day Bush signed the partial-birth abortion ban. Looking on approvingly was a cabal of leaders of the Christian Right that included Adrian Rogers, former head of the Southern Baptist Convention; Louis Sheldon, chairman of the Traditional Values Coalition; Christian talk-show host Janet Parshall; American Center for Law and Justice chief counsel Jay Sekulow; and Jerry Falwell.

When Bush was elected, evangelicals, for the first time in a long time, began feeling good about the state of American politics. The most openly religious president of modern times, George Bush may hail from the mainline Methodist church but the evangelical community knows that in every way that matters, he is one of them. Bush said in the wake of the September 11 terrorist attacks that he believes he was chosen by God to lead the country at this moment in time. While that may send chills down the spines of secular Americans, to evangelicals for whom the idea of predetermination is essential, it is a self-evident truth.

I once asked preacher-turned-political-activist-turned-author Tim LaHaye if the community felt it had as much access to Bush as it would like. "We don't need access," LaHaye told me. "He's one of us. We trust him to do the right thing." National Association of Evangelicals vice president for governmental affairs Richard Cizik put it this way: "You don't need an evangelical lobby. You've got an evangelical in the Oval Office."

The clues weren't hard to find. While he was running for governor of Texas, Bush told a reporter that only believers in Jesus go to heaven. After he'd won the gubernatorial race, Bush proclaimed "Jesus Day" in Texas. During a presidential debate he cited Jesus as his favorite philosopher. He's said he reads his Bible daily. He uses phrases like "Jesus is in my heart," an indication not just of his faith but a signal to evangelicals that he has accepted Christ as his personal savior, which is exactly what makes him one of them. Through Bush, evangelicals have more political influence than they have had at any time in the past thirty years. This is a White House where cabinet meetings are opened with prayer, and where weekly Bible study sessions are attended by roughly fifty White House officials and staff. The administration's first-term political agenda, both domestically and internationally, had evangelicals on their knees thanking the Almighty.

The early presidential speeches were written by evangelical Michael Gerson. Gerson's writings were laden with biblical language that served as coded messages to those who are part of the club. In the wake of the September 11 attacks, Bush was quick to paint the conflict in biblical terms, as "good" versus "evil." In his speech on the first anniversary he said, "Hope still lights our way, and the light shines in the darkness, and the darkness will not overcome it." Evangelicals would have immediately recognized that as a quote from the fifth verse of the first chapter of the book of John, one of the best-known and most often-quoted passages of the New Testament. "The light shines in the darkness, and the darkness has not overcome it," the verse reads, the light referring to Jesus.

In the 2003 state of the union address Bush told his audience, "There is power, wonder-working power, in the goodness and idealism and faith of the American people." Sound like just another patriotic line? Not to the initiated, who will immediately recognize it from their hymnals. "There is power, wonder-working power, in the blood of the Lamb," goes the Lewis E. Jones hymn. The Lamb is how evangelicals refer to Jesus; Christians are the flock. The line is so instantly recognizable to evangelicals that after the speech, Pat Robertson's Christian Broadcasting Network stripped it across the top of its Web page.

There was more of the same in the 2004 state of the union address: "We understand our special calling: This great republic will lead the cause of freedom," Bush told his audience. Evangelicals believe God "calls" them to do certain things; inherent in Bush's statement is the idea that God has called America to spread freedom throughout the world. But Bush didn't need to talk in code that year—it was the plain language in the speech that had evangelicals smiling. Bush pledged to double funding for programs that teach sexual abstinence and, even more important, indicated that he would seek a constitutional amendment forbidding same-sex marriage.

Shortly after he was inaugurated, Bush cut off funds for groups that provided abortions overseas and started giving money to faith-based charities for social initiatives. He quickly appointed Kay Coles James, former dean of Pat Robertson's Regent University, as director of the U.S. Office of Personnel Management, which oversees the entire federal workforce. James is also one of the country's most articulate pro-life advocates. Bush has since restricted stem-cell research and banned late-term abortions. Also at the behest of evangelical leaders, Bush proffered a $15 billion plan to fight AIDS in Africa and promised to pursue a ban on human cloning.

Evangelicals weighed in on Middle East policy as well. Christians have always been staunchly pro-Israel because they believe the Jews remain God's chosen people (although they also believe they will be denied eternal life unless they accept Jesus as their savior), but there is an even more obscure reason. Premillennialists read the book of Revelation to say that Christ will not return until Solomon's temple has been rebuilt on the Temple Mount, on the site now occupied by the Dome of the Rock, an Islamic shrine. The most pro-Israel of the evangelicals call themselves Christian Zionists, and they count among them some very influential politicians (including the disgraced former House majority leader Tom DeLay). It's unclear if Bush adheres to that school of eschatological thought, but he has been careful not to alienate those who do.

Before his downfall DeLay was the putative political leader of the Christian Zionists. He was reported to have had a plaque in his office that said This Could Be the Day, a reference to the inevitability of the rapture. On a trip to Israel, DeLay delivered a pugnacious speech to the Knesset that made clear where he comes down on the issue. "I come to you with a very simple message: Do not be afraid," he said. "Standing up for good against evil is very hard work—it costs money and blood. But we're willing to pay . . . Israel's fight is our fight." The speech was so strident that one Knesset member from the far-right National Union party later quipped, "I told Tom DeLay that until I heard him speak, I thought I was the farthest to the right in the Knesset."

DeLay may be diminished, but the combined forces of the Jewish and Christian lobbies (even those evangelicals who don't call themselves Christian Zionists are pro-Israel) remain formidable. And while evangelicals and Israelis may make an odd partnership because of their theological differences, the Israeli government has been careful to keep Christians sweet, both for their political support and for the money that Christian visitors to Israel bring in. The Israeli Ministry of Tourism sponsors a huge breakfast each year at the National Religious Broadcasters Convention. I attended the 2005 convention in Anaheim, to which the minister of tourism had flown in from Israel to attend. Tourism to Israel had doubled between 2003 and 2005, and Christians were responsible for a big portion of the increase. "Evangelical Christian Americans . . . have been a great comfort for the people of Israel and the State of Israel," tourism minister Avraham Hirchson told his listeners once they had reclaimed their seats after giving him a standing ovation. The breakfast was a love-fest between Christian and Jew, and the audience was a mixture of people wearing suits and yarmulkes and aloha-print shirts. No one mentioned the Second Coming of Christ or the eventual damnation of Jews, but when I sat down privately with Hirchson after the event I asked him if the bedfellows weren't a bit strange given their divergent long-term interests. "They don't patronize us and we don't patronize them," he replied.

Of course, Christians *do* patronize Israel, to the tune of millions of dollars each year. As a show of thanks—and to keep them coming—the Israeli government has pledged to give up a large slice of land near the Sea of Galilee so American evangelicals can build a biblical theme park. The Christian Heritage Center will also include an auditorium and an outdoor theater.

Having flexed their political muscle in the 2004 presidential election, evangelicals started looking to accomplish even more. At the same time, their agenda began undergoing a seismic shift that would have been hard to imagine even a few years earlier. As younger evangelical leaders rise in prominence and immigration makes the church more diverse, the community and, by extension, the Republican Party, is taking on issues that previously were considered the domain of Democrats. In early 2006 a coalition of eighty-six evangelical leaders backed an initiative to fight global warming. At the eleventh hour the National Association of Evangelicals declined to sign the statement, despite NAE vice president Richard Cizik having played a key role in pushing the issue of "creation care" to the forefront of evangelical consciousness in the first place. Other Christian leaders are calling for a renewed focus on social-welfare issues such as caring for those infected with HIV and eradicating poverty.

Evangelicals have also expanded their foreign agenda. The plight of persecuted Christians around the world has always been something the community has cared deeply about; today they are concerned about a wider range of humanitarian crises. They have been active in urging the president to put an end to genocide in Darfur, in trying to stop sex trafficking, and in fighting AIDS. As we saw with Wheaton students, Christians largely ignored the AIDS issue until it became clear that people who hadn't necessarily commited a sin (in other words they weren't homosexual or didn't sleep with a prostitute) were also contracting the disease. In his usual expansive way, Rick Warren announced a global initiative that would help fight the AIDS pandemic, poverty, illiteracy, and other ills. Called the P.E.A.C.E. plan, the initiative calls for planting churches, equipping servant leaders, assisting the poor, caring for the sick, and educating the next generation. Warren has already begun putting his blueprint into action in Rwanda, which he says will be the first purpose-driven nation. Warren's plan is to link the small groups from Saddleback and other congregations to local churches in developing nations to mobilize Christians who can work to address the world's greatest problems, which Warren has identified as spiritual emptiness, corrupt leadership, extreme poverty, pandemic diseases, illiteracy, and lack of education. Warren hopes to enlist 1 billion people to help with the efforts. Never mind that he has no development experience and that he is talking about taking on several overwhelmingly serious problems at the same time—AIDS, illiteracy, corruption, to name but a few. Bigger, more experienced organizations have tried to tackle all of these, and many groups focus on a single issue. Never one to think small, Warren plans to do all of it, and do it better.

Hubris aside, fail or succeed, Warren's elevated status and international pulpit make it very difficult for elected officials to ignore him. Warren and the clout of the evangelical community have helped push the Bush administration into tripling the amount of aid the United States gives to Africa and could be instrumental in turning attention to problems that the developing world has thus far preferred to ignore. Regardless of the efficacy of Warren's P.E.A.C.E. plan, his concern and that of evangelicals as a whole may finally bring about action in the Third World that is long overdue.

Washington may be where the media lens is focused, but the real power of evangelical politics sit out of the public eye in churches throughout the country. Lynne and Richard Ronk, who were decked out in their patriotic best the day I met them, are part of a massive grassroots machine. Lynne was wearing an indigo denim shirt with American flags embroidered on it, half a dozen stars-and-stripes pins, red-white-and-blue earrings, two flag necklaces, a star-spangled bracelet (next to a chain of gold butterflies, her other favorite motif), a flag ring, and a watch with a picture of Old Glory. Richard was somewhat more subdued, wearing a T-shirt with a fluttering flag under his houndstooth jacket. The couple made a special effort getting dressed that morning because they had flown halfway across the country to find out how to help make America the nation God intended it to be.

The Ronks came from their home in Deckers, Colorado, to Coral Ridge Church in Fort Lauderdale to attend the annual conference of the Center for Reclaiming America for Christ, which trains Christians in how to be grassroots activists. Lynne had been involved in political efforts through the Internet for some time, constantly signing petitions and calling politicians, but now that Richard had retired from his job at a medical device company the couple wanted to get more involved. So far Lynne had taken action against abortion, gay marriage, and offensive television programming and she also urged her representatives to approve Samuel Alito's nomination to the Supreme Court. But Richard thinks there is still more to be done, and Lynne agrees. "I'm concerned that if we do nothing, things will continue to deteriorate," Richard said matter-of-factly. "In many ways we're in a downward spiral."

The media may spend a lot of time talking about the accomplishments of the Christian Right in the political arena, but Coral Ridge is filled this weekend with hundreds of people, mainly senior citizens, who think the country is going to hell in a handbasket and that more, much more, needs to be done to change the course. As threatening as evangelicals may be to liberal and secular America, they continue to feel embattled, which makes them want to dig their heels in and fight harder. This conference is all about whipping up the troops.

Over the two days these members of God's army will spend planted in the pews here, they will be told about a link between Planned Parenthood and the Nazis (Planned Parenthood's founder, Margaret Sanger, was a proponent of eugenics), about court rulings that are taking away parents' right to make decisions for their children, and about many other ways that the left and the brand of secular humanism it promotes pose a very real threat to America. For their ninety-nine-dollar registration fee they will learn, in great detail, how to organize their friends, families, neighbors, and church members to battle these forces and turn back the tide of antigodliness that has seized the country. Looking over the mostly white-haired crowd, it would be easy to dismiss them as a bunch of harmless, doddering oldsters with too much time on their hands, but that would be to underestimate them. The potency of evangelical Christians in American politics is derived not from their leaders but ultimately from the worker bees, who operate well under the radar screens of the press.

While the majority of evangelicals have become more mainstream, that is not true of those who are most active in the political arena where the foot solders are drawn from the youth and the elderly—two age groups that tend to hold strong and often extreme positions. Similarly, the generals, as in any movement, are the truest of true believers; thus in the political sphere the old-style leaders of the Religious Right still hold sway. It's only those with the clearest of vision who are able to effectively mobilize followers, but such certitude can make it difficult to see nuance. The leaders of the Christian Right suffer from the same kind of extremism they decry in their counterparts on the left.

James Dobson is perhaps Christianity's most influential political leader. He has been a prominent player on the evangelical stage since the 1970s, first as a Christian psychologist who specialized in the raising of children (his book, *Dare to Discipline,* made him the conservative version of Dr. Spock) and, increasingly as time went on, as the key political organizer of the Christian Right. He is known for his unwillingness to compromise on issues he feels deeply about, which earns him the respect of his base. His political power comes from the 9 million Americans who listen to his radio show each week and who will pick up a phone or write a letter when he asks them to. Indeed, the evangelical community at large is quickly mobilized these days through the technology they have always been so adept at adapting to their needs. There are also thousands of evangelical Web sites and blogs devoted to politics. Evangelicals are skilled at using e-mail as a natural extension of the phone chains they used to put to such good use. I personally get dozens of messages each week asking me to sign a petition or make a phone call, my e-mail address likely having been picked up from a Web page sign-in somewhere.

Evangelicals are increasingly of the opinion that they have a right—an obligation, even—to be involved on the political front. What has changed in the past thirty years is the way in which they do so. National organizations are on the decline as political power moves into the hands of those working on the state and local levels. The Christian Coalition, for example, is a shadow of the hulk it was in the 1980s. "The movement has matured in such a way that it is not a top-down movement," said David Barton, founder and president of WallBuilders, an evangelical group that encourages citizen activism. Thousands of local grassroots groups have sprung up on their own, according to Gary Jarmin, president of Christian Voice and one of the earliest Christian political advocates, putting the real horsepower of evangelical politics on Main Street, U.S.A. "When it gets down to it, it doesn't matter how big or how good an organization you have in Washington," Jarmin said. "It matters how good you are on the street level."

Evangelicals have moved into the mainstream of politics just as they have in other areas of the culture, abandoning their religious organizations in favor of issue-based groups and the Republican Party, where they are now precinct captains and county committee members. Perhaps the most prominent example of this trend is Ralph Reed, who spent eight years as director of the Christian Coalition and built it into one of the most effective grassroots organizations on the political landscape. He left the Christian world to start his own public-relations firm and a few years later became chairman of the Georgia Republican Party. "You're no longer throwing rocks at the building; you're in the building," Reed told the *Washington Post* after leaving the Christian Coalition.

Evangelical grassroots activity is virtually invisible. Unless you're on the blast lists, it's impossible to know what people are saying to each other by e-mail. "It's neighbor to neighbor, mouth to mouth, e-mail to e-mail," Barton said. "That's what you can't measure." An organization can send out a message to a hundred people and in a matter of days that same message could be in the hands of thousands as each recipient sends it to the dozens of people on his or her own distribution list. The process relies on the same principle as viral marketing, which has proven wildly successful in the business arena, namely that messages are better received when they come from someone you know. It's all the more powerful in the political sphere where e-mail is being circulated among people who share a world-view; the effectiveness is heightened because few of the messages are likely to fall on infertile ground.

This kind of local activism gives evangelicals a backdoor influence. For example, school districts around the country are picking up the new textbook published by the Bible Literacy Project, *The Bible and Its Influence,* at the behest of Christian parents and other people who aren't waiting for the state they live in to officially add the textbook to the curriculum but instead show up at their local school board meeting and make their case there. While use of the Bible at school in a devotional context was outlawed by the Supreme Court in 1963, schools are still allowed to teach it as an academic subject. The new textbook discusses the Bible's role in history, literature, and the arts. The Bible Literacy Project is very careful to portray itself as a nonpartisan organization—and it is—but the impetus for it came from evangelicals, as does much of its support on a local level. The group went to such great lengths to stress its ecumenical background and academic bona fides that it eventually had to pull back a little. Word got out—erroneously—that the book was supported by the American Civil Liberties Union. Far from a good thing, such an endorsement is a kiss of death in evangelical circles where there are few more loathed organizations than the ACLU, because it fights for things such as gay rights and to keep God out of the public square.

The Bible Literacy Project eventually issued a disclaimer on its Web site saying the ACLU had not, in fact, endorsed the book.

If seniors make up one significant bloc of Christian activists, young people make up the other. Ned Ryun is the director of a group called Generation Joshua, a national program for Christian youth between the ages of eleven and nineteen who want to "become a force in the civic and political arenas." A big part of GenJ, as it's called, is educational, with online courses on the founding fathers, constitutional law, the Declaration of Independence, Revolutionary War–era sermons, the Federalist Papers, and other, similarly patriotic subjects. There are also courses on successful campaigning and how to run for Congress. Much of the program, though, involves boots-on-the-ground activism, conducted through the GenJ clubs that members can form in any congressional district or county. There is an initiative that "coordinates churches and civic organizations into a mass voter registration drive." And there are student action teams, which give kids hands-on experience working in real elections. In the 2004 election GenJ put about a thousand kids out on the campaign trail working on congressional, senate, and even the presidential races. They're brought in from as far as eight hours away and given housing and food. They help with get-out-the-vote efforts, waving signs, making phone-bank calls, and walking through communities making targeted literature drops. The kids are an invaluable asset to the Republicans, accounting for a signficant percentage of the party's volunteers. As homeschoolers, they are free to campaign right up until election day, when other youth volunteers are already back in school.

When I spoke to Ryun, the group was already making plans for the 2006 elections. They hadn't made any final decisions but were looking at providing volunteers for at least three candidates for the U.S. Senate: Mark Kennedy in Minnesota, Michael Steel in Maryland, and Ed Bryant in Tennessee. Ryun also thought they'd lend some volunteers to Geoff Davis, a candidate from Kentucky whom they helped win a seat in the House of Representatives in 2004. Ryun said Generation Joshua would probably identify about twenty races they wanted to support. They typically work on open or challenger seats and look for candidates who are pro-life and pro–traditional marriage and who are fiscally conservative—a hot-button issue among youth. Kids are clearly eager to get involved. GenJ is only two years old and already five thousand young people have come through the program. "Some of the kids want to have meaningful lives and they see this as making a difference," Ryun said. And as pollster John Zogby pointed out, the kids' political engagement has an effect on their parents' views as well.

Churches provide a key element of organization to the Republican Party that can be seen as a counterbalance to the Democrat-controlled unions, according to Gary Jarmin. "What the evangelical community brought to [the Republican Party] was a vast infrastructure," he said. "They had the capacity to provide . . . buses, child care, a ready-made network, phone lists, and people who know each other." Christian Voice teaches people how to mobilize within their church. First, they instruct, a member should ask the pastor for permission to start a good government committee in the church to handle things such as voter registration. Next, the church volunteer should distribute score cards that show where candidates stand on important issues. Finally, they should organize get-out-the-vote campaigns and find ways to provide transportation and child care so people can make it to the polls. Jarmin encourages an incremental approach that will almost imperceptibly, as he puts it, bake the frog. "As long as it's done sort of under the church radar, not an official activity of the church, it's just sort of an ad-hoc effort, the pastor can stay above it," he said. Staying below the sight line is a crucial part of this kind of activism, Jarmin said, and he tells his volunteers to avoid the media altogether. If not, he explained, their opponents can make an issue out of the activists' involvement, painting them as "radical theocrats trying to ram religion down the throats of the public," he said. "They try to drive fear by tagging us as being extremists and thus diminish the status of the politician we're trying to support."

At the Reclaiming America for Christ conference in Fort Lauderdale, Barbara Collier, the organization's national field director, gave attendees a blueprint for being a "one-person army." She listed things they could easily do to make a difference: research the issues; write letters to the editor; call radio and television stations; attend and speak at county, city, and school board meetings; monitor school board agendas regarding textbooks and classes; visit the offices of elected officials; call elected officials; volunteer to serve on local school and state education boards, particularly textbook review boards; volunteer for local civic boards; organize voter registration drives; and encourage good attorneys to seek judicial appointments. She asked that everyone do one thing on this list each week. "This is a Christian nation and we need to take it back," she entreated.

Collier then urged the crowd to make it personal. She encouraged the audience to develop relationships with elected officials so they would take their phone calls, and to talk to their friends and neighbors about important issues. At election time, check that those people are registered to vote and, on election day, make sure they know where to vote and offer to take them to the polls. While conferences like this garner media coverage, the work their attendees do when they get home often does not. But through churches and churchgoers, evangelicals—and particularly the Christian Right, by far the most organized wing of the community—are pressing their agenda from the local school board on up. "You can't understand the evangelical movement into politics without understanding that it is so related to churches," said Richard Land, president of the Southern Baptist Convention's Ethics and Religious Liberty Commission. "There are lots of players and they have circles of influence." Some churches are becoming more open about the role they play in politics, having come to regard civic engagement as a God-given responsibility, and now sponsor "Citizenship Sundays" on which they invite local elected officials to the church and hold voter registration drives.

One of the most robust examples of church-based grassroots activism for the 2006 election is in Colorado, where Christians are pushing for an amendment to the state constitution that would ban gay marriage. John Paul, executive director of Coloradans for Marriage, said his organization plans to put layers of coordinators in place. The top layer will be on the district level, the next on the county level and finally there will be coordinators in individual churches across the state. Once there's a coordinator in place, that person will approach the church's pastor to ask for permission to set up a petition table in the church lobby or perhaps outside the front door. The table will be a place to garner signatures and to make information available. The real advantage to getting to churches, though, is that they hold reservoirs of manpower that can be applied to tasks such as passing out fliers, planting yard signs, and making phone calls. Paul says they recommend the coordinators utilize church functions as much as possible. For example, they might ask for ten minutes to speak to a Bible study group. Paul said youth groups could also be used for volunteer activities.

Paul's blueprint is in use across the country. Local activists leverage the church infrastructure as the base for all their organizing. Through his Center for Moral Clarity, pastor Rod Parsley, who played a critical role in turning out Ohioans for President Bush in 2004, has helped build a network of churches in each of Ohio's eighty-eight districts that are constantly in touch through the Internet. "It's a very powerful thing, that you can send an e-mail and hit one hundred thousand homes in Ohio in a matter of minutes," Parsley said. His organization also trains activists to have monthly voter-registration drives in their churches. "We believe that good Christians are good citizens," he said. When necessary, they encourage churches to bus people to the polls, but in many Ohio districts that's not necessary because the churches *are* the polling places. He said his organization uses "every means available" to inform people about important issues that are coming up on the ballot, including its television broadcast, radio, print, phone trees, mailing lists, and the Sunday morning church service, where Parsley and other pastors can speak out on moral issues. Parsley's latest venture is Restoration Ohio, which merges religion and politics even more overtly. Its stated aim is to "bring the Buckeye State what it needs most—the love of Jesus Christ," and, indeed, evangelism is its first of three goals. Its second is to serve the needy and its third is to increase the state's voter registration rolls by forty thousand.

There are plenty of pastors, though, who are afraid to talk politics from the pulpit because they're fearful of bringing the IRS's wrath down upon themselves—and, ironically, it's Parsley who has them quaking. In early 2006 a group of clergymen filed a complaint with the IRS charging that Parsley had violated the rules that govern non-profit religious institutions by improper politicking. When I spoke to Parsley several weeks later, though, he still hadn't been contacted by tax officials.

The IRS has promised to clamp down on political activity in the churches, leaving many pastors uncertain of how much they can legally do, although Christian activist organizations are working hard to educate them. Pastors are allowed more political engagement than one might imagine. While a religious institution cannot endorse a specific candidate, an individual—even a pastor—can, so long as he makes clear it's a personal preference, not an institutional one. They are also free to discuss issues, and pastors will frequently deliver a well-timed sermon on a subject that correlates to a measure on the ballot. In late 2004 there was a plethora of Sunday morning homilies about the sacred tradition of marriage, and churchgoers in Colorado can expect the same this fall.

The flip side of all this grassroots activism is that, without a central organizing body, there is no cohesive strategy driving the work. South Dakota's near-total ban on abortion, passed in March 2006, is a prime illustration of this. Pro-life activists from that state are delighted with what they were able to accomplish. Christian strategists, on the other hand, are concerned the ban might end up scoring a point for the opposition. If a challenge to the law makes it to the Supreme Court, the court could find legal reasons to overturn the ban that could come to serve as more legal precedent reinforcing Roe v. Wade, particularly with Chief Justice Roberts's deep respect for the power of precedence. (On the other hand, points out John Green, senior fellow with the Pew Forum on Religious Life, if the ban is upheld, it could become its own self-fulfilling precedent working to overturn Roe.)

That tension exposes a generational gap in the world of evangelical politics. Dobson and his contemporaries are still the most visible political leaders, but their stars are on the wane as a younger, more sophisticated and more mainstream generation of leaders is beginning to take their place. The old guard in Christian politics wants to throw caution to the wind and take what it can get. The new guard is shrewder and believes the incremental approach may well be the most effective. "We realize this is going to be a long-term process," said GenJ's Ryun. "We have to be steady." And where older evangelical leaders tend to be alarmist and appeal to their constituencies on an emotional level, the new generation is more cerebral and relies more on reason and persuasion.

On that front, the old-style Christian Right leaders may be on to something. It's tough to mobilize a constituency that doesn't think it has reason to fight. The old guard's warnings that licentiousness lurks around every corner may border on—or even cross into—paranoia, but that's what gets people to start writing letters, picking up the phone and, most important of all, showing up to vote come November.

The deep suspicion that simmers between the Religious Right and secular Americans stems from a disconnect between Christians' stated goals and how those goals are perceived. Secular America worries about theocracy and the erosion of the separation of church and state. Evangelicals believe the doctrine was intended to keep the government out of religion, not religion out of the government, and point to the many times God is mentioned in a civic context, including in the Declaration of Independence and on our currency.

Where the rest of us may think evangelicals are trying to legislate morality, they say—and truly believe—that they are all about freedom, religious and otherwise. They feel that they are the ones under attack and that they are being forced to accept things such as gay marriage and the destruction of innocent, unborn lives—a breach of their freedoms. In their minds, they are under siege and are being prevented from practicing their religion. A conversation with any evangelical activist will be dotted with anecdotes about school fairs and multicultural days at which Muslims and Hindus and, worse, gays and lesbians were represented but at which the Christian faith was not. They don't see their status as the majority culture in America as something that might be oppressive to minorities; they see it as something that should be recognized and celebrated. It's tough to overstate how great a motivating force this is for the community. They feel that their ability to worship how they please, to live their lives and to raise their children in a moral fashion is under threat. These are things worth waging a cultural war to defend.

Evangelicals around the country echo that they want to protect freedom, and yet that claim seems incongruous with an agenda that would, in fact, limit people's actions. In their minds, there is a difference between liberty and license, and there are things that simply are bad for the health of the nation and should therefore be prohibited. Murder is one of these—and so, by extension, is abortion; gay marriage is another. John Green points out that evangelicals have a somewhat different definition of freedom than secular America. Their notion of freedom includes deliverance from the bondage of sin, which would include liberation from pornography and homosexuality. They believe freedom is inherent in our contract with God, who allows us to choose between accepting and rejecting Christ.

The biggest threat to the values they hold dear and upon which they believe this nation was built, in the estimation of evangelicals, comes from the judiciary. The march toward the legalization of liberal values that they see taking place is being presided over by judges. Taking God out of the Pledge of Allegiance, prayer out of schools, legalizing abortion and gay marriage were all things authorized by courts, not by legislators. "Stop activist judges" is the war cry of the Christian Right. Everyone from James Dobson to Pat Robertson has declared that nomination and confirmation of federal judges is the most important issue before the American people today. At the end of the day, it all comes down to constitutional interpretation. Evangelical Christians tend to be strict constructionists and believe all judicial decisions should be made with the framers' original intentions in mind. It's the logical position for them to hold since they believe the country was founded on Christian principles that it has been moving away from ever since. So far, Bush has given them what they want, particularly where it matters most, on the Supreme Court. Evangelicals are elated over the two justices the president has been able to appoint to the bench; they are hopeful he will be able to grant them one more before his term is over and thus give them a chance of finally overturning Roe v. Wade.

Evangelicals may seem to walk in lockstep with the Republican Party yet they insist they are not partisan but rather are issue-driven and focused on morality. That is simultaneously truth and subterfuge. The statement is accurate in that the *reason* most evangelicals are Republicans is the party's stance on the issues of morality that evangelicals care about. What's disingenuous about the statement is that it conceals the deep distrust most evangelicals now have of the Democratic Party and all things liberal, and their well-developed relationships with the GOP that go a long way toward keeping them in that party's tent. Saddleback's pastor Rick Warren states publicly that he is apolitical, but shortly before the 2004 election he sent an e-mail to 150,000 pastors reminding them of five issues that need to be nonnegotiable for evangelicals: abortion, gay marriage, stem-cell research, human cloning, and euthanasia. In his message he urged the pastors to encourage Christians to vote. He may not have mentioned the president's name but the message left no doubt about which candidate he was supporting. Shortly after the election Warren was invited to the White House.

But as the ubiquitous Jim Wallis reminded the country, God is not a Democrat or a Republican. On the other hand, Wallis, author of *God's Politics: Why the Right Gets It Wrong and the Left Doesn't Get It,* is—a Democrat, that is—as is a small but significant group of evangelicals. While it's unclear if these born-again liberals are growing in number, they are certainly growing in prominence and could portend change for the Republican-evangelical alliance. Said John Green: "From a historical point, we're at the high point of Republican voting . . . Whether this is the tippy-top remains to be seen."

CHAPTER TEN

What's Next?

I N HOUSES THROUGHOUT Darien, Connecticut, people are gulping down coffee, straightening their ties and smoothing their hair. It's seven fifteen a.m. on a Friday morning and soon those people will be getting into their cars or hopping onto commuter trains to make their way into work. At nearby St. Paul's church, though, a few hundred men have already packed the sanctuary and are waiting for the weekly meeting of the New Canaan Society to start as they wipe the crumbs from the hot buffet breakfast they've just finished off their suits and sweatshirts. This week's turnout is particularly robust because the speaker is pastor Tim Keller of Redeemer Presbyterian in Manhattan, a popular figure who is known as the thinking man's evangelical, but even on a slow week the New Canaan Society does not suffer from lackluster attendance.

The society was started more than ten years ago when its founder, Jim Lane, returned to the United States after spending four years in London and realized that men have a harder time making friends than women do. The lone male among his wife and three daughters, Lane decided he needed more masculine companionship in his life, so he started a Bible study with a few other men in his neighborhood in New Canaan, Connecticut. Initially they met in Lane's living room; eventually the place was packed to the rafters as NCS became quietly famous in Christian circles. Finally the group became too big for Lane's house, so it now meets in the wood-paneled, chalet-style sanctuary of St. Paul's.

I expected NCS to be populated by a bunch of buttoned-down Wall Street types, and there are certainly many of those here. There are also young hipsters in jeans and T-shirts and white-haired retirees in khakis. The atmosphere is relaxed and convivial, but, as I quickly find out, the men take their weekly worship session very seriously. They are more intense and more focused than the congregations at most church services, and there is an ease and lack of self-consciousness that comes from knowing most everyone in the room feels equally passionately about his faith. As the men turn to the business of praise, I'm surprised to see that even in this all-male environment some of the attendees raise their arms in supplication as they sing. There's much less macho posturing than I had anticipated; instead the focus is on fellowship and worship. It's immediately apparent how close this group is, in spite of its size. The opening prayer is personal, addressing particular needs of members of the group and their families.

After my host, cofounder Eric Metaxas, an author and humorist, warms up the room and kindly tells the group that the woman in their midst (me) is an invited guest, Keller takes the podium. His address is delivered as a sermon, rather than the casual talk I would have expected on a Friday morning, but it is not the message of a megachurch pastor. Rather, it is weighty and scholarly. Keller refers to the words used in the original text of the biblical passages he is exploring and explains the different ways in which they can be translated. His talk is refreshingly intellectual and well-suited to this crowd who, given their willingness to turn up week after week in the cold hours of the morning, clearly are committed to learning. Today's discussion is, in fact, a study of the importance of fellowship and points out how, through all their differences, the people in our lives help us better understand God. He uses the example of a group known as The Inklings that included C. S. Lewis, J. R. R. Tolkien, and Charles Williams. They got together regularly at the Eagle and Child, a local pub that they dubbed "the bird and baby," and every Thursday night in Lewis's rooms at Magdalen College, Oxford

University. They'd discuss Christianity and mythology and read portions of their writing to one another. They became very close friends.

After Williams died, Lewis wrote that there was a side of Tolkien he would never see again because only Williams could bring it out in him. Similarly, Keller said, different people help us perceive aspects of God we can't see on our own. After Keller wrapped up, the men stood and started filing out of the room, now bathed in a warm amber hue cast by the ascending sun. Some of them left immediately; others continued their conversations in the adjoining space where coffee and breakfast sandwiches were once again laid out on a table. As I made my way out of the sanctuary I noticed several men hugging each other.

Researcher George Barna says the men at New Canaan are part of a new breed of Christian he dubs "revolutionaries" who want a more authentic spiritual experience and are looking in places other than their local church to find it. As he puts it, they are intent on "being the church rather than merely going to church." Barna says they number about 20 million, and he believes they will reshape the Christian world over the next two decades. The younger two generations, which he calls baby busters and mosaics, are involved in the changes, but surprisingly it is baby boomers who are most represented in this new trend. Barna's research shows that these Christians are more committed to their faith than their congregational counterparts. "There's this big movement of people who are now pretty much turned off by local church. They want more God and less institution so they're developing this whole network of faith-based activity," Barna said. "It was almost like the coming out of the gay community." (Ironically, evangelicals constantly liken themselves to gays, the group they most loathe for its lifestyle choices but most respect for the way it has been able to transform itself from a community that was disparaged to one widely accepted and even celebrated. The frequency with which the comparison is made is indicative of a level of envy on the part of evangelicals that gays have been able to make inroads that they, as yet, have not.)

Despite the continuing success of megachurches, as they get bigger and blander some people are starting to look for a new kind of experience, one more immediate or transcendent. They're finding it in some unlikely places, in the podcasts of sermons they download from the Internet, in cyberchurches, and in Bible studies at their workplaces, what Barna calls "marketplace ministries." Many have left the church building and are meeting in parks and in houses. In fact, the house church movement, in which several families meet on a regular basis in someone's home, often to be led by the same person each week, is growing by great leaps.

This is a seminal time for the church, a moment of reflection and self-assessment such as hasn't been seen in decades. Its attempts to be germane to society have been so successful that the church is in the midst of an identity crisis sparked by its own achievement. Long accustomed to being on the fringes, evangelical Christianity has become so big, so powerful, and so mainstream that many on the inside are wondering if they've lost their flavor and have abandoned what made them distinctive.

The response to these concerns has taken several different forms. Many Christians are looking to put the sanctity back in church and are returning to the traditions that the megachurches abandoned. Where churches such as Willow Creek and Saddleback desanctified the physical church, others are looking to resanctify it, placing new value on incense, stained glass, candles, and other high-church trappings. They are reintroducing liturgy to their services, or moving into denominations that never abandoned it, such as the Episcopalian church (although there they opt for conservative congregations that are on the restrictive side of the split over gay clergy). Megachurches were invented by baby boomers and designed to appeal to that generation. They rely on the notion of choice and individualization and on the tools of marketing to hone and promote their product. This comes, though, at the cost of the idea that the church is a body, the needs of which supersede those of the individual. Along with defecting boomers, younger generations, which are remarkably religious, are beginning to rebel against the church of their parents' generation and are looking for more direct encounters with the divine. They don't need the pat answers megachurches provide but are willing to embark on their own personal spiritual journeys.

The changes run to even those denominations that are traditionally more conservative. One of the most forward-looking churches I visited was Mosaic in Los Angeles, presided over by an immigrant from El Salvador. The congregation is young, urban, and multicultural. On Sunday four services are held in different venues across the Los Angeles area; the one I attended was in the evening in a downtown theater called the Mayan, which is one of the city's hottest Salsa clubs on the weekends and was also the venue where the *Rock Star: INXS* reality show was filmed each week. All of the churches I visited during the course of my research were trying to be relevant and current. Mosaic was the first place that was genuinely hip. The lights in the theater are kept low, and the walls are adorned with Mayan motifs and fake lanterns with flapping orange cellophane mimicking flames. Easels stood on either side of the ground-level floor, flanking the band playing off to one side of the stage. A young man approached one of the easels and started painting; a few moments later pastor Erwin McManus took the stage. McManus is young and good looking, his delivery direct and ardent. People sat at round club tables while they sipped Red Bull and sodas. In the balcony upstairs, a few young men tinkered on laptops while they listened to McManus. The crowd was young, primarily single, and very attractive; more than a few audience members were checking each other out.

The look of Mosaic is modern and trendy, but the church belongs to the Southern Baptist Convention and its theology is, at its very core, conservative. McManus, though, is taking his church to places of which other Southern Baptist Convention congregations have likely never dreamed. His main argument is that Jesus was countercultural and bold but the church has allowed itself to become tame and institutionalized. "The greatest enemy to the movement of Jesus Christ is Christianity," McManus wrote in his book *The Barbarian*

Way. When they started trying to tell non-Christians the right way to live, Christians lost sight of their faith, McManus argues. At Mosaic, McManus takes the emphasis off the institutional and places it on God. The church is deeply mystical. Instead of trying to prove logically that the Bible is true, McManus urges people to look inside themselves for answers to their questions about God.

While Mosiac doesn't look like the traditional Southern Baptist church, it may represent the denomination's future. Historically white, today one out of every five SBC congregations is ethnic, according to Richard Land, president of the Southern Baptist Convention's Ethics and Religious Liberty Commission. The SBC is growing at a rate of 10 percent a year outside the South and 2 percent a year in the South; half of that growth is made up of churches that are primarily ethnic. The influx of people with different cultural perspectives is sure to alter the SBC, just as it is bound to remake the church at large, whose demographic is being altered by immigration.

The most interesting development in Christianity is a new movement called the "emergent church." As recently as two years ago, many conservative Christians were dismissing the emergent church—or, "the conversation," as adherents like to call it—as a flash in the pan that would soon burn out. Those predictions were well off the mark and the movement continues to grow; an entire subgenre of the Christian publishing industry has sprung up around it. Over the past few years, doctrines that were once on the edge of acceptability—if even there—have become part of evangelical thought.

This diverse new movement is really an amalgamation of minimovements lumped together under the emergent church heading. Some of these are just a repackaging of current beliefs, but many of them are hewing radically new paths. These minimovements are going in different directions, but what they all have in common is that they are reactions to westernism and modernism, neither of which, proponents point out, were elements in the early church. McManus identified four main threads in the movement, any combination of which can be represented in these churches. They are liturgical, confessional (adhering to set creeds and beliefs), experiential (such as the Charismatics or those who include performance in their services) or mystical (mysticism having been abandoned by the church during the Enlightenment).

There's a thread of the emergent church that takes its rejection of currently established norms one step further: the postmodern church. Its devotees argue that rationalism is a modernist structure that was imposed on the church during the Enlightenment and they rebel against the idea that truth is demonstrable. They are deconstructing the spiritual experience and many of them want to return mysticism to their worship.

The emergent groups, to varying degrees, model their activities on those of the first-century church, which they consider the most authentic since it got its marching orders from Jesus himself. They all are looking for a genuine experience, rather than the scripted, prepackaged one found in many evangelical churches today; they emphasize what they call "missional living"—mixing with the world rather than isolating themselves behind church walls—and they have refocused their attention specifically on the life of Jesus Christ. Over the course of the past year I have increasingly heard people contrast the action of Christians with those of Jesus Christ. While "What would Jesus do?" has long been a consideration of evangelicals (there was a moment when it was trendy for teenagers to wear bracelets with the letters WWJD woven into them), the recent comparisons have been different, more incisive. Instead of wondering if Jesus would get angry at the driver of the red Camaro cutting people off on the freeway, today people are remarking that Jesus would not be as judgmental as Christians tend to be, as phobic of people with alternative lifestyles, as focused on the acquisition of material wealth and that he would be much more concerned with the poor, the sick, and the suffering. Those inside the emergent church tend to be less dogmatic about theological issues and more accepting of divergent views, both in the spiritual and social domains.

These emergent churches come in all shapes and sizes. At the interactive services at Solomon's Porch in Minneapolis congregants sit on comfortable chairs arranged in the round. The worship gatherings, as the services are called, have an arty, countercultural tone and consist of music, prayer, and discussion. The songs they sing are written by people who belong to the community; they read the Bible and share personal stories. Their prayers take different forms, including silence, singing, reciting creeds, and body prayers, in which parts of the body are used to express emotions. The worshippers use something historical in each gathering to connect them with the ancient church, and they take communion every week, unusual in evangelical churches where communion is typically administered once a month.

Cedar Ridge Community Church in Spencerville, Maryland, which was founded by Brian McLaren, one of the key thinkers in the emergent movement, has a more traditional feel—despite being located on the site of a former horse farm. Sunday services are modeled on the Episcopal service and are divided into two parts, word and sacrament. Services begin with a sermon—the word—and communion is taken every week—the sacrament. During the sacrament portion music plays and people roam freely around the room. Someone might light a candle, another person may write a prayer, some people might pray together, and still others may sing. The sanctuary is adorned with a cross and other artwork. Art is an important element of the emergent church. In the Middle Ages the church was the center of the arts but with the rise of rationalism the church abandoned its creative side and became largely cerebral. Emergent churches want to reintroduce imagination into their spiritual lives.

Some of these emergent churches have moved dramatically beyond what we today think of as church. One of these is Monkfish Abbey, which describes itself as a soul-care community in Seattle, Washington. "We consist of a family living in a home, a few people gathered in their living room, neighbors and co-workers of the folks who hang out here, and an extended tribe of invisible friends who are floating around out there in the World Wide Web," their Web site explains. This is the antigrowth model of church, consisting of somewhere between five and fifteen people. They have abandoned the in-or-out distinctions of evangelical Christianity: "Most of us are Christians, or were Christians, or at least dig Jesus—but not everyone would hang their hats on any of these etymological pegs and that's okay, too," their Web site goes on to say. In the terms of the postmodern movement they describe themselves as a "neomonastic incarnational community." Neomonastic because, while they don't all live together and haven't taken vows of chastity or poverty, they regularly share a common meal and conversation and celebrate communion together. Incarnational because they "believe the thumbprint of the divine is present in all things and all people." For some that is the presence of Jesus within them, for others it is an internal divinity that exists in everyone.

One of the most innovative and radical thinkers in the emergent/postmodern realm is Spencer Burke, a longish-haired laid-back surfer type who runs a Web site called TheOoze, which describes itself as a "conversation for the journey." Burke used to be a pastor at Mariner's Church, an influential megachurch in Irvine, California, a few miles west of Saddleback. Unfulfilled by the big-church experience, he left Mariners and began shepherding a small group of people who did church in a new way. They'd meet in a local park, in someone's home, or would visit other religious gatherings, perhaps an African American church in Los Angeles or a nearby Buddhist temple. Eventually, though, Burke moved away from that, too, when he realized that a house church has many of the same organizational challenges as a big church, all distractions from learning and worship. Burke finally abandoned house church in favor of home church, which he likened to homeschooling. He worships with his family, wherever, whenever, and however they feel led.

"I think there is a major transition afoot in the church," he told me one August afternoon as we sat in the cluttered garage—his makeshift office—in the alley behind his Balboa Island cottage.

Burke says there's a new focus on spirituality, not just in the church but in the country at large. He points to the attention that the media lavished on Billy Graham's last crusade in New York City and to the spirituality seen in the lives of people such as Oprah, Bono, and the Dalai Lama. Ironically, that is one area in which Burke and Saddleback's Rick Warren share common ground. Warren told a gathering of journalists at the Pew Forum's biannual Faith Angle conference in Key West, Florida, that he sees the signs of a spiritual resurgence, a possible Third Great Awakening or a new Reformation—although he envisions it happening in a different way. Where Burke interprets this spiritual growth as something that occurs in people's lives outside of the structures of the church, Warren believes it will take place through the small groups at Saddleback and other churches.

Burke sees the recent emergence of evangelicals not as a sign that the organized church is getting stronger but as an indication that it's about to burn out. "Is that the new trend, or is it that the sun is brightest before it sets?" he asks rhetorically. "It's going to fail . . . I'm actually predicting that not only is evangelicalism going to go away but even Christianity as a brand is going to go away. This is part of the final movement of the Age of Enlightenment." Burke sees a move into general spirituality where labels aren't important, where the idea that there is one right way to worship will be rejected, and where the focus is put back on the Bible. He believes there will be a new collaboration among factions that have long been divided. Admittedly, Burke is an idealist whose views are, for the time being, at the cutting edge of the evangelical community, though he is viewed as an important voice in the emergent movement. "Absolute truth is Jesus. Everything else is up for grabs," Burke expounded. "Instead of finding what divides us we're moving together toward what unites us."

On that front Warren agrees. "The first Reformation actually split Christianity into dozens and then hundreds of different segments," he said at the Pew conference. "I think this one is actually going to bring them together." While Christians are still separated by doctrinal differences and likely always will be, they are beginning to agree on the purposes of the church, Warren said. He thinks that whereas the last Reformation was one of creed, this will be one of deed and will prompt the church to think more about its behavior and what it does in the world.

While Burke comes out of the evangelical tradition, what's particularly important about the emergent movement is that it isn't confined to that world; on the contrary, about half the people involved come from mainline denominations and a good portion of emergent churches still belong to those denominations. On one level the emergent movement represents a move toward the middle, with mainline churches adopting the emphasis on personal salvation that in recent history had been claimed by evangelicals, and evangelicals returning to the social concerns of the mainline. But Brian McLaren says what's happening goes beyond the merging of two previous traditions. "It feels like evangelical and mainline Christians are moving toward something new together."

Many emergent evangelicals have begun going to Catholic retreat centers to seek an ancient spirituality, something unthinkable a few years ago. Over the past several years, evangelicals have been increasingly finding common ground with Catholics, which has helped reintroduce them to scholarship and intellectualism. If they are able to overcome the differences they have with mainline denominations and other Christians, there are sure to be other dividends. One that is likely is a return to the liberal ideals of the social gospel, a move already under way. Of course, there are always going to be ultraconservative, right-wing, born-again Christians, but if the trend to ecumenicalism continues they could become less dominant within the evangelical world, which may leave the overall body more moderate.

McLaren pointed to a verse in the Old Testament, Micah 6:8, which says God requires us to "do justice, to love kindness and to walk humbly with your God." Christians have long emphasized the "walk humbly" part. Evangelicals have jumped in on the "love kindness" part of late, as demonstrated in their rapid and continued response to the Hurricane Katrina disaster and their efforts in Africa. The next step, McLaren said, will be when evangelicals start to care about justice, as other factions of Christianity already do. Little germs of concern are apparent, but they haven't yet taken root. You can pull people out of the ditch, McLaren said, but eventually you have to stop them from being pushed into the ditch. Evangelicals may not be all the way there yet, but McLaren is optimistic that they are moving in the right direction. Many Christians on both sides of the evangelical divide feel that the Christian Right has hijacked the religion and polluted the term "evangelical," and, indeed, more and more evangelicals are dropping the label, much as the community abandoned the "born again" moniker in the early 1990s. McLaren believes this is a historical moment in which the disjoined church can come together as a body looking not at dogma and what divides them but focusing on the life of Christ and the example he set.

This new trend in evangelical Christianity could have political ramifications as well. As evangelicals turn their attention to issues such as AIDS and global poverty, their interests more naturally align with those of the Democratic Party; as the evangelical agenda becomes broader and the community more diverse, the issues evangelicals care about may no longer be best addressed by the GOP. Abortion and same-sex marriage still rank high on the list of evangelical priorities, but Christians are expanding their definition of "morality" to include more than just lifestyle. Ignoring poverty is a moral issue; so is caring for the sick and exploited here and around the world. "There's going to be quite a tussle within the evangelical community, because the people advancing the broader agenda are going to try to sell it to the rank and file," said the Pew Forum's John Green. "That could move the community."

Already some of the most visible evangelical leaders are signaling their discontent with the GOP. Richard Cizik, vice president of the National Association of Evangelicals, lamented to *Washington Monthly*'s Amy Sullivan that when there's a conflict between the interests of business and religion, the GOP chooses business every time.

"We need to stop putting all of our eggs in one basket—that's just not good politics." he told Sullivan. In the same article Sullivan spoke with Dr. Randy Brinson, who conceived Redeem the Vote as an evangelical alternative to MTV's Rock the Vote and turned out huge numbers of young Christians for the GOP. Disillusioned with what he felt was a Republican Party that preferred conflict to actual change, he has started collaborating with the Democrats on faith issues.

Evangelicals who have been cheerleaders for the Bush administration's efforts to spread democracy in the Middle East are beginning to rethink those policies. Evangelicals have been among the most vocal proponents of the country's nation building, but the case of Abdel Rahman has them rethinking that support. Rahman is an Afghan man who converted to Christianity and faced the death sentence because the law in now-democratic Afghanistan deems apostasy—the abandonment of Islam—a capital crime. After loud protests from Christians on the grassroots level all the way up to the White House, the case was dismissed and Rahman was granted asylum in Italy, but the incident gave American Christians pause. "Abdul Rahman's imprisonment has revealed a major fault in our foreign policy," Family Research Council President Tony Perkins said in a statement. "If we can't secure the most basic of human rights, Americans will increasingly question whether we should continue the expenditure of lives and resources in these countries." Americans pushed for democracy in Afghanistan and got a constitution that recognizes the dominance of Islamic law. We pushed for elections in the Middle East: Palestinians voted for Hamas when given a chance, Egyptians showed their affinity for the Muslim Brotherhood in their elections, and the introduction of democracy to Iraq has ushered in lawlessness and chaos. Evangelicals are realizing that if America creates free societies in other parts of the world, those societies may well choose to persecute Christians.

Democrats have been bending over backward to try to convince the country that they, too, love God, but words alone are unlikely to be enough. If the Democrats want to steal evangelical voters from the right they're going to have to take concrete steps to do so. To begin with, they will have to at least open the door to pro-life candidates, a move that could go a long way with evangelicals but is sure to anger the Democratic base. McManus believes that if given a choice between two pro-choice presidential candidates, evangelicals would choose the Democrat in huge numbers. "Abortion is the only issue that keeps Christians voting Republican," he said. "The last two elections are not really reflective of how strong the Republicans are but of how weak the Democrats are."

There are signs that the Democrats have already started down that path. Hillary Clinton, for example, hasn't gone as far as saying she's pro-life, but she has said she would like to see fewer abortions performed each year. While that's not going to be enough for evangelicals on the far right, it enables moderate Christians to find common ground with her. Working with Randy Brinson, Democrats also outflanked Republicans in Alabama by introducing legislation to include *The Bible and Its Influence* as part of that state's curriculum in a bid to appeal to voters of faith. Republicans there found themselves in the awkward position of opposing the textbook for political reasons, even though conservative evangelicals in other states had lent it unswerving support. Still, there's a long way to go before large numbers of evangelicals are going to feel comfortable in the Democratic Party. In a poll conducted by the Pew Research Center for the People and the Press in August 2004, 40 percent of people surveyed said the Democratic Party was friendly toward religion. A year later that number had dropped to 29 percent.

McLaren thinks that each time the White House is revealed to have been less than completely honest and open with the American people, the prospect of defections becomes more likely. I spoke to him the day after it was reported that Scooter Libby had leaked classified information at the behest of vice president Dick Cheney, who had said the president had okayed such actions. "The world could change incredibly fast if enough people in the Religious Right felt they had been manipulated," McLaren said.

Increasingly they do. Like Richard Cizik, many in the evangelical community are beginning to feel that the Republican leadership pays lip service to their issues but hasn't delivered. The honeymoon that Bush enjoyed with evangelicals lasted into the beginning of his second term of office, but finally the bloom is off the rose. Evangelicals in all parts of the country have been expressing disappointment with the president of late. African American evangelicals who voted for Bush in 2004 are upset that they left the Democratic bosom but weren't given the marriage amendment they were promised. Moderate evangelicals feel deceived about the country's reasons for going to war in Iraq, and there are even staunch social conservatives who feel the president hasn't done enough to fight abortion. Bush and, by extension, the Republicans could be dying a death of a thousand cuts. With margins as tight as they were in 2004, even a slight dip in these groups' support of Republicans could have decisive consequences.

It is therefore no exaggeration to say that the future of American politics may well depend on whether evangelicals begin to move to the Democratic Party, whose focus on poverty and other social issues is actually more in line with the broader evangelical agenda, or whether the Republicans will respond to their concerns and truly become the compassionate conservative party they purport to be. "Behind an agreement on traditional morality, there's a lot of disagreement on other matters," Green said. "That gives people . . . hope that they can eat away [at Republican dominance]. But if there weren't people trying to eat away, you wouldn't see the Republicans try to hold them."

The issue of immigration legislation has also proven to be a divisive one. When it was taken up by Congress in early 2006, Hispanic and liberal evangelical groups came out immediately calling for humane reform, but conservative groups largely sat out the debate. The ultraconservative American Family Association sent an online poll to those on its e-mail blast list trying to gauge its community's views on the issue. While conservative, white evangelicals overwhelmingly feel that the borders should be sealed tighter, other more moderate groups cast the debate in humanitarian terms. Depending on the form of the bill that is finally passed, Hispanic evangelicals could walk away from the GOP in large numbers and at the same time fracture the evangelical community.

But there are potentially mitigating forces for all these scenarios. An evangelical move to the left could well be neutralized by simple demographics. Red states have higher birth rates than blue states, which means that over time the country should become increasingly conservative. *Wall Street Journal* columnist James Taranto points to what he calls "the Roe effect." He says the right to abortion has diminished the number of Democratic voters because it is, de facto, pro-choice women who have abortions and children tend to gravitate toward their parents' values. If pro-choice women are having fewer babies than pro-life women, there will be fewer pro-choice voters in the next generation, the argument goes. The effect is heightened, Taranto holds, because the racial groups that have the most abortions proportionately—blacks followed by Hispanics—also have higher rates of Democrat voting than non-Hispanic whites.

The Supreme Court is another factor likely to keep evangelicals in the Republican camp. As long as there is the chance of another vacancy on the high court, evangelicals are going to want to be on the team they know will provide them with a chance to outlaw abortion. Republicans also show signs of responding to the new evangelical concerns and co-opting an agenda that traditionally belonged to the left. The increase of aid to Africa is but one example.

Just as evangelicals have influenced the country, so, too, has America made its mark on evangelicals. They now look, sound, and, in many areas—though obviously not all—think like the rest of us. This mainstreaming of the evangelical community has ramifications for everyone. Politically, it will likely mean either a softening or over time a possible diminishing of the Republican Party. If evangelicals leave the GOP and return to their Democratic roots—many of them were, after all, Democrats until just a few decades ago—they will demand that the party abandon its central pro-choice stance and become open to pro-life candidates, a prospect that worries the most liberal in the party to no end. That shift is not beyond the realm of possibility. The Democratic Party's position on abortion was once so firm that Pennsylvania Governor Bob Casey was prohibited from speaking at the 1992 Democratic Convention because of his pro-life beliefs. Less than fifteen years later that same party actively recruited his son, Robert Casey Jr., to run for the Senate in Pennsylvania, despite his sharing those pro-life views. Ardent Democrats were roiled at the overture; once it became apparent that Casey had a shot at pushing out the Republican's rising star Rick Santorum, they quieted down. Furthermore, Democrats named Harry Reid their leader in the Senate; Reid is a vocal opponent of abortion rights. The real indication of evangelical power, then, is not that they are molding the Republican Party, it is that they are beginning to shape the Democratic Party, too.

The role of evangelicals in America has been cyclical throughout this nation's history; so, too, have societal trends. As today the tide of evangelical prominence surges, the tide of societal progress ebbs; the two have always been inextricably linked in one way or another. Despite all their modernist trimmings, evangelicals at the heart are deeply traditional and they have been able and continue to impose their values on America to an astounding degree. Almost imperceptibly the clock is being turned back to a prefeminist, pre–sexual revolution era. People are getting married younger, and rising numbers of educated women are choosing to stay home to raise their children. Hollywood is producing more and more wholesome entertainment, much of which would have fit right in with the other fare flickering on silver screens in the 1950s. Sex and drugs no longer rule rock and roll. The Bible is back in the classroom. Evangelicals feel America has abandoned its Christian roots; in truth there is ample evidence that it is the advancement of the secular lifestyle that is being turned back and that the country has done a regressive about-face that will return it to the norms of half a century ago. Evangelicals are pushing a nostalgic, even anachronistic, view of what it means to be an

American. Even their steps toward a more liberal agenda represent a move back to a point in their history when the social gospel reigned. Yes, evangelicals have donned the trappings of modern culture and have come to resemble secular America. And in doing so, they have redefined the mainstream.

Acknowledgments

THIS BOOK IS based primarily upon original reporting and I must thank the hundreds of people I spoke to along the way who let me into their lives, despite knowing that there would likely be things with which they strongly disagree in the finished product. They are far too numerous to name individually here. I also relied on the work and ideas of many academics, and owe a debt of gratitude to all of them. I feel I must give special thanks to Edith Blumhofer, Larry Eskridge, Larry Lyon, John Green, Mark Chaves, and Darrell Bock for their time and their insights.

Along the way many people opened doors and made introductions for me, affording me access to people and places I wouldn't have had on my own; among them are Kevin Palau, Larry Ross, Brad Taylor, Velvet Kelm, Lori Isaacs, Leslie Bates, Lou Taylor, Cally Parkinson, Drew Ryun, Catherine Ryun, Ned Ryun, and Eric Metaxas. Thanks also to Jim Lane.

My friends have been alternately supportive and cajoling along the way, as the occasion saw fit. Many of them provided me with a place to write, others read early versions of the manuscript, still others provided needed encouragement; on more than one occasion it was the enthusiasm of a friend that kept me going. A few people need to be mentioned by name: Emily Won, Selina Pandolfi, Jon Auerbach, Maggie Jones, Deb Kogan, Hilary Reyl, Claire Shipman, Sharon Carlstedt, Brent Britton, Elyse Weiner, Stan Pottinger, Joe

O'Neill, Colleen Curtis, Diane Karnett, Jonathan Freedland, Lisa Dallos, and Jordan Tamagni. Elyse Cheney pointed me in this direction in the first place and Mary Jane Fine helped me find a title.

Gillian Blake was a rock throughout this process. She is an insightful, hands-on editor who improved this book immeasurably. I feel truly fortunate to have been able to work with her. Oversize thanks also are due to Benjamin Adams at Bloomsbury.

When Tina Bennett began representing me, I quickly realized I had found the best agent a writer could hope for. She is a steady advocate and an astute editor. She has also become something even more important to me: a trusted friend.

My parents have both contributed significantly to this book. My father allowed us to turn his tranquil existence upside down for months at a time during my long reporting trips to California, on which I brought my whole family. My second son was born while I was writing this book and my mother provided countless hours of babysitting both in her home and in mine. Whenever things threatened to fall to pieces, she flew in and quickly restored order. Thanks to her, my family ate many more home-cooked meals than they otherwise would have. The past few years would have been much bumpier without her help.

My children tenaciously endured several years seeing less of their mother than they, or I, would have liked and were remarkably understanding for their tender years. I am grateful to Daphline Maloney and Yoly Brito for making sure they were well cared for. Berly Riquetti also helped keep things running smoothly.

My deepest gratitude is reserved for my husband, Oliver, who for the past several years has drawn from a seemingly bottomless reservoir of support. I'm exceptionally fortunate to be married to a man who fills so many roles so extraordinarily well. He gamely let me drag him to church services and Christian events across the country and, during the many trips I took alone, served as daddy extraordinaire to make up for my absence, all without a word of complaint. I'm sure that in the past two years he got more middle-of-the night feedings and diaper changes under his belt than most men accumulate in a lifetime. He also read numerous drafts of the manuscript and provided invaluable insight. It's no exaggeration to say this book could not have been written without him. Our children and I are enormously blessed to have him in our lives.

Notes

INTRODUCTION

Attendance figures for Times Square Church are taken from their Web site, www.TimesSquareChurch.org/about. Information about megachurches throughout the country is available at the Web site of the Hartford Institute for Religion Research, http://hirr.hartsem.edu/org/faith_megachurches_database.html.

The high estimate of 100 million evangelicals comes from the Institute for the Study of American Evangelicals and can be accessed at their Web site, at http://www.wheaton.edu/isae/defining_evangelicalism.html.

The *Christianity Today* editorial "We're Prime Time, Baby!" was posted on July 28, 2005, and can be accessed at http://www.christianitytoday.com/ct/2005/007/20.23.html.

George Marsden's pithy definition of a fundamentalist comes from his book *Understanding Fundamentalism and Evangelicalism* (Grand Rapids, Mich.: Wm. B. Eerdmans, 1991).

For a detailed profile of Christian Exodus and its founder, see "God's Brand-New Country" by Guy Lawson, *GQ* magazine, July 2005, pp. 56–63.

A few examples of the investigative work done on Benny Hinn and Paul Crouch: *Dateline NBC* has aired several investigative pieces on Benny Hinn, including one on March 6, 2005, and one on December 27, 2002. William Lobdell at the *Los Angeles Times* has written numerous stories about Paul Crouch and his Trinity Broadcasting Network, including "Televangelist Paul Crouch Attempts to Keep Accuser Quiet" (September 12, 2004), "Crouch to Stay Chief of TBN Despite Gay Sex Allegation" (September 14, 2004), and "The Prosperity Gospel: Pastor's Empire Built on Acts of Faith, and Cash" (September 19, 2004).

Finally, to read more about the new face of Christianity, see Donald E. Miller's *Reinventing American Protestantism: Christianity in the New Millennium* (Berkeley and Los Angeles: University of California Press, 1999).

CHAPTER ONE

The apocalyptic Left Behind books are published by Zondervan, in Grand Rapids, Michigan.

For the history of Calvary Chapel I relied on Chuck Smith's account as laid out in his book *Harvest,* which is available on Calvary's Web site, at http://www3 .calvarychapel.com/costamesa/high_bandwidth.htm. The material I used comes primarily from the first chapter, entitled "In the Beginning." Much of the biographical information on Chuck Smith himself comes from Randall Balmer's comprehensive *Encyclopedia of Evangelicalism* (Waco: Baylor University Press, 2004), which I relied on for factual material throughout this book.

The history of the Crystal Cathedral has been documented in many places. I relied upon a profile of Philip Johnson that Calvin Tomkins wrote for the May 23, 1977, issue of the *New Yorker.* Much of Robert Schuller's story is also available on the Crystal Cathedral Web site at http://www.crystalcathedral.org/about/history .html. Pastor Bob DeWaay's criticism of Schuller is taken from the January/February 2000 issue of *Critical Issues Commentary.*

This account of the birth of Willow Creek is drawn from *Rediscovering Church,* by Lynne and Bill Hybels (Grand Rapids, Mich.: Zondervan, 1995).

CHAPTER TWO

The quotation from Alexis de Tocqueville's *Democracy in America* is from the 1899 Henry Reeve translation.

To write this chapter I relied on the invaluable work of two of the best known historians of evangelical Christianity, George Marsden and Mark Noll. Specifically, I drew on Marsden's *Understanding Fundamentalism and Evangelicalism* and on Noll's *American Evangelical Christianity: An Introduction* (Malden, Mass.: Blackwell, 2001), also on a conversation I had with Noll in his office. I also relied on D. G. Hart's *That Old-Time Religion in Modern America* (Chicago: Ivan R. Dee, 2002) and referred to *The Beliefnet Guide to Evangelical Christianity* by Wendy Murray Zoba (New York: Doubleday, 2005).

The book that forever divided fundamentalists from evangelicals was Carl F. H. Henry's *The Uneasy Conscience of Modern Fundamentalism* (Grand Rapids, Mich.: Wm. B. Eerdmans, 1947).

I obtained the text of Jonathan Edwards's famous sermon from http://www .jonathanedwards.com/sermons/Warnings/sinners.htm.

The account of the Azusa Street Revival comes from the April 18, 1906, edition of the *Los Angeles Daily Times.*

Statistics on the numbers of congregations in which people speak in tongues can be found in *Congregations in America*, by Mark Chaves (Cambridge, Mass.: Harvard University Press, 2004).

CHAPTER THREE

The Four Spiritual Laws are from *Have You Heard of the Four Spiritual Laws?* by Bill Bright © Copyright 1965, 1994, 2000 Campus Crusade for Christ. All rights reserved. Used by permission. For information on and to read the complete text please visit: http://www.campuscrusade.com/four_laws_online.htm.

A history of the Alpha Course is available at http://uk.alphacourse.org/organisation/origins/index.htm.

CHAPTER FOUR

A history of the Abyssinian Baptist Church can be found at http://www.abyssinian.org/abc/template/page.do?_mid=9.

CHAPTER FIVE

Information on best-selling books comes from www.publishersweekly.com.

The *Time* article on Karen Kingsbury, "That Other Passion: The Queen of Christian Romance Tries to Cross Over" was written by Michele Orecklin and ran in the March 14, 2005, issue.

The recent Christian best sellers mentioned in this chapter include Bruce Wilkinson's *The Prayer of Jabez: Breaking Through to the Blessed Life* (Sisters, Oregon: Multnomah Publishers, 2000); Joel Osteen's *Your Best Life Now* (New York: Warner Faith, 2004); and Rick Warren's *The Purpose-Driven Life* (Grand Rapids, Mich.: Zondervan, 2002).

Information about the launch of *PDL* comes from Greg Stielstra's *Pyromarketing* (New York: HarperCollins, 2005). An account of what transpired between Stielstra, Rick Warren, and Warren's representatives was published in *Publishers Weekly* (Juli Cragg Hilliard, "Purpose-Driven Interference?" July 25, 2005 and " 'Pyro' Goes Ahead; Warren Weighs In," August 29, 2005). An example of Warren's monitoring of what is written about him is available at http://www.lighthousetrailsresearch.com/emailfromrw.htm.

Malcolm Gladwell wrote a detailed profile of Warren and his acumen in the September 12, 2005, issue of the *New Yorker*.

For more on Warren's "stealth strategy," see Tim Stafford's November 2002 article in *Christianity Today*, available online at http://www.christianitytoday.com/ct/2002/012/1.42.html.

CHAPTER SIX

To read detailed profiles of Christian bands and their contributions to the music world, see Mark Joseph's *Faith, God & Rock 'n' Roll* (London: Sanctuary Publishing, 2003).

CHAPTER SEVEN

Film gross receipts come from www.boxofficemojo.com.

Terry Mattingly writes about Christians in film, television, and other aspects of popular culture. His essays have been compiled in *Pop Goes Religion* (Nashville: W Publishing Group, 2005).

CHAPTER EIGHT

For an in-depth view of Patrick Henry, see "God and Country: A College That Trains Young Christians to Be Politicians," by Hanna Rosin (*New Yorker,* June 27, 2005).

The study about the performance of homeschooled students was conducted in 1998 by Lawrence Rudner and was published on March 23, 1999, in the Education Policy Analysis Archives, an electronic journal accessible at http://epaa.asu.edu/epaa/v7n8/.

The first step toward reinvigorating Christian education was Mark Noll's *The Scandal of the Evangelical Mind* (Grand Rapids, Mich.: Wm. B. Eerdmans, 1994).

The growth of Christian Impact at Harvard is described by Collin Hansen in "The Holy and the Ivy" (*Christianity Today,* September 2005).

CHAPTER NINE

Richard Cizik's quote about the lack of need for an evangelical lobby comes from a *Philadelphia Inquirer* article by Matt Stearns, "Robertson's Role in GOP Questioned" (July 27, 2003).

For a look at Christian support of Israel in the United States, see "Apocalypse Soon" by Johann Hari (*Independent on Sunday*, June 29, 2003).

Ralph Reed's comment about throwing rocks comes from an article by Dana Milbank, "Religious Right Finds Its Center in Oval Office: Bush Emerges as Movement's Leader After Robertson Leaves Christian Coalition" (*Washington Post*, December 24, 2001).

The Bible Literacy Project disclaimers about ACLU support can be seen at http://www.bibleliteracy.org/Site/News/bibl_news060302.htm.

CHAPTER TEN

George Barna talks about the changes in the church in *Revolution* (Carol Stream, Ill.: Tyndale House, 2005). Spencer Burke's thoughts and more on the emergent church can be found at www.theooze.com. Information on Monkfish Abbey can be found at http://www.monkfish-abbey.org/who-we-are/.

For more on Erwin McManus's take on what Christianity *should* be, see *The Barbarian Way: Unleash the Untamed Faith Within* (Nashville: Nelson Books, 2005).

The transcript of Rick Warren at the Pew Forum Faith Angle conference is at http://pewforum.org/events/index.php?EventID=80.

More of evangelical discontent with the GOP can be found in Amy Sullivan's article "When Would Jesus Bolt? Meet Randy Brinson, the Advance Guard of Evangelicals Leaving the GOP" (*Washington Monthly*, April 1, 2006).

Tony Perkins's statement about the fault in American foreign policy is available at http://www.frc.org/get.cfm?i=PR06C10. James Taranto's column about the Roe Effect can be accessed at http://www.opinionjournal.com/extra/?id=110006913.

Index

A Note on the Author

Monique El-Faizy is a journalist whose work has appeared in the *Guardian*, the *Washington Post*, the *New York Times*, *USA Today*, the *St. Petersburg Times*, *Cosmopolitan* magazine (UK), *GQ* magazine, *Parents* magazine, *Moscow* magazine, and the *Moscow Guardian*, among others. She has worked at the *New York Daily News*, the *Philadelphia Inquirer*, the Associated Press, and the Bergen County *Record*. She lives in New York City with her husband and their two sons.